THE PARTNERSHIP

GREG SHERIDAN

Greg Sheridan has been Foreign Editor at *The Australian* since 1992 and has written about Australian foreign policy since entering journalism in the late 1970s. He has written four books concerning Australia and Asia, and the interaction with the US in Asia. In researching this book, Sheridan interviewed a wide range of key insiders at the most senior levels of government in Australia, the US and various Asian countries. He spent two two-month periods as a Visiting Fellow at the Centre for Strategic and International Studies in Washington, DC. Sheridan is a contributing editor to the US foreign policy journal, *The National Interest*, a visiting Fellow at the Land Warfare Studies Centre in Canberra and a founding member of the Australian American Leadership Dialogue.

THE PARTNERSHIP

THE INSIDE STORY OF THE US-AUSTRALIAN ALLIANCE UNDER BUSH AND HOWARD

GREG SHERIDAN

NEW SOUTH

I wish to dedicate this book to my wife, Jasbir Kaur Sheridan, the light of my life, and to our son, Ajay, and his wife, Inu, and to our sons Lakhvinder and Jagdave. They are the tightest alliance of all.

A New South book

Published by
University of New South Wales Press Ltd
University of New South Wales
Sydney NSW 2052
AUSTRALIA
www.unswpress.com.au

© Greg Sheridan 2006
First published 2006

This book is copyright. Apart from any fair dealing for the purpose of private study, research, criticism or review, as permitted under the Copyright Act, no part may be reproduced by any process without written permission. Inquiries should be addressed to the publisher.

National Library of Australia
Cataloguing-in-Publication entry

    Sheridan, Greg, 1956– .
    The partnership: the inside story of the US-Australian
    alliance under Bush and Howard.

    Bibliography.
    Includes index.
    ISBN 0 86840 922 7.

    1. Howard, John, 1939– - Military leadership. 2. Bush,
    George W. (George Walker), 1946– - Military leadership. 3.
    War on Terrorism, 2001– . 4. Australia - Foreign relations
    - United States. 5. United States - Foreign relations -
    Australia. I. Title.

    327.94073

Text design Ruth Pidd
Cover design Di Quick
Front cover photograph Newspix/Brett Faulkner
Back cover photograph Author with Condoleeza Rice, March 2006
Print Griffin

CONTENTS

Acknowledgments 9

Introduction: why do we have an alliance with the United States of America? 11

CHAPTER 1 Council of war: the White House, April 2003 18

CHAPTER 2 The bonds of terror 32

CHAPTER 3 Afghanistan: the first Aussie Bronze Star since Vietnam 40

CHAPTER 4 Diggers to Iraq: Howard joins the Bush family, Australia plays its red card 57

CHAPTER 5 Inside the belly of the beast: the Bush foreign policy from the inside 74

CHAPTER 6 In the neocons' lair: a season in Washington, an encounter with Wolfowitz 86

CHAPTER 7 Sexing up the intelligence relationship: Washington opens the golden door, Canberra walks through 97

CHAPTER 8 Iraq: a general's story 111

CHAPTER 9	The Australian Defence Force: redesigned for global power	128
CHAPTER 10	Howard's love affair with the soldiers	141
CHAPTER 11	Defence cooperation with the United States	152
CHAPTER 12	Australia's standing in America	161
CHAPTER 13	Indonesia: helping with leviathan, or deputy sheriff?	172
CHAPTER 14	The Asian giants: China, agreeing to disagree; Japan, Australia's strategic partner	188
CHAPTER 15	Commander of the Gulf: a sailor's story	206
CHAPTER 16	The United Nations: mangling multilateralism together	214
CHAPTER 17	Howard and Bush as national security heads of government	228
CHAPTER 18	Two case studies in the new partnership: the tsunami and climate change	237
CHAPTER 19	The Americanisation of Australian politics	249
CHAPTER 20	The Free Trade Agreement: making dollars and sense	261
CHAPTER 21	Lord of the skies: a fighter pilot's story	271
CHAPTER 22	Labor and America: out-thought, out-muscled, out-voted	279

CHAPTER 23 Why does everyone hate America,
            but love it too?   290

CHAPTER 24 Secrets of the alliance: Roosevelt,
            Spender and Scanlan   302

CHAPTER 25 The new alliance   319

            Index   324

ACKNOWLEDGMENTS

I wish to record my thanks to the editor-in-chief of *The Australian*, Chris Mitchell, for the outstanding leadership he has given in ensuring *The Australian's* commitment to understanding and reporting Australia's place in the world at all levels, and to the editor, Michael Stutchbury, for enduring leadership. I would also like to thank my colleagues who are especially concerned with national security issues, especially Paul Kelly, Dennis Shanahan, Patrick Walters, and Cameron Stewart, and our former colleague, John Kerin. The work environment at *The Australian* is collaborative, collegial and full of the clash of ideas, facts and opinions.

Similarly I am indebted to the section editors for whom I most work – Tom Switzer, the opinion editor, with his encyclopedic knowledge of American foreign policy, Patrick Lawnham on Inquirer and Louise Evans on features. All three manage writers with that mixture of direction and patience which is so helpful.

I am particularly grateful to Kurt Campbell of the Centre for Strategic and International Studies in Washington, DC, who invited me to become a visiting fellow in his International Security program, which in turn allowed me to conduct many of the US-based interviews for this book. Kurt and Dr John Hamre, the head of CSIS, ensure a supremely stimulating and productive work environment at CSIS.

I am also grateful to the Chief of the Australian Defence Force, Air Marshall Angus Houston, who approved my requests to interview numerous serving soldiers. Similarly I am grateful to General Peter Leahy, Chief of Army, for making it possible for me to talk at length to a number of SAS men. As well I would like to record thanks to Lieutenant Colonel Malcolm McGregor who invited me to take up a visiting fellowship at the Land Warfare Studies Centre in Canberra.

I must also thank John Dauth for wise counsel and long friendship. Appreciation is also due to John Elliot of UNSW Press who took on an unusual project and managed it with forbearance, skill and commitment.

Hundreds of people spoke to me for this book. Some are named, most are not, because that is the nature of their position. To everyone who did agree to talk to me, I am most grateful. Naturally, no one mentioned above is in any way responsible for the book's opinions, judgments or mistakes.

Finally I must thank my family. An author's family puts up with a great deal in the gestation of a book, and my debt to my family, especially my wife, Jasbir, is immeasurable.

INTRODUCTION: WHY DO WE HAVE AN ALLIANCE WITH THE UNITED STATES OF AMERICA?

It was just before the war against Saddam Hussein's regime in Iraq was to kick off. A huge US force, a substantial British force, a small but lethal Australian group and a tiny Polish contingent were to join together to invade Iraq, topple Saddam Hussein and disarm him of the weapons of mass destruction he was believed to possess.

Just before the invasion was to begin, the United States called a high-level military planning meeting. It was convened in Qatar. Even though attendance was restricted to the most senior officers – one participant joked that you had to be a full colonel to carry anyone's briefcase – there were too many invitees for a conventional meeting room. So the US hosts held the meeting on an indoor basketball court. They had another reason for that choice, which would become apparent as the meeting got under way. Then Brigadier (later General) Maurie McNarn, the Australian commander, was the senior Australian present among the couple of hundred officers called together.

As the meeting was called to order, everyone was there in their appointed place except for US General Tommy Franks, the trash-talking Texan who had been at high school with Laura Bush and was overall commander of the coalition force. Suddenly the lights went out. On the big, bare wall of the court a flickering image appeared, then took definite shape. Several minutes of the movie *Gladiator* were shown. At the end of a segment of fierce fighting,

Russell Crowe was left standing on a pile of bodies, knee-deep in blood and gore. The film was stopped at that point. The United States contingent, the vast majority of those present, began a raucous chant: 'Hoo Ha! Hoo Ha! Hoo Ha!', a common enough US military war cry.

The noise was deafening. McNarn leant across to a senior Brit standing near him. 'You know the moral of that film?' McNarn asked. 'No', said the Brit. 'What's that?' Because of the noise of the American chant, McNarn had to shout his reply. Just as he began answering the Brit, the chant stopped and Tommy Franks walked in. Across the silence, McNarn's voice, accent unmistakably Down Under, rang out: 'If you want a bloody job well done, make sure you put an Australian in charge!' Franks looked daggers at McNarn, who had inadvertently executed Operation Stolen Thunder. The course of a true alliance never does run wholly smooth.

The vast majority of Australian-US cooperation in Iraq was highly productive and deep connections were made or reinforced between the two militaries. But the incident above, trivial in every way, reminds us that the Australian and American styles are quite different, and the Australians are more than willing and able to speak up for themselves. The idea, common enough, that in the Australian-US alliance the Americans say what they want and the Australians follow suit is absurdly mistaken. It is the thesis of this book that in the Australian-US alliance, as in many vastly unequal relationships, the power may lie with the bigger party, but the initiative most often lies with the smaller party.

This book examines the Australian-US alliance during the period when John Howard has been prime minister of Australia and George W Bush has been president of the US, technically since Bush's inauguration in January 2001, but effectively since Bush's election in November 2000. It is not a book about Iraq, though of course Iraq figures heavily in it. It is not a comprehensive treatment of Australian foreign policy, some aspects of which are less influenced by the alliance than others. As such there is a lot that is not in this book, which is concerned with the Australian-US alliance, and the inside story of that alliance under Howard and Bush.

This book asserts four main propositions: that most of the initiative in the relationship has come from the Australian side during that time, that Howard has had more of the running of the relationship than Bush; that Howard and Bush have transformed the alliance from a predominantly regional affair to a truly global partnership; that Howard has got most of what he wanted from the alliance at, for him, very little cost either politically, militarily or economically; and finally that the US alliance greatly enhances Australian national power.

What has Howard wanted from the alliance and what has he got from it? Howard wanted: an enhanced intelligence relationship; enhanced defence cooperation; greater Australian influence in Washington's decision making; a free trade agreement; increased US involvement in the region, especially in Indonesia; the greater prestige in Asia that comes from being close to and able to influence Washington; and the enhanced prestige for his government with Australian voters that comes from the same source.

Howard, an unlikely international statesman, has been successful to a substantial extent in all these objectives. As such, the story of the alliance over these years is one of the most remarkable, complex, broad-ranging diplomatic and security initiatives in the history of Australian government. Of course it has been much more than just Howard. It has been the whole Australian system that has produced this, including Howard's senior ministerial colleagues, especially the foreign minister, Alexander Downer, but also, crucially, the Australian Defence Force, the Australian embassies and consulates in the US, the foreign affairs and prime minister's departments more generally, the intelligence agencies, the business community and even some entrepreneurs of private diplomacy.

But the Australian system has been driven from the top, from the political level, in particular from Howard. He came into office in 1996 determined to intensify the Australian-US relationship across the board and, in time, that's what he's done, not through a preconceived plan but by taking advantage of opportunities as they have come along.

Alexander Downer has been Howard's most important political partner in this. As a young man Downer joined the Department of Foreign Affairs and Trade in the mid-1970s. At the end of his first year his supervisor in the department wrote: 'Alexander Downer has the potential to become the outstanding diplomat of his year, but will have to control a tendency to bumptiousness.' That was a shrewd assessment then as it is now. Downer stumbled badly a few times early in his stint as foreign minister. But he showed great resilience and a capacity to learn. He has matured into an effective foreign minister and an effective domestic political operator. Second only to Howard, he became the dominant face of the government in national security, foreign policy and Australian-US alliance matters.

The new intimacy in the alliance has also come about because of the American system. Once Bush realised, especially in the context of the war on terror, that Howard had something to offer, the American provided reciprocal political leadership. And the American system more broadly under Bush, with so many old friends of Australia in positions of influence within it, has been open to the Australian initiative.

This book is based on hundreds of interviews over the past four years in both Australia and the United States, and on years of work on the alliance before that. Most of the interviews were not for attribution. Where I refer to books I cite them in the text. Much of the information in this book is new. I hope that even those who disagree with the book's judgments or analysis will find this new information useful or interesting.

But in a sense all this comes after you have answered an earlier question – why do we have an alliance with the US at all? In the end, how you feel about the moral worth of the alliance reflects how you feel about the United States as a force in history.

One of the reasons I always hated Marxism, which was fashionable when I was an undergraduate, was because of its determinism: its view that history had an inevitable course that it must follow. I don't believe anything is inevitable, and think that history is enacted, unpredictably, by independent human beings who make unpredictable judgments.

For all its sins, the United States has stressed in its founding and defining documents, in its highest public leadership, and in most of the life of the nation, qualities which accord with the deepest nature of human beings – liberty, self-determination, democracy, hard work, the rule of law, civic equality, religious equality. It doesn't always live up to these virtues, of course, sometimes spectacularly so, but it's always trying. Abstract values are much less important than concrete actions and the balance sheet of the US's concrete actions is vastly in credit, while of course there are grave debits. But that's a big argument, and another book.

Australian policy makers, and the Australian people, while alert to the US's many faults, have mostly accepted that it is a force for good rather than bad, certainly a force we want to be associated with, from Alfred Deakin successfully inviting Teddy Roosevelt to send his fleet to visit Australia in 1908, through the joint fighting in World War I, through John Curtin turning the military running of the country over to US General Douglas MacArthur during World War II, through to Howard and Bush today. And in all that time no one ever won an election in Australia with an anti-American platform, not even Gough Whitlam in 1972, who supported the alliance and correctly said his policies were compatible with it.

But the Australian debate, except for a tiny class of commentators hypercharged on the rhetoric of moral extravagance, is normally conducted in less heroic terms than the vast sweep of history. The most defining characteristic of the Australian public temper is pragmatism. That was Bob Hawke's signature word. Howard has grasped the same insight and pressed into service his own word – practical, which he has elevated into the most powerful rhetorical instrument: 'this is a practical approach to reconciliation'; 'this is a practical view of the China relationship', and so on.

In that spirit of practicality, Australian policy makers have found countless benefits in the US alliance, ANZUS to give it its formal title. Under ANZUS, the Americans are committed to respond to an attack on Australia, and Australia is reciprocally committed. Of course, their response to any specific historical circumstance would not be governed by the wording of ANZUS but by their judgments at the time. But can anyone really doubt that the US would help an ally if that ally was in real trouble?

The Americans take their alliances very seriously. Richard Armitage, a former US deputy secretary of state and one of the best human beings I have met, put it starkly when he told an Australian audience: 'An alliance means I'll fight and die for you, and you'll fight and die for me.'

If Australia were ever in any real security trouble, there are countless ways the US could make a decisive difference short of sending in ground troops to help. If you are allied with American air power, for example, if the Americans are acting as your air force, you more or less cannot lose if you have any kind of ground force at all. Similarly, operational intelligence – has the enemy's air force left its base, is the ship at sea – logistics, planning and a thousand other tasks of war are areas where alliance cooperation in conflict could be crucial.

Short of these apocalyptic scenarios there are many military benefits for Australia in the alliance. Access to US defence technology allows Australia, with a small population, to keep a technological defence edge in the region. Access to the vast US military operational intelligence network is a massive force multiplier for our powerful but small defence force.

But the alliance should never be limited to its military aspects. It is an asset Australians can use to help the region, and to help ourselves in the region – whether it's Paul Keating helping to shape US thinking on APEC (Asia-Pacific Economic Cooperation forum) or John Howard urging Bush to engage Indonesian president Susilo Bambang Yudhoyono. For the alliance undoubtedly gives Australians a standing in Washington they wouldn't otherwise have. And that standing, that access and influence, are a plus in Asia. Similarly, it's unlikely that Australia could have negotiated a free trade agreement so speedily with the US in the absence of the alliance.

This far from exhaustive laundry list of benefits has been important to Australian policy makers and to the Australian people. But undoubtedly the moral argument about the role of America has also given them a certain level of existential comfort about the pragmatic benefits.

The chief costs of the alliance are generally reckoned to be either that because of the alliance Australia becomes a higher priority target for the US's enemies, or that Canberra might be associated with unpopular US policies. Australian policy makers should not associate themselves with any policy they think is wrong just because of alliance solidarity. As to being targets, certainly during the Cold War Australia was a higher priority target for a potential Soviet nuclear strike because of its alliance with the US. But in the war on terror Australia's enemies have, in their eyes, ample grounds for hostility entirely independent of the alliance with the US.

But you cannot finally divorce the alliance from the idealism – high-falutin', brash and sometimes ungracious idealism in the American case, muted, shame-faced, rather embarrassed idealism in the Australian case – that underlies it. All through the Cold War, as Australian policy makers readily calculated that the benefit of having the alliance far outweighed the extra risk involved in it, there was also a sense that this was one way Australia made its contribution to the global order, this was one way Australians tried to make the world a little better, as well as look out for themselves.

I think it was a sound calculation then. This book investigates whether it's a sound calculation now.

Chapter 1

COUNCIL OF WAR:
THE WHITE HOUSE, APRIL 2003

Washington in April, a cool, crisp spring day. The snow is all gone and by the Potomac River the cherry blossom is just beginning to flower. The tourists are coming in numbers, so are some protesters. For this is April 1, 2003, and Washington is a city at war.

Just under two weeks ago the United States had launched a war against Saddam Hussein's regime in Iraq. On the night the first shot was fired in anger the Australian ambassador to the United States, Michael Thawley, John Howard's former foreign policy adviser in Canberra, received a phone call from his good friend US Deputy Secretary of State Rich Armitage. 'Michael, can you come over here?' Armitage asked.

Thawley travelled the short distance from the Australian embassy on Massachusetts Avenue to the State Department building on C Street. From the outside, both the embassy and the State Department are two of the most non-descript structures in Washington. That night Thawley followed the early military moves blow by blow from the office of Armitage's boss, Secretary of State Colin Powell, with Powell and Armitage and a few others. While there, Thawley used his mobile phone to ring Howard in Canberra to tell him the balloon had gone up. Washington was at war. So was Canberra.

For that little period Howard may have been one of the best informed leaders in the world, as for a short time Thawley gave him minute-by-minute accounts of what was happening.

The Australian Special Air Service (SAS) regiment went into action in Iraq straight away. It would bring glory and honour on the nation in the western desert of Iraq, engaging the enemy almost as soon as it entered the territory, moving at lightning speed through almost continuous hostile engagements, knocking out Iraq's air force and controlling vast chunks of territory. It would vastly enhance Australia's standing in the US, and perhaps globally.

The first night of the war was exhilarating for Thawley and the other watchers in the State Department. It looked as though Saddam Hussein might have been killed in an early US bombing raid. Even I got a phone call to this effect in Sydney. There was a chance the war would be over quickly.

Today, April 1, in the (Teddy) Roosevelt Room at the White House, Australia's foreign minister, Alexander Downer, is to meet President George W Bush. But at first Vice President Dick Cheney, Bush's consigliere, takes the meeting. With him are National Security Advisor Condoleeza Rice, who was to become secretary of state in the second Bush administration, and Scooter Libby, Cheney's chief-of-staff, later to be charged over allegedly lying to a special prosecutor in the Valerie Plame case. This was the case in which the Bush administration was accused of revealing Plame's identity as a covert agent for the Central Intelligence Agency, allegedly as retribution for her husband, Joseph Wilson, writing articles damning of the administration. Libby, who had been extraordinarily influential, had to resign from Cheney's office when charged.

Next to Libby was the sandy-haired Steve Yates, an open-faced, perennially youthful figure, intellectually a hard-line hawk, but personally avuncular and, like the other Americans in the room, very pro-Australian. Yates worked on Cheney's national security staff. There were a couple of other Americans present as well.

Downer was accompanied by Thawley, suave and somewhat saturnine in his perfect suit, and Dr Ashton Calvert, the head of the Department of Foreign Affairs and Trade, bald with patches of white hair at the sides of his head. Calvert was a characteristically

Australian combination of cerebral intellectual, bureaucratic obsessive and plain-speaking hardhead. One or two other Australians rounded out the meeting.

The account that follows of the conversation that day in the Roosevelt Room comes from a number of people who were present. The general sequence of the remarks has been confirmed and direct quotations have only been used for remarks for which there are authoritative sources. The conversation gives a unique insight into the extraordinary intimacy between the Australian and American leaders at the time, as well as what their political, diplomatic and military priorities were.

Cheney had come straight from watching the daily press briefing with Secretary of Defense Donald Rumsfeld and Chairman of the Joint Chiefs of Staff General Richard Myers. A few times a week Cheney and Bush spoke via video conference with General Tommy Franks, the commander of the US forces in Iraq. Franks was confident the military operation was going well. Cheney shared that view. History indeed would vindicate Cheney and Franks in this judgment. The conventional military phase went exceptionally well. It was the post-war phase that became an awful mess.

Downer told Cheney that every morning in Canberra the National Security Committee of Cabinet met and was briefed on what the Australian military had done in Iraq.

Downer was quick to talk about domestic politics to Cheney. As the war progressed Bush, Howard and Britain's Tony Blair, and their respective ministers, would do whatever they could to help one other politically. They would also discuss their domestic political situations with one other, swapping lines of argument, coordinating announcements, working through the politics of the war as well as the military and diplomatic aspects. Downer said to Cheney: 'The (Howard) government has been through a particularly rugged time over the Iraq issue given the opposition to the war in Australia. But opinion polls have now turned around.'

At this moment, Bush came in to join the meeting. The busiest and most powerful man in the world had few enough allies at this point and Downer was one of them. Like everyone who spends any time with Bush privately, Downer, who had met Bush well before the 2000 presidential election, had formed the view that Bush was smart and tough and funny. Bush was highly intelligent but he didn't intellectualise things. He always had a very clear idea of what he wanted to do.

Bush too was upbeat in his assessment of how the Iraq campaign was going. He wanted to be gracious with Downer and told him he thought he hadn't spoken often enough to Howard since the beginning of the war. He'd like to call Howard in the next few days. Downer was appreciative of the gesture and told Bush that Howard felt a great sense of empathy with the president. He repeated that as the war had gone on Australian public opinion had come around to support it.

But Downer also expressed some concern at how effective the Iraqi government was in its propaganda efforts, especially its use of civilian casualties to undermine Western support for the war. Bush concurred. He himself wanted a better effort in the public relations campaign by the coalition forces and their governments.

Then a bit of a smile played around the president's lips: 'Of course it's hard for Saddam Hussein to speak if he's dead. If he isn't dead, at the very least he has a big headache.' Bush was referring to the mistaken view the Americans held at this time that they might have killed Saddam on the first night of bombing. Downer noted it was certainly strange that Saddam hadn't made a public effort to rally the Iraqi people. Bush noted that the US had got a pretty good shot at him on the first night. Bush repeated the formulation that obviously appealed to him – if Saddam wasn't dead, he sure had a big headache.

The president then moved on to a favorite topic – the media: 'It seems like the media has only one thing to do and that's to write speculative pieces about the direction of the war campaign.' Bush, often the sunniest of personalities, was bitter about the media, saying that a lot of people in the American media 'want the United States to lose the war'. This was an extraordinary charge to make and yet there was such hostility to the Iraq campaign in the liberal media that Bush's remarks are not unreasonable. After the war *The New York Times* and other parts of the liberal media establishment would engage in much self-flagellation over allegedly believing too much of what the Bush administration told them about Iraq. But from inside the White House it didn't look like they were getting an even break, much less support or trust, from the media.

Bush wanted to concentrate on the main game. The only important thing was winning, Bush said. He waxed philosophical. War was tough and each war was different. This war was breaking new ground. Twenty-four-hour coverage of the war meant it seemed like it had been going on for ages, whereas only a little while ago he'd been sitting in the Oval Office pondering with colleagues whether to take a shot at Saddam. Downer commented on the US loss of life and noted that there had been relatively few US fatalities given the scale of the operation. Bush was sombre – he said Australia had not yet lost any lives in Iraq but was likely to do so at some point. Iraqis were losing lives more because of other Iraqis' actions than because of the coalition.

Bush wanted Downer to tell Howard that the war was going well and the coalition would win. Downer replied that it was important to win as soon as possible and with the smallest possible number of civilian casualties. Bush thought it was likely that the US would need to kill thousands of Saddam's security forces in order to secure victory in the war. Saddam's security forces, he said, are 'a bloodthirsty group'.

Downer told Bush the coalition needed to get more stories into the media about Saddam's appalling human rights record. Downer then matched Bush on the media. Downer said he had given up watching CNN, it was just too biased in its coverage of the war. Fox News was much better.

Bush went one better. He was on a news blackout, he said, and didn't watch the media at all, getting his information from his regular briefings on how the war was going.

Downer wanted to tackle Bush on the question of United Nations involvement in post-war Iraq. Christopher Meyer, the UK ambassador to Washington at this time, in his enthralling memoir, *DC Confidential* (Weidenfeld & Nicolson, 2005) identifies Britain's Blair, Spain's Jose Maria Aznar and Australia's Howard as the three pro-Bush prime ministers who were pivotal in convincing Bush to seek a second resolution from the United Nations Security Council explicitly authorising war against Iraq. The US of course was unsuccessful in its attempts to get a second resolution. Downer's comments in the Roosevelt Room indicate that despite the Howard government's well known and deeply felt scepticism towards the UN, it recognised the political importance of the UN and sought to maximise its role with the Americans.

In any event, Downer reassured Bush that the Australian government didn't want the UN to take over all of Iraq. But he knew the question of the UN role was being considered in the administration, he said. Bush was outright hostile to the UN. The US, he said, would get blamed for destroying Iraq and it didn't want others coming to rebuild the place. He didn't want non-coalition countries to be able to say that because of a US-led war innocent lives had been lost and then they had had to come in and rebuild the country.

Bush got blunter as he warmed to his theme: 'The UN can't manage a damn thing.' Bush recalled visiting Kosovo to observe the US military and he found the UN personnel there 'a bunch of drunks'. Bush continued: 'It's like they took the most inefficient bureaucrat in the world and gave him a senior UN post.' Kosovo had made a big impression on Bush. Bush said he accepted that there would need to be a UN role in post-war Iraq but he didn't want the UN managing Iraq and 'nor would prime ministers Blair and Howard'. Downer countered that it would be important to have UN agencies like the IMF and the World Bank involved.

Downer asked Bush how he saw the question of further UN Security Council resolutions on Iraq. Bush said the US was only going back to the UN when it could do so from a position of strength. The unsuccessful effort to gain a second security council resolution, which had wasted so much time, was 'all for Tony Blair'. Bush paused a second: 'John Howard wanted it too.' This seemed to be Bush's polite way of blaming what he considered to be a blunder, of seeking a second Security Council resolution, partly on Howard. There is no doubt that Blair was more influential with Bush than Howard, but Howard was also substantially influential in his own right. Bush saw him as a fellow conservative, he'd been in office longer than either Bush or Blair and he's an older man. The conversation in the Roosevelt Room certainly confirms that the Howard government pushed hard for the Bush administration to exhaust all UN procedures before it went to war, and then to involve the UN to the maximum degree possible after the war.

At this stage of the discussion Downer displayed a certain psychological and conversational elegance. He thanked Bush for trying to get the second resolution. Downer told Bush not to consider the effort a failure. It was important to Australia that the US and its allies be seen to have exhausted the UN processes. It was better to have tried and failed at the UN than not to have tried at all.

Bush was taken by the first part of Downer's comments, noting that Downer was the only person who had ever thanked him for making that effort at the UN. Downer jumped in to say that the US had isolated the French, meaning that the failure of the second resolution was a failure of the UN, not a failure of the US. Downer said that now 60 percent of the Australians believed it was the UN which had failed on Iraq. The president replied with his only bout of sarcasm in the conversation. 'Yeah', he said, with obvious and mordant irony, the way the second resolution was handled was a 'brilliant strategy'. The whole episode obviously still rankled with Bush. He said America and its allies had 'begged' the Security Council for a resolution. Now the war had started there was no need to go back to the Security Council until after the war was won. Of course, Bush said, he understood that some governments would need some kind of UN blessing if they were going to donate money for the reconstruction of Iraq. Bush said there was 'an insidious plot' by some people, whom he did not name, who could not stand what the US had done in Iraq and who would do everything they could to make sure the whole venture failed. Nonetheless, the United States agreed that there was a need for a UN role in Iraq and there already was a role for the UN.

Downer reassured Bush again that Australia didn't want the UN to run Iraq and Bush agreed that the Iraqi citizens wouldn't want the UN to run Iraq either. The whole exchange indicates the high level of sensitivity, indeed hostility, which Bush personally felt towards the UN, as did Bush's subsequent remarks.

The conversation turned to France, a subject which often comes up in Australian-US conversations, and in US-UK conversations. Bush said the French position on Iraq was 'motivated by money if you looked way down deep'. The French had financial transactions with Iraq which they didn't want to see the light of day, Bush said. The Russians were the same. In these matters, Iraq was 'a lot different than Afghanistan'.

Bush then told an intriguing tale. Before the war, he said, there had been indications that Saddam was trying to get out of Iraq early with US$1 billion. America was not going to agree to Saddam robbing the Iraqi people. Bush went on to say that it's impossible to rule a country by fear, and once the grip of fear is broken the regime would lose all support. The US, he said, understood that some Iraqis felt let down by their experience with the US-led coalition in 1991. It would take some time to win back their confidence.

Downer understood and agreed with this sentiment but pointed to the strong support for the coalition from the Kurds. Not only the Kurds, Bush replied, but the Shia in the south, especially around Basra, were now helping the coalition's 'hunter-killer teams', pointing out areas where Saddam's paramilitary forces were taking shelter.

Bush returned to one of his key frustrations. The media, he said, didn't show 90 percent of the positive things in the war. When coalition leaders and briefers told the media about these things, the media didn't believe them. The coalition had been very cautious about bombing civilians, Bush said, and as a result people didn't feel like they were at war. 'It must be quite surreal', the president said.

Michael Thawley, at the height of his powers and self-confidence after several years as ambassador in Washington, observed that 90 percent of Baghdad was mostly unaffected at this stage. Downer asked whether there was any intention of putting Iraq TV off the air. Bush replied that if there's no electricity you can't watch TV and the US was considering whether to cut off the power supply. However, Bush said, there is one thing the US will not do. The US will not bomb civilian areas.

Thawley intervened again, saying that one effect of such careful targeting in the bombing campaign was that the war would last longer and this was poorly understood. Downer told Bush that Howard had been making this point in the public debate.

Bush then moved to what for him was one of the main purposes of the meeting. The president thanked Downer for the Australian contribution to the coalition and its overall support on Iraq. 'Australians are brave, skilled fighters', Bush said. He noted that they were operating out in Iraq's western deserts. In a crucial exchange, he pinpointed what he thought was the key strategic contribution of the Australians. Before the war, the Americans were very worried, Bush said, about the possibility of Iraqi attacks on Israel. The president did not elaborate, but such an attack, and the subsequent Israeli retaliation, would have massively complicated Middle East politics and the Iraqi campaign. Thanks to the Aussies, Bush said, the Iraqis had no capacity to do that. By this, Bush meant the Australians had knocked out Scud missile launching sites in the western desert and had captured the huge Iraqi Al Asad airbase. Meanwhile, the president noted, Australian frogmen were clearing Iraq's waterways and Australian fighter pilots were in the thick of the bombing campaign.

Bush was obviously well briefed on the Australian military contribution, and Downer wanted to encourage him in this line of thinking. Downer commented that Australian Hornets (F/A-18 aircraft) were involved in combat air patrols, combat support and close air support. Downer recalled that on the first day of the conflict the Australian SAS had come upon an Iraqi military communication base and killed the ten Iraqis guarding it and blown up the facility. Bush said he knew exactly when that had happened as it was the first significant military engagement of the war.

Downer wanted to place the Iraq commitment squarely in the tradition of the Australian-US alliance. He told Bush Australia was pleased to be involved in Iraq as an active member of the coalition. Australia, he said, valued its alliance with the US 'enormously'. The alliance was of great value to Australia in pursuing security in the Asia-Pacific region. The North Korean issue demonstrated this.

Bush said he believed there would be 'amazing after-effects' in the Middle East when the Iraq war was won. He also believed that the US-led effort could make a serious dent in the proliferation of weapons of mass destruction (WMDs).

Downer wanted to use his access to Bush, Cheney and Rice to discuss North Korea, where, as with the discussion on Iraq, he had a few key points he wanted to get across. Downer opened up by telling Bush that Australia remained very concerned about North Korea. Bush said North Korea was a serious example of the consequences of non-action. Bush didn't draw the connection, but this is a key point the neoconservatives, especially Paul Wolfowitz, then US deputy defense secretary, made in relation to Iraq and it underlay much of their intellectual approach more generally. Doing nothing about a serious problem, or doing nothing effective, just drifting along with the usual diplomatic falderol, held its own risks. There are risks in action, but there are also risks in doing nothing.

Bush was explicit about his options on North Korea. The United States, he said, had the option of taking military action there and it was important not to take that option off the table. Of course, he said, this is not a pleasant prospect for South Korea and it certainly isn't a pleasant prospect for North Korea.

Bush then described North Korea's leader, Kim Jong-il, as being like 'a child who throws his food on the floor and expects all the adults to rush over and pick it up'. The US policy, Bush said, was not to pick up the food. The other aspect of US policy, Bush described, was increasing the number of 'adults' involved. China, especially, had to 'learn to be an adult'. Bush said he had spoken to China's then president, Jiang Zemin, and told him that China needed to do more to settle the North Korea problem. Bush had told Jiang that he was reviewing military options. Bush said he had wanted to demonstrate to the Chinese how seriously he took the problem and the potential consequences for China if it did not help in resolving it. Bush said South Korea also needed to 'grow up' and ditch its messianic desire to transform Kim into something he wasn't. Japan on the other hand had been 'great'. Bush complained about the complacency of the international community on North Korea, saying it would be wonderful if somebody besides the US was determined to try to change North Korea.

Downer had one key point he wanted to make with Bush. The Chinese had to understand, Downer said, that what they did on North Korea would affect their relationship with the US. This was not a casual remark from Downer. It proceeded from analysis within the Department of Foreign Affairs and Trade that the best way to move North Korea was to move China and the best way to move China was to get the US to make it an issue in the bilateral relationship.

Bush replied that he had been very blunt with the Chinese on North Korea and they knew what was at stake.

Somewhere around this point Bush had to leave the meeting to attend to other matters. He had had a substantial meeting with Downer, sent a message to Howard, heard first-hand the Australian concerns about both Iraq and North Korea. There were the usual friendly felicitations from Bush as he left. The meeting, however, continued, with Cheney now taking the lead. Rice, Libby and the other Americans stayed in the room.

Cheney turned the discussion straight back to weapons of mass destruction, which underlay both the Iraq and North Korea issues. Cheney said one of the primary considerations which had driven the US to go back to the UN was concern about the UN's 12 years of inaction in enforcing Security Council resolutions on Iraq's WMD programs. The WMD issue was bigger than Iraq, Cheney said. He wanted to believe the UN could help stop the spread of WMDs but if it couldn't deal with Iraq that cast doubt over whether it could deal with other WMD issues. Nonetheless, Cheney said, this didn't mean the US wouldn't deal with the UN at all.

The conversation turned back to another favourite topic – the French. Downer said it looked like the French want to be a counterweight to the US. Cheney said that's just what it looked like. Cheney then moved on to Germany. He said that during a visit to the US in 2002 the then German chancellor, Gerhard Schroeder, had looked Bush in the eye and told him he would support the US on Iraq. However, Cheney said, Schroeder shared Chirac's vision of a united Europe following the French lead and acting as a counterweight to the US. But, Cheney said, most countries in Europe don't want to follow France. France's main weight came from its membership of the Security Council, which was merely a result of historical circumstances.

Downer in this conversation was happy enough to criticise the French but put in a good word for the Germans. Downer told Cheney that he had been in Germany recently and he believed the Germans did value their relationship with the Americans and would now work to improve that relationship. This was evident, Downer said, in Germany's helpful attitude to issues currently before the UN.

Downer, like Howard, has a very keen appreciation of which tunes play well in Washington, how to sugar-coat a point so the Americans swallow it more easily. He told Cheney that the Europeans owed the Americans an enormous debt for the great things the US had done for Europe over the course of the previous century. Downer said it was entirely unreasonable for the Europeans to be so difficult on helping to resolve the WMD issue.

Cheney said the expansion of NATO to Eastern Europe was 'very positive' because the East European nations know what the stakes are.

Cheney and Downer at some point had a further exchange on WMDs which throws light on both Australian and US thinking about Iraq. Cheney said the proliferation of WMDs was 'an enormous issue' on which the world needed leadership, and the US was providing that. The key was getting Iraq right. If the coalition got Iraq right this would help a great deal later on in dealing with other nations without having to resort to military force. Downer agreed. He said it was necessary to draw a line on WMD proliferation. While some things could be dealt with through the Comprehensive Test Ban Treaty or the Non-Proliferation Treaty, these treaties themselves did not stop all countries from acquiring or passing on WMD technology. Cheney could not have agreed more. He said the treaties did not work for that two or three percent of rogue states that you had to deal with.

What the exchange on WMDs demonstrates is that both the Americans and the Australians, privately as well as publicly, regarded WMDs as the heart of what they were doing in Iraq. We now know the intelligence on Saddam's WMDs was faulty. But we also know that both the Bush administration and the Howard government believed that Saddam had WMDs and that this belief was at the core of their reasons for undertaking the Iraq operation.

This conversation is a snapshot of American and Australian thinking at the highest levels at a particular point in time, although many of the concerns were abiding and would animate Washington and Canberra for the next several years. It should not be seen as outrageous that Bush was upset with the media, as was Downer to some extent as well, that Bush spoke disparagingly of the United Nations, that both the president and Downer spoke disparagingly of the French, or that Cheney felt betrayed by Schroeder. What is surprising is how blunt Bush had been with Jiang Zemin over the North Koreans. The conversation demonstrates the intimacy and comfort level the Australian and US leaderships had with each other. This intimacy and mutual comfort would grow as the conventional military campaign in Iraq wound up in triumph but then the difficult stabilisation phase unfolded.

The conversation also shows Downer's approach to the Americans at the highest level. Downer had a couple of key messages he wanted to communicate – the importance of maximising UN involvement, the need to get the Chinese pushing North Korea, the military significance of what the Australians were doing in Iraq. Not all of these, especially the UN bit, were what the Americans wanted to hear, so he sweetened the medicine a bit. He also wanted to score some face time with the president and underline Australia's military and political contribution. He didn't try to perform some verbal tour de force of strategic sagacity, just communicate a couple of key, clear messages, absorb anything the Americans wanted to tell him and make sure they were registering Australia's contribution and Australia's views.

The exchange illustrates the range of issues occupying Australian and US government leaders at the time: the substance of the Iraq war; future policy on WMD issues; media management; domestic politics; the perennial perfidy of the French; the baleful necessities of the United Nations; Asia-Pacific issues such as North Korea; the formal interaction of Australia and the United States and their militaries; and personal greetings and messages.

It is a revealing picture of an alliance in the process of getting much closer. How much closer we shall see in the following chapters.

Chapter 2

THE BONDS OF TERROR

Every Australian cabinet minister in his or her office in Parliament House has a hot line to the prime minister. When the PM wants to talk urgently to one of his cabinet ministers, a light flashes on the cabinet minister's phone console and the cabinet minister takes the call straight away.

It was December 2000 and the call was no emergency. It was celebratory. It was about 5 pm and through the day it had become apparent that the challenger, George W Bush, had beaten the incumbent vice president, Al Gore, in the US presidential election. The results had been close and hung on disputed returns in Florida. The Australian prime minister, John Howard, was ringing to invite his foreign minister, Alexander Downer, down to his office for a drink of champagne to celebrate Bush's victory. The two men, Howard and Downer, as tight a partnership as has existed between a prime minister and a foreign minister in Australian political history, were delighted that Bush had won. Back in June of that year, the Office of National Assessments had been predicting a Gore victory.

Neither Howard nor Downer liked Gore much. They had a good relationship with US Secretary of State Madeleine Albright and Secretary of Defense William Cohen, and a fair if patchy relationship with Clinton himself. They found Clinton an episodic president. He would declare the birth of a new Pacific community but then fail to turn up to the APEC summit in Kuala Lumpur. He had bursts of attention on different issues but there was often no follow through. Gore they found much worse. They felt he had no significant interests or connections with the Asia-Pacific region. He was critical of Canberra's position on environmental issues and evoked no warmth from anyone in the Howard government. They found him personally remote and unrealistic in some of his policy positions. Downer felt Gore lacked any real strategic sense.

Howard and Downer believed if Bush won it would be very good for Australia. They knew the leading figures in the Bush administration well. Downer had been to see Bush when Bush was governor in Texas, way back in 1997. After the visit, Downer got a letter from Bush, saying in part: 'Australia is a very important ally of the United States, and should I ever be in the position to confirm that alliance, I look forward to doing so'.

Howard had a telephone conversation with Bush when Howard visited the US in 1999. Dick Cheney, Bush's vice president, had several times visited Australia when he was head of Halliburton, while Clinton was president, and Howard always made a point of seeing him. Bob Zoellick, who as United States trade representative would be a member of Bush's cabinet, had come to Australia on a Special Visitor's Program sponsored by the federal government. Downer had often met Rich Armitage and Paul Wolfowitz at sessions of the Australian American Leadership Dialogue and he knew the future US secretary of state, Colin Powell, as well.

Even at that early stage, Howard and Downer thought they might interest Bush in a free trade agreement. They certainly thought they could get more and higher level attention for the Asia-Pacific region, especially southeast Asia. The Bush team held as core doctrine the strengthening of key alliances. Surely defence cooperation could be ramped up. Howard and Downer drank most of a bottle of champagne together. It wasn't just social imbibing. They were working out what they might take to cabinet's National Security Committee in the way of initiatives to intensify relations with a Bush presidency.

They began the new relationship with telephone calls and messages and visits. Downer in Britain a little while later rang Powell and mentioned it had been kind of lonely being almost the only centre-right government around. 'Well, Alex', Powell said, 'you're not alone any more.'

Howard and Downer had wanted to intensify the US relationship since they were first elected but it hadn't really quite clicked with the Clinton administration. It was helpful to Howard and Downer that they were leading an experienced government several years in office by the time Bush was elected and that they had a series of ideas and propositions to put to the new Bush team.

Howard can hardly have guessed that his relationship with Bush would result in his sending Australian troops into battle in Afghanistan and Iraq. He can hardly have imagined either some of the personal experiences he would have – such as being invited to stay at the president's ranch in Crawford, Texas, the ultimate sign of approval and intimacy from Bush.

For Howard one of the most extraordinary scenes of his prime ministership came in May, 2003, shortly after the end of the conventional phase of the war in Iraq, when he visited Yankee Stadium in New York for a baseball game. Howard's presence was announced over the microphone. The Australian flag was paraded. The Australian anthem was played. And the New York crowd stood and applauded Australia, as represented by Howard. New Yorkers, like Parisians, are generally a hard crowd to impress. It's difficult to imagine a scene like that playing out for Howard in Australia, or for any other Australian prime minister in New York for that matter.

For all that the two governments had in common, the tempo between Howard and Bush really accelerated just before the terror attacks on September 11, 2001. In an amazing bit of timing, Howard was in Washington giving a press conference at the Willard Intercontinental Hotel as one of the jets hijacked by the terrorists crashed into the Pentagon and the smoke rose, visible in the windows behind him. He had had his first meeting with Bush the day before. In an apposite piece of timing, Howard was in America to celebrate the 50th anniversary of the signing of the ANZUS treaty in San Francisco in September 1951. The bonds of terror would draw Howard and Bush close. They would also draw Howard and the UK's Tony Blair close as Howard was in London when the July 7, 2005, terrorist bombings took place. In a joint press conference with Blair that day, Howard probably addressed a worldwide audience as big as any ever addressed by any Australian prime minister.

But it is the 9/11 attacks that have become the modern iconic moment. Everyone remembers where they were and what they were doing when the attacks took place. Downer recalls he was at home in Adelaide watching ABC TV's *Lateline* when Joshua Frydenberg, then a Downer staffer who worked on national security issues, rang him and said: 'Mate, switch over to CNN.'

Downer rang his then chief of staff, Mike Smith, and told him: 'This will change the world.' The then deputy prime minister John Anderson, who was acting prime minister while Howard was away, rang and Downer told him the Department of Foreign Affairs was getting a consular response in place to look after Australians in New York. Looking after Australians on the ground is always the first priority.

Downer woke his wife Nikki to come and watch the TV. They woke their children, who also got up to watch the unfolding events. Downer saw the second plane crash into the World Trade Center and the building subsequently collapse. The son of family friends was in New York but the Downers weren't able to get through to anyone in the US to help them locate him that night. Eventually Downer went to bed about 2.30am and was woken early next morning by TV trucks turning up in his garden.

I was actually in the middle of a telephone interview from my Sydney home with BBC Radio in London, denouncing the Howard government for its treatment of the refugee-filled boat the *Tampa* when the interview was interrupted by news of a plane crashing into the World Trade Center. Like Downer, I assumed at first it was a light plane in a terrible aviation accident, but when I switched on CNN I found it was something altogether different. I spent the next few hours watching and writing, in touch with my newspaper, *The Australian*, and putting together an analysis piece saying the obvious: this will change the world. My paper's editor, Mike Stutchbury, and a team of journalists worked all night, updating continuous special editions of the paper.

For Howard in Washington, events were moving rapidly. The US ambassador to Canberra, Tom Scheiffer, had gone back to the US for Howard's visit. His first priority was to make sure, with the Australian officials, that Howard was safe and properly looked after. Howard, his wife and senior members of his party were evacuated to a bomb shelter underneath the Australian embassy. Howard had been due to address Congress. Instead he was welcomed almost tearfully onto the floor of Congress in what was seen as a gesture of solidarity.

All planes in the US were grounded but the US provided Air Force Two to take Howard and the senior members of his party back to Australia. It was on that plane ride that Howard rang Downer. Both of them had come up independently with the idea of formally invoking the ANZUS treaty for the first time in its history. The NATO treaty similarly was invoked. On September 13, the National Security Committee of the Cabinet met in Howard's absence to consider the ANZUS question, but naturally left a final decision until Howard returned. Then, on September 14, the cabinet met and decided formally to invoke ANZUS.

It was a historic moment in the development of the alliance and it underlines the now global nature of ANZUS. The Howard government invoked ANZUS under Clause IV, which states: 'Each Party recognises that an armed attack in the Pacific area on any of the parties would be dangerous to its own peace and safety and declares that it would act to meet the common danger in accordance with its constitutional processes.'

Howard received near-universal support for the move. It was an Australian initiative but the Americans were very happy about it.

It was both symbolic and practical. When the Americans decided to take action against the Taliban regime in Afghanistan, which had sponsored Osama bin Laden and al-Qaeda, Canberra sent the SAS, which, as we shall see in the next chapter, performed magnificently and in one operation clearly saved the Americans a substantial loss of life at enemy hands.

But almost no one remarked that the wording of the ANZUS treaty did not in fact specifically cover the circumstances. The terrorist attacks occurred in New York, Washington, DC, and Pennsylvania. By no stretch of the geographical imagination could those locations be regarded as 'the Pacific area'. Clearly it would have been open to any Australian government to offer help to the US without invoking ANZUS, as Australia did in the first Gulf war and in the Vietnam war. ANZUS specifically talks of an attack in the Pacific. Therefore it is fair to conclude that ANZUS has been effectively reinterpreted to mean an attack on any of the parties anywhere.

This illustrates two important truths. One, the precise wording of a security treaty doesn't really matter very much so long as the broad intent, for the allies to help each other, is clear. No one will ever be limited, or compelled, by the wording of a security treaty but they will be influenced by the spirit and expectations which have grown up around it, and the accompanying political and military habits of consultation and collegiality. And of course they will be influenced by public opinion and their own assessment of what is right and wrong. And secondly, ANZUS may have started life as a regional pact for the Pacific but it is now a global pact, and the US and Australia, always remembering the limits imposed by Australia's size, are global security partners.

There was another way in which 9/11 brought Australia and the US together. Australians died in the World Trade Center. An attack on the US was also an attack on innocent Australians. Australians would die in many of the subsequent terrorist atrocities – in Istanbul, in London and of course in Bali where, in the first bombings in 2002, 202 people were killed, 88 of them Australians.

Paul Wolfowitz told me that many Americans considered Bali to be 'Australia's 9/11'. Howard was profoundly affected by being in America on 9/11. He saw first-hand the sense of shock and outrage and sudden vulnerability which the Americans felt. It helped him make the intellectual transition into the new strategic environment. He and Downer understood that 9/11 ushered in a new strategic era. Whether it caused a new era to be born or simply revealed something which had already quietly come about is not important.

There are three essentials of the new strategic environment. One is the existence of a global terrorist movement organised on an unprecedented scale and able to mobilise sympathisers in many parts of the world. Two is the existence of rogue states, semi-rogue states and divided states which are prepared to lend at least part of their state apparatus to the aid of the terrorists. And three is the growing ease of the technology of destruction, as 9/11 showed, and the ultimate possibility of terrorist nuclear strikes.

The strategic environment is also changed fundamentally because the mind of America is changed. It cannot tolerate the same risks as it tolerated in the 1990s.

The formulation used above is my own but it reflects the broad strategic sense of the government. In realising the degree to which 9/11 changed the strategic environment, Howard and Downer were well ahead of most of the community of strategic analysts and commentators in Australia, who were fiercely wedded to paradigms they had spent a professional lifetime developing.

The change in the American strategic mind was given further expression in the Quadrennial Defense Review released in February 2006. It makes clear that for the first time the US military is taking the war on terror as a central organising principle even for force structure. The decision in this document to substantially increase the size of US special forces surely owes something to the experience of working so closely with Australian special forces who were so effective in both Afghanistan and Iraq. The Pentagon calls the war on terror 'the long war' and compares it with the Cold War rather than World War II. In an interview with me, US Defense

Secretary Donald Rumsfeld dryly remarked: 'You won't see the war on terror finish with a signing ceremony on the USS Missouri.' He fully expected the war on terror to last decades.

The Pentagon's Quadrennial Defense Review also hailed the US's 'unique relationships' with the UK and Australia. It lauded the fact that those two nations' forces 'stand with the US military in Iraq, Afghanistan and many other operations'.

The decision by the Howard government to send Australian troops to Afghanistan aroused almost no partisan controversy. It was warmly supported by the Labor Party. In choosing to send the SAS, the government sent the most militarily useful contribution it could. Their extraordinary performance will be examined in the next chapter, but it is worth noting here that the US National Security Strategy of September 2002 (which became famous for outlining the doctrine of the occasional, presumably rare, need for pre-emptive war to stop terrorists from mounting attacks on the US) specifically drew attention to the Australian SAS, while at the same time recognising the significance of ANZUS being invoked. It commented: 'The attacks of September 11 energised America's Asian alliances. Australia invoked the ANZUS treaty to declare that September 11 was an attack on Australia itself, following that with the dispatch of some of the world's finest combat forces for Operation Enduring Freedom.' This is a level of tribute which, in the US National Security Strategy, is not even paid to the UK's forces. But for the purposes of this chapter these words also show clearly the way the US now interprets ANZUS – an attack on one ANZUS partner is an attack on the other.

The bonds of terror, certainly of the war on terror, drew Howard and Bush ever closer together, a process which only intensified as the years wore on. The bonds of terror also clarified, if they didn't altogether transform, the meaning of the ANZUS treaty. This is now a global treaty and it is as close a security alliance as there can be.

Chapter 3

AFGHANISTAN: THE FIRST AUSSIE BRONZE STAR SINCE VIETNAM

Operation Anaconda in Afghanistan was a turning point in the modern history of the Australian-US alliance. It was a minor turning point in US military history and a major one in Australian military history. It was certainly a pivotal and extraordinary moment in the life of the Australian Special Air Service Regiment (SAS). The SAS is the cream of the Australian military, Australia's special forces. The most hard-headed military men I've ever met, from the former US deputy secretary of state, Rich Armitage, who was himself an American special forces officer in Vietnam, to the former Israeli prime minister, Ehud Barak, one of the most decorated soldiers in Israeli history and also a special forces officer (men who are almost pathologically protective of their respective nations' claims to military competence and who don't give out military compliments freely) have told me plainly that the Australian SAS is as good as any special forces formation in the world.

Right after the end of major combat operations in Iraq in 2003, Armitage told me in an interview: 'The Australian SAS are shit-hot, and our people love to work with them.' The American coalition commander in Afghanistan, Lieutenant-General Frank Hagenbeck, said in a television interview: 'The Australian SAS displayed those kinds of things that make them the elite, in my view, of small-unit infantrymen throughout the world. And that's an autonomy, independence, tenacity that they will never ever be defeated.'

The National Security Strategy of the United States, issued in September 2002, described the Australian SAS in Afghanistan as 'some of the world's finest forces', a level of compliment not afforded to any other ally in that document.

An earlier American commander in Afghanistan put it a little more colorfully in a letter to the then commander of the Australian SAS, Duncan Lewis. US Marine Corps Brigadier General James Mattis wrote: 'We Marines would happily storm hell itself with your troops on our right flank.' And that letter was written just *before* Anaconda.

The significance of Anaconda lay in the fact that it was one of the largest conventional military operations in the war on terror, it all went terribly pear-shaped and could easily have resulted in the loss of many American soldiers and undoubted military humiliation for the US, and this tragic outcome was averted by the exceptional performance of the Australian SAS.

The Australian commander of the SAS in Afghanistan during Anaconda, Colonel Rowan Tink, was awarded the Bronze Star – the first Australian to receive this American award since Vietnam. The Bronze Star is awarded for distinguished combat service or conspicuous bravery in battle.

Tink's Bronze Star citation reads: 'For exceptionally meritorious achievement while serving as commander (of the Australian Task Group), Australian Defence Force, with Coalition Task Force Mountain in Bagram, Afghanistan. The commander's outstanding leadership, strategic and tactical proficiency, dedication to duty and commitment to mission accomplishment in a combat zone under the most extreme of circumstances greatly contributed to the success of Operation Enduring Freedom. The commander's performance of duty reflects great credit upon him, the Australian Defence Force and the members of the Coalition Task Force Mountain.'

But lest all this American praise seems like polished brass-stroking, not necessarily reflecting reality on the ground, consider this image. It's a peaceful image, from Afghanistan just after

Anaconda. The battle is over. Everyone's back at base. The dead are being mourned, the lessons of the battle learned. A large group of US soldiers is lined up at the mess for food. It's a fairly sound rule in life not to come between a soldier on active deployment and his food. But this day something very strange happens. A few Australian SAS men arrive and join the food queue. Suddenly the marines recognise them and the food line breaks up, the Australians are applauded and ushered to the front of the food queue. The Australians are served first. In its way this is as eloquent a testimony as ever you could find.

So just what was Anaconda? By now, the basic story line of Anaconda has been told several times in Australian and American books (not least in John Birmingham's well written *A Time of War*, Black Inc, 2005). It is in the process of entering Australian military folklore. But the bare bones of what happened are summarised here once more so that we can consider their significance to the Australian-US alliance, and to Australia's military disposition.

Before Afghanistan, Australian governments since the end of the Vietnam war in 1975 had been extremely reluctant to deploy Australian ground forces overseas for combat. Australia's commitment to the first Gulf war, in 1991, had been made by the Hawke government early. This was a shrewd move, in part designed to let Canberra off with a very light load. Early commitment, with its political assistance in generating international momentum for the American coalition, was traded against Australia not having to send ground troops or even air force assets to the combat zone. Canberra sent a couple of ships to steam menacingly around the bottom of the Persian Gulf and Washington was perfectly happy with that.

Since Vietnam, Australia had many times deployed its under-resourced army overseas, but only ever to peacekeeping-style missions, never to close combat in high-intensity environments. Australia still doesn't do that very often, except for the SAS. But throughout the 1990s Canberra was getting closer to doing it. The high prestige Aussie troops had earned in East Timor helped make the Howard government more willing to deploy them again, even though East Timor too was a peacekeeping operation not militarily or diplomatically opposed by the Indonesians. When Bill Clinton had contemplated a significant military strike against Iraq in the late 1990s, Canberra committed the SAS, but the American military action was called off.

After the September 11 terror attacks in the US the need to remove the Taliban regime in Afghanistan, which sheltered and sponsored al-Qaeda and its leader Osama bin Laden was obvious. The US military action against Afghanistan was entirely justified in self-defence, but also had the sanction of the United Nations, which helped with the domestic politics. The Australian deployment was supported by the Labor Party. Even the traditional anti-military minor parties were muted in their criticism. It was as bipartisan as could be.

Canberra ultimately sent three rotations of SAS troopers to Afghanistan, each comprising about 150 men. Both the Afghanistan and Iraq campaigns were waged by US Central Command, CENTCOM, which is headquartered in Florida but has responsibility for the Middle East. Australia, because of its geography, naturally interacted mostly with US Pacific Command, PACOM, based in Hawaii. So a lot of CENTCOM folks didn't have an intimate knowledge of Australian land forces and what they were capable of, especially given that most of what interaction Australia had had with CENTCOM was naval interaction, patrolling the Persian Gulf.

So many US allies are, in technology and training, so far behind the US that the US military often views allies, even NATO allies, as slightly Third-Worldish. The primary exception is the UK, whose armed forces are renowned the world over for their quality.

The Australian SAS in Afghanistan very quickly established its competence. It was the one part of the Australian army (an army which had been monstrously starved of resources over the years, as is explored in chapter 9) which was kept up to world's best standards, in a high state of readiness, given adequate equipment and superb training.

The Australian SAS has a mystique about it and this mystique itself is a valuable military asset. Not to put too fine a point on it, the SAS is feared by potential adversaries. It is modeled on the British SAS and until the Afghanistan campaign the Australian government was almost obsessively secretive about it. Its personnel and its methods were not to be known. One of the many consequences of Anaconda was that the Howard government somewhat changed this policy, in part because the Americans were themselves describing Anaconda in detail to their own media and did not omit the Australian role. Canberra ultimately decided that the feats of arms of the SAS were so remarkable that they needed to be told. Undoubtedly the government also saw a political advantage to having such an important Australian institution publicise its achievements. Thus the News Ltd journalist, Ian McPhedran, was given great access to SAS personnel for his ground-breaking book *The Amazing SAS* (HarperCollins, 2005). And in the preparation of this book I also interviewed a number of serving and former SAS men, on and off the record.

The Australian public love their armed forces. Polls consistently show the Australian Defence Force (ADF) as the most trusted institution in Australia. Nonetheless the ADF has a lot of trouble recruiting enough people even to meet its modest targets. A lot more people apply to join, or at least make inquiries about joining, than get let in. Many don't meet the physical or educational standards required. One of the few cohorts from which recruitment is very high is the sons and daughters of servicemen. The ADF in many ways really is a family. Its men and women disproportionately marry each other, and their sons and daughters disproportionately enlist. Another group that enlists disproportionately is rural Australians, especially the sons of farmers. The other cohort that tends to enlist in big numbers is school cadets.

Rowan Tink fits these profiles to an astonishing degree. I met him at *HMAS Kuttabul*, the naval base somewhat oddly located in Sydney's red-light district, Kings Cross. He has a great deal of military in his DNA. His uncle, having survived Tobruk in 1941, was killed at El Alamein in 1942, a victim of friendly fire, that is, misdirected fire from his own side. Tink's great uncle was killed in World War I. Tink himself grew up on the family farm at Dubbo, but the farm was sold half-way through his schooling. He was a student at Sydney's elite Scots College and an enthusiastic member of the school cadets. Almost all the boxes ticked.

Tink is a bit bigger than most Australian SAS men that I've encountered. The day I met him he looked tanned, muscular and supremely fit, having earlier that day been for a run around the Opera House. The average body shape for an Australian SAS soldier is a bit different from that of the US special forces. A British defence minister once described the American special forces to me as being like super infantry, bigger, stronger, tougher and certainly with specialist skills. They specialise in smashing down a wall, smashing an enemy, rescuing a hostage or whatever the mission is, achieving their goals very fast, going in and coming out very fast. The Australian SAS, like its British progenitor, really emphasises an altogether different role and produces a somewhat different soldier.

The Australian SAS is really designed for the traditional task of long-range reconnaissance and patrol. The emphasis is on durability, endurance and independent action. As one SAS man put it, having a sense of an internal locus of control is a key psychological trait for an Australian SAS man. Thus the Australian SAS is trained to operate in very small units and infiltrate behind enemy lines to undertake covert patrols and surveillance for as long as necessary. Real big blokes are not necessarily perfect for this, because they need too much food, whereas a key requirement is self-sufficiency in the field. As far as I can see from contact with an admittedly small sample, the typical Australian SAS man is lean and wiry and can survive on almost nothing for as long as it takes.

The Australian SAS did a lot of long-range patrolling and surveillance, often in hostile territory, throughout their involvement in Afghanistan. They very quickly won the respect of the Americans. Apart from anything else, they had their own equipment, especially their tough, durable, long-range patrol vehicles, which the SAS men could keep going in all conditions. One Australian patrol in Afghanistan stayed out for a very extended period, weeks and weeks, sending back invaluable intelligence.

Another difference between the cultures of the US special forces and the Australian SAS is the US emphasis on technology. The typical Australian description here can be self-serving but it goes something like this. The Americans can tend to be a bit entranced by their own technology, as they have so much of it and it is so advanced compared to everyone else's. The Australian culture, though naturally wanting the best technology it can get, tends to focus more on the soldier than the machine, especially in the SAS. The Australian way is more inclined to have human eyes gather the intelligence, the American way is more inclined to have a spy plane taking pictures.

As well as long-range reconnaissance and surveillance, the core tasks of the SAS include offensive operations, recovery operations and counter-terrorism in all environments – at sea, in the air, on land.

Finally, the American system is just so big that it understandably tends to go in for very precise specialisation, even among its special forces. Thus there are US special forces trained for the sea, others for the snow, others for the desert. The Australian SAS is so small that it has to be generalist, it has to train for everything. The SAS does mountain and cold-weather training in Australia and New Zealand, although these conditions are not to be compared with Afghanistan. It also trains in the snows of Norway. Those who argue for the narrow Defence of Australia doctrine – that our forces should only be configured and trained for the narrow continental defence of Australia – would regard this as a ridiculous waste of time and money. But as it turned out, the SAS had to operate extensively above the snow line in Afghanistan and the training they had done saved their lives and the lives of others as well.

All these factors would come together in Anaconda.

Tink was the right man to be in charge of the SAS in Afghanistan at the time of Anaconda. Even by military standards he is blunt and plain-spoken, not at all crude, but he gets to the point quickly, and insists on the point if he thinks he's right. It is a quality that hasn't universally made him friends, even in Canberra. Some of the Americans found him too feisty for their taste, insisting that the Australians would do things the Australian way. US Major Paul Wille, who was involved in planning Anaconda, described him as 'a pain in the butt sometimes'. In one published American account of Anaconda, Tink is described as 'difficult'.

Tink has even been known to make a political comment. During a media visit to Bagram in 2002, Tink was asked about what motivates him. He said in part: 'On September 11, 2001, the world saw the depths to which a terrorist organisation will stoop. Let no one doubt that an organisation like al-Qaeda is evil. Given the chance, they will kill you, they will kill me, they will kill our families, they will kill our friends, they will kill our countrymen and they will kill the freedom-loving people of this world.' There is nothing exceptional about these comments except that they come from a senior serving soldier. Tink clearly has a tendency to speak his mind.

It's important not to misconstrue all this. Tink had an excellent relationship with the Americans. At all stages they wanted him there and they wanted the SAS there. They came to have the highest possible regard for Tink, as is evident in the award of the Bronze Star. But anybody who thinks Australian commanders dealing with Americans simply do as they are told, or are overawed by the Americans, has just never encountered Rowan Tink. He was concerned above all to ensure that the operations he was involved in were effective, and that his men were not exposed to unnecessary risk. While he was in command, Sergeant Andrew Russell was killed when his vehicle ran over a landmine. This was a tragedy. That there were no other Australians killed in Afghanistan under Tink, and specifically none killed in Anaconda, is much more than good luck. It reflects the high quality of the SAS soldiers themselves, and the high quality of Tink's leadership.

The basic story of Anaconda is simple enough. Anaconda took place in late February and early March 2002. It was an operation named after the giant snake, because it was supposed to crush the enemy to death between different, converging coalition forces in Shahikot Valley, where it was believed some high-value al-Qaeda and Taliban leaders were hiding. It was the main conventional coalition military operation after the fall of Kabul. In fact it was the biggest coalition operation of Afghanistan, involving nearly 2000 coalition troops, including about 100 Australians. It was designed to root out and destroy elements of the Taliban and al-Qaeda taking shelter in the Shahikot Valley. The idea was that a combined force of Americans, Afghans and other coalition partners, including a very few Australians, would drive at night with lights out into the valley to attack the enemy. In a precisely coordinated move, the enemy's positions would be pounded from the air. Then helicopter-borne US troops, again with a very few Australians, would be delivered by air and join in the fight. Those enemy combatants not killed in the first encounters would try to escape through various tracks and trails, and across one main sector of these in the south the main body of the Australians would be waiting for them.

The operation went wrong from the first. The Afghan vehicles were no good and the convoy soon got bogged down and separated from each other. It came under withering attack from an enemy force much stronger and more numerous than anticipated. The early aerial bombardment of the enemy, who were well entrenched in tunnels and caves, was ineffective. The first American helicopter was driven off by ferocious enemy fire, but not before a US soldier fell from the helicopter. He was immediately captured by Taliban forces and shot. Other American helicopters came back to rescue their fallen comrade and two helos were shot down, with six Americans killed and about a dozen others wounded. The intensity of enemy fire meant that another daytime rescue bid was out of the question. So 36 Americans, essentially surrounded by a substantial Taliban force, had to wait until nightfall to be rescued, all the time fighting off fierce attack.

The Australians distinguished themselves in several critical ways in this battle. First, and perhaps most important, small SAS patrols had entrenched themselves high in the mountains above the valley to provide, as the SAS call it, 'overview of the battle'. This meant that they could observe what was happening much more comprehensively and much more accurately than anybody else. They could see not only the fallen Americans, they could also see the different Taliban forces heading in for the kill. This was critical. As a result, thousands of feet higher than human beings are supposed to operate at, in extreme cold, suffering altitude sickness, with frozen water bottles and bloodied noses, the SAS patrols remained undetected throughout and called in precise American air strikes to engage the Taliban and al-Qaeda forces away from the trapped Americans. In the conditions, the US spy planes could not see the Taliban and al-Qaeda in sufficient detail to be effective. In this particular situation, American technology would not do the job. Only a highly trained and supremely fit human being could do the job, although it is worth noting that the SAS men were not specialists in operating at those sorts of altitudes. It is a perfect illustration of the utility of what the SAS is classically trained to do – long-range, hidden, independent, constant surveillance – to see, hear, know and understand your environment. The American reliance on technical surveillance has diminished that capability in their own special forces. The Americans in the valley were vastly outnumbered. Without the SAS patrols they would certainly have been massacred in what would have been not only a human tragedy but a colossal disaster for the US military.

In another incident in Anaconda an American company with two Australian SAS men attached became isolated on a steep slope and came under ferocious fire. Many men dropped their heavy packs and ran for cover, literally ran for their lives. SAS trooper John Wallace, with all the extreme physical fitness, training, presence of mind and capacity for instant judgment that an SAS man should have, kept his pack and made it to cover. Keeping his pack kept him and the Americans with him alive, as in his pack was the radio equipment needed to keep in communication with the base. This allowed Wallace to inform the base of precisely where he and his comrades were located and where the attacks on them were coming from, which in turn enabled precise air strikes to continue all through the daylight hours until they were rescued under cover of darkness. Wallace was awarded the Australian Medal for Gallantry.

Anaconda lasted more than two weeks. The main body of the Australian SAS were there for the whole show and did everything that was required of them in the south, including directing American air fire into the valley and participating effectively in what combat came their way.

Anaconda changed the relationship between the Australian and US militaries. It marked the moment at which the Americans decided they wanted the SAS with them as a matter not of coalition politics but of operational priority. However, the military politics in the lead-up to Anaconda were important because they affected the outcome of the operation.

'I arrived in Afghanistan on January 29', Tink recalled. 'At this stage we had one SAS squadron and a regimental headquarters (in Afghanistan) and a logistics tail back in (a nearby regional country) for a total force of about 150. I was there six months and left on July 20. I was in Afghanistan the whole time and in command for that whole period.'

Tink and his men were initially working with a US Marine Expeditionary Unit. Most of the American special forces were in the north, operating with the Northern Alliance. As usual, the Australians got on very well with the marines. Later, shortly after Tink arrived but before Anaconda, the marines pulled out and the Australians were put in with a command called K-BAR, a US-led assembly of several nations' small special forces and sometimes just ordinary infantry units. The Australians didn't like this arrangement very much. It was too ad hoc and the forces were too diverse. Some didn't have suitable vehicles and had to be given everything by the Americans. Others had their own vehicles but didn't want to deploy them. Others were notionally special forces but in reality their nations had lost the special forces culture. With the British special forces by this time gone, the Australians were unique in being the only non-Americans who were fully equipped and didn't need anything more from the Americans.

'The marines were in the process of leaving. Maybe they saw Anaconda coming and didn't want to be part of it. Maybe it was because they'd completed the insertion phase and that's their primary role. The direction I got about mid-February was that we should pick up sticks and return to (a nearby regional country) for an operational pause.'

The military is such a big beast that it is always complicated. Tink had three lines of reporting – to Brigadier Ken Gillespie in Kuwait, to General Duncan Lewis in Sydney, and in-country, first to Mattis and then to K-BAR. It would have been reasonable for the Australians to take an operational pause at that time. They'd already done good work in Afghanistan, demonstrated Australia's commitment and earned the Americans' trust. Many of their number had worked through severe Afghan winter conditions. The marines they had worked with were going.

'We were approaching the end of operations deadline of February 10 and waiting for ministerial approval for the pause. At the end of January the US started to obtain information that al-Qaeda was concentrating in the (Shahikot) Valley area. On at least two occasions the Russians had tried to attack in that valley and got badly hurt.'

Tink's men were the only significant non-American force left in the area and the Americans didn't want them to go away: 'I was insisting on the operational pause because those were my orders. There was also a lot of scuttlebutt at the time to the effect that the SAS might be deployed to other countries with concentrations of al-Qaeda. Then I picked up the first hint that Anaconda was in the wind.

'On February 13, I was given access to the draft operational order for Operation Anaconda, a five-phase operation to eliminate al-Qaeda and the Taliban in that area. There was a request for Task Force 64, that's us, to participate, to use our knowledge of the area and our vehicles. We used long-range patrol vehicles. The Americans lacked long-distance vehicles in this area. Our vehicles gave us the capacity to stay in the field for weeks.

'I'm picking up that this will be a major operation and going back to Gillespie and Lewis saying the operational pause is not a good idea. The Americans were offering me a front-row seat. Some officers would get excited about a front-row seat. Let me tell you, I was one of them. Some would be less keen because major operations are likely to produce casualties.

'The way it was shaping up, I could be an independent force in Anaconda, not just part of K-BAR. I was keen to pursue the idea of an independent task force.

'On February 14, I took a Black Hawk helicopter flight from Kandahar to Bagram to attend a planning session for Anaconda and provide advice. I did not yet have permission to participate in Anaconda so I was walking a fine line. The flight was freezing, flying at low levels all the way through snow fields. I took an Australian intelligence officer. My offsider and I were the only foreign (non-American) participants in that conference. D-Day at this stage for Anaconda was scheduled for February 22 – eight days away. I sent my 2-I-C to Bagram to join the planning group because this was moving so fast.'

A New Zealand operational concept was rejected because the New Zealand forces lacked the necessary equipment. The Germans were well equipped and had their own vehicles but had really lost the special forces culture.

Even though a great strength of the Australians was that they were self-sufficient in equipment, nonetheless Tink said: 'The US was attempting to push assets at us at this stage, such as J-Stars, an airborne sensor capability of very limited use to us. I had to be resolute and say to them, we've got what we need.'

As Tink grappled with operational planning, he confronted an issue his uncle who died at El Alamein would have understood only too well: 'I didn't want my guys in unnecessary danger. Our prime concern was coalition fratricide – friendly fire from the Americans.

We very easily could have had blue-on-blue incidents where the Americans could have fired on us. I was dogmatic on our having our own area of operations and that we control what comes into it and even control US aircraft if they're going to drop anything.'

Tink was in an unusually strong position. The Americans wanted meaningful coalition participation. The Australians were their only option. Tink could insist on what he wanted. He was vindicated in the end. Tink is quite clear what the success of the SAS's efforts in Anaconda meant to the alliance: 'The Americans viewed us differently after Afghanistan.'

Preventing friendly fire incidents was an abiding obsession with Tink for his whole time in Afghanistan, even long after Anaconda: 'During a contact on about May 16 a single American gunship came in to support us. I sat myself in the air shell and listened to all the communications. I exercised where needed the power of veto. At the end of it, the Americans were so impressed with our methods of control they implemented them themselves.'

That particular incident, however, was very fraught. The American gunship saw a group of people it thought were enemies and wanted to fire on them: 'Our squadron leader said don't give him that authority, and it turned out they were friendlies. I didn't want to give this guy permission to fire on anyone more than necessary. Otherwise there would have been a lot more people killed.'

These kind of split-second decisions are unavoidable in warfare. Part of what made Tink a good leader in Afghanistan was his determination to know everything it was possible to know, in real time, and take responsibility for the decision himself.

The lead-up to Anaconda was frenetic and proper joint planning suffered partly as a result. Tink's commanders still wanted him to pull out soon. They gave permission for Anaconda thinking it would end more quickly than it did. Meanwhile the kick-off date for Anaconda kept slipping. Ultimately, the Australian SAS operational involvement in Anaconda ran from February 26 to March 13: 'The Australians were the only ones who stayed the whole time.'

The feats of endurance were incredible. One Australian sergeant, for 10 days straight, directed American strikes into the valley for 22 hours a day. It was performance like that, at the very breaking point of human capability, which saved many American lives.

It was not until midnight on February 21 that Tink actually got formal permission to participate in Anaconda but he was told he had to be out by March 10. As we have seen, the battle did not allow that. The role of the main body of the SAS was in the south of the area: 'Our role was to provide a screen or blocking force on the south to prevent al-Qaeda from escaping. We initially sent in two troops of 25 and then sent in the third troop as well. We knew it was difficult to go in without being compromised so we held back about 30 kilometres behind our positions. We went in at night on about February 28. Then on March 1 we moved our vehicles in an overt fashion as back-up. We wanted al-Qaeda in the valley to know we were there so they'd think twice before coming our way.'

Given the small number of troops he was dealing with there was a bit of bluff involved.

At one point, before Anaconda kicked off, a US task force wanted to withdraw through the Australian area. Tink wouldn't operate the areas until the Americans were gone and some Americans were affronted by this: 'The American officer involved offered a time and space separation (of US forces from Australian forces). The US officer believed the measures I was insisting on were not necessary and were just against the proper pecking order. The answer is I did not operate our positions until they withdrew. I wanted better than just to wait for an hour. They ultimately withdrew to positions we were going into, not in the direction they said they were going to. If we'd gone in as they said we'd have hit each other head-to-head.'

It was difficult negotiations like these that led some Americans to describe Tink as difficult, or 'a pain in the butt', but the Americans also came to respect his judgment: 'Once the Americans realise we are not the typical run-of-the-mill foreign military they're used to dealing with they'll treat us with the level of respect we believe is appropriate. There have to be certain issues you won't compromise on, such as safety.'

The SAS has an exchange program with the Americans and the British, and it is yet another example of this extraordinarily intimate three-way partnership that this should be the case. The special forces of each country highly guards its operational secrets, yet these are freely shared among the three via the most intimate process of all, having the special force soldiers of one nation serve in the forces of the others. Tink himself spent two years in the early 1980s with the renowned US Navy SEALS. At any one time there are normally two Americans and one Brit serving in the Australian SAS. The Australian on exchange with the Americans is normally stationed with the US First Special Forces Group, which trains for southeast Asian conditions. The level of trust has risen over the years so that it is now much more common to have soldiers from one country on exchange actually deploy into missions with the other country. Each such deployment has to be approved at the highest level in each country, but such approval is nowadays generally forthcoming. These are not just training deployments.

This chapter has focused heavily on Anaconda but of course the Australians did many other things in Afghanistan. After Anaconda the Americans were keen for the SAS to stay involved and Canberra sent a third rotation in and kept the SAS in Afghanistan until the end of 2002. They would go back on another rotation a couple of years later.

The coalition headquarters the Australians reported to in Afghanistan was not a special forces headquarters but a conventional headquarters. That's unusual in the culture of special forces but it actually had the effect of broadening the impact of the SAS's actions and changing the Australian-US army-to-army relationship. Australian-US military cooperation has a long history, going back to World War I, and in some limited senses even beyond that.

In the great scheme of history, Anaconda was not a huge battle but it was a pivotal moment in modern Australian warfare. It convinced the Australian government just how good the SAS really is and how effective deploying them can be. It convinced the government to be more open about the SAS. It was the largest and most significant land battle Australia had been involved in to that point since the Vietnam war. It paved the way for the even more extraordinary performance of the SAS in Iraq. It also convinced the Americans of how good the Australian SAS is, that in some ways it does things that even the Americans don't do themselves. It changed the American outlook to one of wanting the Australians there whenever possible. It also led to the Americans doing some soul-searching about their dependence on technical means of gathering battlefield intelligence. The US Quadrennial Defense Review released in early 2006 announced a big increase in US special forces, and it is not drawing too long a bow to suggest that the experience of working with the Australian SAS played some role in this.

Anaconda itself was hard to judge in strictly military terms as a coalition operation, as opposed to the Australian element, which was clearly a success. A great deal went wrong with Anaconda. It didn't go anything like to plan but the best estimates are that it left 200 al-Qaeda and Taliban fighters dead and routed them from a stronghold. It was a fierce and bloody and terrible encounter. For a long time it hung by a thread. That thread was the Australian SAS. And that thread didn't break. And all the world saw.

Chapter 4

DIGGERS TO IRAQ: HOWARD JOINS THE BUSH FAMILY, AUSTRALIA PLAYS ITS RED CARD

How could an Australian foreign minister resist? The US secretary of state, accompanied by the assistant secretary of state for East Asia and sundry ambassadors, locked eyes with Australia's foreign minister, Alexander Downer. This was a serious moment and a serious request. The US was poised to take military action against Iraq and wanted Australia's support.

The Iraqis had not abided by what they agreed to, the secretary of state said. The US 'will not put up with it'. Iraq was 'jerking the US around'. If the US gave in now it would find itself in exactly the same position in three months' time.

Downer said Australia would support the US but he wanted to know what the US planned for 'post-Saddam'. The Iraqi opposition, Downer pointed out, was very divided. The secretary of state didn't answer the point directly but was more concerned to stress the pressure the US would put Saddam under. The US was working with the Iraqi opposition groups and planning for the future, the secretary of state said, but did not offer any details. Finally the secretary of state stressed the US was going to 'do it big and do it right'. The US would be 'screamed at' by the international community and would welcome Australia's support.

You can count on us, Downer said, or words to that effect.

Madeleine Albright was relieved. The date was November 15, 1998, and she had, she said, been speaking to the president, Bill

Clinton, about Iraq every five minutes. The conversation here recounted that she had with Downer took place at Kuala Lumpur, in Malaysia, where Albright and Downer were attending the annual Asia-Pacific Economic Cooperation (APEC) forum meeting.

The point in recounting this conversation is to demonstrate what a complex, difficult problem Iraq was for US governments all through the 1990s, and to demonstrate two subsidiary points of the highest importance. It was the Clinton administration, not presumably in thrall to neoconservatives, which changed US policy to one seeking regime change in Baghdad. And everyone across the Clinton administration, and across the international intelligence communities, believed that Saddam Hussein had WMDs (weapons of mass destruction).

Of course the military action which Albright was referring to in her conversation with Downer, which Clinton characteristically postponed, was to be a sustained bombing campaign ('do it big and do it right'), followed up by intimate work with Iraqi opposition groups to help topple Saddam, not a full-scale invasion.

Bush and his administration did not come into office determined to mount a ground invasion of Iraq. The thing that changed for the Bush administration was the 9/11 terror attack and the prospect of Iraq cooperating with terrorists, especially in the provision of WMDs. Even though that was a small possibility it was too big a chance to take after 9/11. It is easy to find plenty of anti-Saddam articles and speeches from the 1990s by the people who were to lead the Bush administration. That doesn't prove there was a conspiracy from day one to invade Iraq. It just shows that Iraq had been a big foreign policy issue for a long time and a lot of people had been chewing it over. Republicans generally were urging Clinton to be stronger on Iraq than he had been. But while alternative histories are by their nature unknowable, it is unlikely that the Iraq invasion would have taken place without 9/11.

History is likely to judge the Bush presidency predominantly on the way Iraq turns out. Assessments of the Howard prime ministership will also be influenced by the ultimate judgments on Iraq, but not to the same extent. Howard supported Bush for a slightly different combination of reasons from those which motivated Bush himself. That is another way of saying Howard legitimately took into account questions of managing the US alliance as one part of his matrix of decision making. Naturally, that was entirely different for Bush.

The former deputy secretary of defense, Paul Wolfowitz, the intellectual driving force in the Bush administration behind the invasion (whose views are considered in detail in chapter 6) has been pilloried for a magazine interview in which he said that the WMDs which Saddam Hussein was believed to hold were not the only reason for the US-led invasion, but the only reason all arms of the US bureaucracy could agree on, so that was the public justification. Really, Wolfowitz was only speaking commonsense in that observation. Any operation as big as the Iraq invasion will have a complex strategic context and a multiplicity of factors, a consideration of some of which argue for, and some against, the action in question.

As argued elsewhere in this book, the Bush administration was undisciplined and dysfunctional in the way its warring tribes kept arguing, publicly and semi-publicly, their divergent interpretations of Iraq and everything else, even after a common administration position had been reached. But that doesn't mean they acted in bad faith, or that their actions were unreasonable given all the facts as they, and most other governments in the world, thought they knew them. From all the comments and all the debate involving all the administration figures and the plugged-in think-tank people, it's clear there were several reasons for the Iraq operation.

The first was weapons of mass destruction. There had been a history of Saddam lying and cheating about his WMD programs through the 1990s. The United Nations inspection process had discovered large quantities of WMD materials which later Saddam could never convincingly account for.

Given the history of Saddam's lies and deceptions, intelligence agencies all over the world tended to interpret whatever evidence they got on the basis that Saddam was lying, because he was clearly not cooperating with the UN inspectors. The evidence, we now know, was not conclusive, but the only explanation of all the evidence that made sense at the time was that Saddam was concealing his WMDs. There was a compelling logic to that assumption. In 1991 at the end of the Gulf war, Iraq had been given 90 days to disarm itself of WMDs (Saddam was allowed to keep conventional weapons, with some restrictions). If Saddam had disarmed in terms of WMDs he could have exported as much oil as he wanted, kept his army fat and happy, and in due course begun clandestine redevelopment of his WMD programs.

Instead Saddam encompassed the destruction of his own regime by convincing his enemies that he was more dangerous than he really was. This is an extraordinary and bizarre thing to have done. It is a most unusual historical circumstance, although it is not absolutely unique. The Australian specialist on the Vietnam war, Steven Morris, a few years ago wrote a wonderful book, full of original scholarship, entitled *Why Vietnam Invaded Cambodia* (Stanford University Press, 1999). It established beyond any doubt that the Vietnamese were ideological supporters of Pol Pot and the Khmer Rouge until the latter began to attack them on their borders. Vietnam was a much bigger state than Cambodia and the Cambodian government ensured its own destruction by continually provoking the Vietnamese. It was irrational and self-destructive behaviour by the Cambodian government. Morris finds the explanation for Pol Pot's fantastic miscalculation in the deep reaches of Khmer Rouge ideology, which held that it was bound to triumph. In other words, some regimes behave against even the narrow interests of regime survival, which makes them almost impossible to interpret or predict.

Saddam was almost certainly not as irrational as Pol Pot. His internal hold on power, with a Shiite majority which despised his secular Sunni regime and a substantial Kurdish minority which also despised him, was based on the terror he inspired. This terror arose partly from the times when he had used chemical weapons against his own people. Similarly, a portion of his regional prestige – he was partly loathed, partly feared, partly admired in the region – came from the notion that he had defied the Americans on WMDs and survived. Thus he undertook specific actions which reinforced the international view that he had WMDs, when by cooperating properly with inspectors he could have established that he did not have WMDs.

Because Saddam ran such a tight, clan-based system of government it was extremely difficult to get intelligence informants from the top of his regime. He held knowledge so tightly anyway that many of his own senior people believed he had WMDs. Everybody of consequence internationally thought that Saddam had WMDs.

This is a point Howard has often made. Even France's Jacques Chirac thought Saddam had WMDs. There was, before the Iraq war, little disagreement about that but big disagreement about the way to cope with it. Ken Pollack, a former senior US national security official under Clinton, had at first supported the war but later became a vociferous and important critic of Bush's policy towards Iraq and the Middle East. He wrote a withering and much quoted article in *The Atlantic Monthly* (January/February 2004) decrying the failure of US intelligence in estimating Iraq's WMDs. But Pollack made the point in that article that the big European intelligence agencies were actually more alarmist than the US agencies. They believed Saddam had WMDs. Generally, they believed he had more WMDs than did the Americans, but their governments decided that containment was the way to deal with this.

A senior Australian official has told me that the intelligence on mobile biological laboratories, which turned out to be wrong, came from German sources. Germany and France thought that Saddam had WMDs but could be contained. The US and its allies and supporters thought he had to be confronted.

I have several times interviewed Martin Indyk, assistant secretary of state for the Middle East under Bill Clinton and later a fierce critic of the Bush administration. Although a partisan Democrat, Indyk stayed on for the first six months of the Bush administration to help with the transition and to maintain vital continuity on Middle East policy. He told me that on all the information he saw, including all the intelligence, he believed Saddam had WMDs. Sandy Berger, Clinton's last national security advisor, declared at the end of the 1990s: '(Saddam) will use those weapons of mass destruction again, as he has ten times since 1983.'

Pollack has written of attending a Washington meeting in 2002 on Saddam, a meeting which included more than a dozen former UN weapons inspectors. One of the senior people at the meeting asked if anyone present believed Saddam was not operating a secret centrifuge plant (part of a clandestine nuclear weapons program). No one did. (This account was reproduced in *Commentary* magazine in December 2005.)

It would be easy but tedious to produce a long list of those who opposed the war – governments, analysts, politicians, UN officials, intelligence agencies – who nonetheless shared the view that Saddam had WMDs. It is unreasonable to accuse the Australian agencies of an intelligence failure on this subject. To have got the matter right definitively, which no one else in the world did, the small Australian agencies, focused as they are on Asia and the Pacific, would have had to masterfully out-perform the intelligence agencies of the US, the UK, France, Germany, Israel and all the other experts on the Middle East. Official inquiries in the US, UK and Australia have cleared all three governments and their leaders – Bush, Blair and Howard – of fundamental misrepresentation of the intelligence. The three governments stretched some of the facts to breaking point, some specific points were highly coloured, they drew the maximum implications from the intelligence, but the basic question is: did the intelligence agencies sincerely believe Saddam had WMDs? The answer is yes.

These inquiries made many other ancillary criticisms of their governments and the relevant intelligence agencies, but they established conclusively that, in terms of genuinely believing Saddam had WMDs, Bush, Blair and Howard acted in good faith. The decision to go to war was not an intelligence decision but a political decision, but it would not have been taken if the governments had known the truth of Saddam's WMD capacity.

So the assessment was a mistake, but in all the circumstances it was a reasonable mistake. Nonetheless, the fact that the chief justification for the war turned out to be wrong undoubtedly compromises much of the rationale for the war. Western publics don't pay their governments to make honest mistakes on vital national security matters but to get it right. This whole experience will make it much harder if the US or anybody else ever again needs to take urgent action based on intelligence.

What, then, of the other reasons for going to war? The connection between Saddam and terrorists was, so the former US deputy secretary of state, Rich Armitage, told me before the war, 'at the top' of American concerns. There was never, as far as we know from all the evidence, a causal connection between Saddam and 9/11. But Saddam had long sponsored other arms of terrorism. Abu Nidal, the renowned terrorist of the 1970s, lived in Baghdad until he was murdered. Saddam sponsored the families of Palestinian suicide bombers. His regime cooperated with Ansar al-Islam, an extremist group with substantial connections with al-Qaeda active in northern Iraq, which Saddam did not control, before the war. It is still unclear how deep Saddam's connections with al-Qaeda were, although there were certainly connections. The fact that he ran a secular regime which al-Qaeda did not approve of does not mean they would not have cooperated against the larger common enemy – just as the Nazis were for a time in alliance with the Soviets, despite their hatred of communism. History is replete with such alliances. As more documents from Saddam's government are translated, his connections with terrorists appear greater than was commonly thought immediately after the war.

The former head of counter terrorism on the US National Security Council under both Clinton and Bush, Richard Clarke, believed the US was wrong to invade Iraq and in his post-war writings downplays the association between Baghdad and al-Qaeda. Nonetheless, in his book attacking Bush, *Against All Enemies* (Free

Press, 2004), Clarke records that he, like everyone else of consequence, believed Saddam had WMDs. Clarke also believed Saddam had connections with terrorists, and had engaged in some sponsorship of al-Qaeda.

There was also the problem of sanctions. Saddam was subject to sanctions because he refused to verifiably disarm in accordance with his own promises and United Nations Security Council resolutions after the Gulf war in 1991. But the chief victims of the sanctions were the Iraqi people. Saddam used their suffering for propaganda. It was often claimed in the Western media that 500 000 Iraqi children had died because of the sanctions. US policy makers came to the view that sanctions could not be sustained indefinitely, morally or practically. If they were removed unconditionally Saddam would have won a great victory and been free to resume at full pace his WMD programs. But if sanctions continued his people suffered. Driving him from office was an alternative to the suffering caused by sanctions.

There was also undoubtedly among some in the Bush administration a feeling that US credibility had been dented by Saddam's long defiance.

There was a wider geo-political view, associated most widely with Wolfowitz, that an Iraq free of Saddam could quickly become a tolerable semi-democracy, as the quasi-independent Kurdish areas in the north had been for some time. This, it was hoped, would introduce a democratic contagion to the broader Middle East political culture. Wolfowitz in particular argued that this political culture was so dysfunctional that it needed to be changed. This is not to suggest the US ever contemplated a series of Iraq-style wars. Iraq was always sui generis.

Connected to this was the general view that Saddam was one of the most brutal and totalitarian tyrants of the 20th century and it would be a blow for the human rights of Iraqis to liberate them from his rule. Undoubtedly, too, some US strategic optimists hoped that Iraq would become an ally of the US and offer it an alternative to its dependence on Saudi oil.

Howard's justification for the action in Iraq was always fairly narrow. He was clear that the primary justification for action was the threat of Iraqi WMDs. He and Downer also did argue the human rights case and they did argue that part of the Australian decision was about alliance management, but they were explicit that the main justification was WMDs. There is absolutely no evidence that they ever thought the WMD claim untrue. I have interviewed a number of Australian soldiers who were deployed to Iraq. Chemical and biological weapons hazards were prominent in their minds. The Australians took every possible precaution against such weapons and much of their preparation involved dealing with these potential hazards.

Howard's alliance management considerations had two dimensions: one, earning credit from the Americans for a relatively small but effective military commitment to a cause which Howard believed to be just; and two, reassuring the Americans that they did not have to undertake every difficult task alone, thus encouraging them to continue to shoulder the burden of security. Howard, as described elsewhere in this book, was influential in convincing Bush to try to get explicit United Nations Security Council approval for the Iraq action. Bush and Howard and Blair argued that approval was implicit in pre-existing UN Security Council resolutions on Iraq, but Bush mounted an effort, which failed spectacularly, to get a 'second' UN resolution authorising action.

Howard, and every part of the Australian system, especially the Australian Defence Force, had much less success in trying to influence US post-war planning.

The failure in US post-conflict planning for Iraq was the most egregious American failure in the entire Iraq operation, worse even than the intelligence failure over WMDs because it was entirely avoidable. The worst single scandal of the war for the Americans was the shocking abuse of Iraqi detainees at the Abu Ghraib prison. But the state of the prison, undermanned and badly run, was a part of the overall planning failure.

Australian leaders were shocked that before the war the US military headquarters under General Tommy Franks was in Qatar and the US civilian headquarters, which would temporarily run Iraq after conventional conflict was finished, was in Kuwait, under Jay Garner, and the two headquarters did not have a direct electronic link.

Investigations for this book showed that Australians made repeated efforts to get the Americans to focus on post-conflict planning in a more coherent way, but were unsuccessful. Indeed the conversation quoted above between Downer and Albright prefigures many conversations Australians would have with US officials in 2002 and 2003. As late as February 25, 2003, a month before the war began, Downer met with the then US secretary of state, Colin Powell, at the Hyatt Hotel in Seoul, South Korea. Both men had a raft of officials and ambassadors with them. The conversation confirms that while Australia had pre-positioned troops and was always overwhelmingly likely to go in with the Americans, it had not made a formal, final decision to join the operation. Downer told Powell that when the time came it was important for Bush to ring Howard and request a contribution to the military effort. Then the Australian cabinet would make a formal decision.

But Downer wanted to talk about Phase Four – the 'postbellum' period, the peacekeeping and nation-building phase, about which Americans were so uncomfortable. Downer urged Powell to maximise the role of the United Nations. Downer understood that this was sensitive and the US inter-agency process was in full swing on it, but a UN role would help answer the concerns of countries like Indonesia and Malaysia. Malaysia's leader, Dr Mahathir, was a 'write-off', Downer said, and best ignored.

Powell said Mahathir was 'so far out on the edge, he has made himself irrelevant'. Powell even thought that if Mahathir was going to be bad, it was good that he was being as bad as he was.

Downer told Powell that Indonesia was a more serious country. Downer argued that the more the UN was involved, the more many countries would embrace the new order in Iraq. Otherwise it would be a 'hard sell' internationally. Downer knew the UK was already putting this position to the US. Downer cited the case of East Timor, where the UN had been effective.

Powell said General Franks would be in command in Iraq for a short while. (As it turned out Franks left almost as soon as the conventional fighting was over.) Powell admitted the debate inside the US administration was between those who wanted to hang onto the administration of Iraq and those who wanted to internationalise it. In a badly mistaken judgment, Powell thought those arguing for internationalisation were winning. But the endpoint was clear: Washington did not want a US general commanding a Muslim nation, Powell said. The US army itself, he was sure, did not want to hang around Iraq. Powell didn't go so much for the East Timor comparison, pointing out that Iraq was a bit more complicated than East Timor. He also said it was important the US not just let the nation fly to pieces.

This was a significant conversation. It showed Downer in a coordinated push with the UK to get a particular outcome – the greatest UN involvement possible in post-war Iraq. It showed Downer's concern with the post-conflict planning. It showed the confusion and indecision in the Bush administration regarding the post-conflict phase, with Powell believing wrongly that the UN would be heavily involved early, that Franks would run Iraq for a short while and that the US would not be in post-war Iraq for long.

Downer went to Iraq itself in May, 2003, shortly after the finish of major combat operations. He met the head of the Coalition Provisional Authority, Paul Bremer, the man then in charge of Iraq, at the Australian Representative Office (later the Australian embassy) on May 23. The two had a meaty, lengthy meeting. Downer got on OK with Bremer but he had some clear messages he wanted to give him: the coalition should leave Iraq as soon as it could while leaving Iraq in a decent state; Australia believed expatriate Iraqi leaders who had spent long years abroad could not win the hearts and minds of the Iraqi people; and finally de-Baathification should not be overdone.

The Baath Party had ruled Iraq for decades and had been Saddam's political instrument, but Downer was against getting rid of too many of the top layers of the Baath Party. Downer said that 'slicing off the most egregious champions of an appalling regime' had to be done. But, as with the former Soviet Union, many former officials, Downer believed, would go with the flow of political change. Baath Party members, Downer told Bremer, should not be excised if they could contribute meaningfully to moving Iraq forward. Many Baath members would only have joined to advance their careers and protect themselves.

Bremer didn't entirely agree. A strong de-Baathification policy was popular, he said, and he envisaged de-Baathification affecting 15 000–30 000 people.

Downer also told Bremer it was important to consult the Saudis and Jordanians on how to manage Iraq because they were 'on our side'. Bremer agreed, but said Saudi-based Wahhabi organisations had been very unhelpful in Fallujah. He asked Downer if Australia could speak to the Saudis about this. Presumably the Americans were talking to the Saudis directly on this subject, but, as is so often the case in international diplomacy, they wanted friends and allies to reinforce the message.

Downer also suggested a political way forward to Bremer, emphasising local town representatives and governing councils. Bremer was sympathetic but non-committal.

Downer that day also met most of the Iraqi Leadership Council, including the future prime minister, Ibrahim Al-Jaafari and the future president, Jalal Talibani. Downer told them the coalition wanted to hand over power to the Iraqis as soon as possible and in particular Australia did not want to participate in the long-term running of Iraq. The Iraqis in turn complained about the political difficulties the Americans were putting them in by being slow about moving the political process forward, handing more power to Iraqis

These discussions were important because they showed Downer trying hard, despite the limited Australian resources committed at that time, to influence the outcome in Phase Four in Iraq. The Howard government's view of post-war planning and policy was closer to the State Department's than to the Pentagon's, and it didn't prevail. It has to be judged that although Australia tried hard it was not successful here, either before the war or during the occupation.

One area where it was much more successful was in its influence on coalition military policy during the conventional combat phase. The Australian forces themselves performed magnificently. The Australian SAS was among the first coalition forces to enter Iraq, it fought the first significant engagement. The regiment's weaponry, speed, precision and mobility saw it sweep across the western desert of Iraq, identifying targets for US air power, knocking out Iraqi installations, making sure no Scuds could be fired into Israel and destroying Saddam's command-and-control capabilities in their area. One of its main accomplishments was taking the huge Al Asad airbase, in which were discovered 57 Soviet-built Mig aircraft. Intelligence had indicated there would be just two such aircraft at the base. The SAS also found a great deal of WMD paraphernalia, although, of course, no actual stocks of WMDs.

In an episode of which their AIF forebears would have been proud, the SAS chopped up one of the Migs to ship home to Australia, with the idea of its becoming an exhibit at Canberra's War Memorial. However, word came from Canberra that this was not on. Don't bring home trophies like that. We have already seen (chapter 1) George W Bush thanking Australia for the work of the SAS in western Iraq. The decision announced in the US Quadrennial Defense Review, published in February 2006, to vastly increase the US special forces capability almost certainly owes something to the example of the Australians, for whom the Americans came to have the very highest regard. In terms of the alliance, Iraq drew the Australian and US militaries very much closer together.

However, it was not just the SAS: Australia played a crucial role in the coalition's targeting policy. This was done through then

Brigadier (later General) Maurie McNarn, who was the overall Australian force commander in the Iraq operation.

Critics sometimes ask whether the Australian Public Service ever produced a full scale evaluation of what the Iraq operation would mean for Australia's national interests. The answer is the Australian Defence Force did just that, in part so that they could propose operations and deployments, including a timeline and an exit strategy which would serve the national interest. It hardly need be said that this did not usurp the role of government, it merely provided the fullest and most coherent range of options to government.

For the duration of the conventional fighting McNarn was based in coalition military headquarters in Qatar. Among other things, McNarn served on the final targeting board, which approved what targets the coalition could hit, what individuals it could go after and what weapons it could use. This is an aspect of coalition war-fighting that is too little understood. In a coalition you are responsible not only for what your forces do, you are to some extent involved in a corporate responsibility for your allies. Of course, Australia had so much smaller a force involved in Iraq than either the Americans or the British that this should not be exaggerated. But each of the coalition partners, the US of course, the Brits and the Australians, had what became known as the red card. This was an ability to veto any target.

Things often moved at incredible speed. On one occasion there was a request for Australian F18s to hit a particular 'high-value' target straight away. Everything was checked out and approval given by McNarn and the F18 was on the job and firing within 23 minutes. But in some ways it was the acts of restraint where Australia made the biggest contribution to the Americans. There was a list of individuals the coalition partners designated as legitimate targets in their own right before the war began. The US had initially proposed a bigger list, but the UK and Australia substantially whittled it down. It speaks well to the credit of the US military that they stuck by coalition agreements, including the coalition veto, the red card.

Every night at headquarters in Qatar a group of the most senior commanders would gather. They would hold a secure video teleconference with all the other commanders in the different headquarters and of the different services (air force, navy etc). Each commander participating would have some staff backup with him. At this conference they would go through the list of targets nominated for the next day. McNarn had, among others, Australian intelligence officers and military lawyers with him. An independent intelligence assessment capacity was essential, and without the military lawyers he could barely have done his job at all. On a number of occasions McNarn played his red card. The first time he did it, it was a great shock to the Americans he was dealing with. But it also liberated some participating Americans who may have been uneasy about a particular target but did not themselves possess the red card power and may even have been cautious about speaking up against a plan devised by a fellow commander, or perhaps even someone more senior to them. Once or twice McNarn put his objections in writing, saying the proposed action was against the coalition's strategic objectives, militarily unnecessary and against the laws of armed conflict.

'Shit!' one American exclaimed when he saw this document. 'What if this leaks?' ... To which the Australian replied, well it won't matter if you don't take the illegal action, or words to that effect.

Once McNarn had put his objections in writing there was absolutely no question of the action being carried out. This became known as 'the Australian option'. Having put his objections in writing once or twice, McNarn didn't need to do so again. People wouldn't push him that far, in part because they didn't want the piece of paper. A lot of proposed targets were cleared by lower targeting boards before they came to the top targeting board, on which McNarn sat. This allowed a good deal of caucusing between the UK and Australia, who often had similar views. 'Do you want to take the lead on this?' was often a question one asked the other. On a couple of occasions McNarn's objections went all the way up to General John Abizaid or General Tommy Franks, but Australia's red card, the Australian option, was always respected.

Sometimes McNarn acted without the UK. Or with the UK merely remaining silent. Towards the end of the war the coalition was expecting a nasty fight to enter Baghdad, which did not eventuate. But the coalition was prepared for a serious battle. In one set of proposed operations McNarn vetoed three of five proposed US air force weapons systems. These were mainly huge bombs of different types. This led to an explosive reaction from one of the US air force officers present, who called McNarn a 'pencil dick'. McNarn in reply read from the US air force's own *Concept of Operations* document, which said that the particular bomb under question was not accurate for a radius of less than 16 metres and was unsuitable for use in a built-up area. The most senior American commanders ultimately ratified McNarn's judgment.

The story of the red card, or the Australian option, is not one of conflict between Australia and the US. It is a positive story about the effectiveness of coalition warfare. The Australians and the British involved in the targeting boards, especially the final targeting board, helped the Americans produce a more effective and ethical targeting policy. This is not because the Australians and the Brits were more effective or ethical soldiers than the Americans, but because they came in at the level of review with fresh and independent eyes and with decisive authority. Because they were operating as national commands in a formal military coalition, they had levels of authority which only their most senior American colleagues had. All military systems are hierarchical and it can be difficult for a military officer to challenge one of his seniors in a line of command. A friendly foreigner, an ally, enjoying the absolute confidence of his own government, can do so more readily and more effectively.

The Australian option, the red card, reflects well on Australian independence, forthrightness and expertise, but it also reflects well on the Americans and their willingness to make a coalition a meaningful arrangement. By committing to Iraq the Howard government gave the US military and political assistance which no one else in the world except the British replicated. The Australian and US militaries became powerfully closer as a result. Howard and Bush also became infinitely closer as a result. Howard, it might be said, joined the Bush family.

In an interview for this book Howard said he had worried a great deal in the lead-up to the decision on Iraq, and he was certainly surprised that no WMDs were found, but he had never regretted the decision on Iraq. Removing Saddam was moral justification enough, and it was important the Americans not think they had to do every difficult thing alone. That's another Australian option.

Chapter 5

INSIDE THE BELLY OF THE BEAST: THE BUSH FOREIGN POLICY FROM THE INSIDE

When George W Bush won his second term as president, the Office of National Assessments (ONA) in Canberra came up with an assessment of what his victory would mean for US foreign policy. It said, in part: 'Buoyed by his victory, Bush feels vindicated in maintaining his policies'. However, it was not very sanguine about Bush's prospects for a successful second term: 'Bush risks declining support at home and diminishing influence abroad. The departure of (Colin) Powell narrows Bush's range of advisers and strengthens Cheney.'

That last judgment has probably proven to be wrong. Condoleeza Rice has emerged as the dominant influence, after Bush himself, in the foreign policy of his second term, while the key neoconservative intellectual, the former deputy secretary of defense, Paul Wolfowitz, has departed the administration, after having a huge influence.

The ONA is a fine organisation, capably led. Like all of us it is fallible and the genius of democracy sometimes defeats it. This was particularly so in 2004. It mis-forecast the result of the Indian election which brought the Congress Party to power and Manmohan Singh to the prime ministership in May. Nor did it pick the socialist triumph in Spain (though that was certainly forgivable given how late sentiment turned after the Madrid bombings) in March. Then it had trouble analytically with the American election. For, in the months leading up to Bush's decisive triumph in November

2004, the ONA's reports tended to emphasise the difficulties Bush would have in securing a second term. This is not a criticism of the ONA. It just goes to show that even a process as open and as scrutinised as American politics has more than its share of mysteries and unpredictabilities.

If politics is like that, policy can be even more so. One Washingtonian once told me that policy inside Washington is like a football inside the biggest rugby ruck or maul you've ever seen. There are a lot of players exerting influence on it from a lot of different directions. Nobody is really controlling it until the ruck breaks up, although often you get rolling rucks and mauls. And from the outside, and from the inside too for that matter, it can be exceptionally difficult to see where the ball is.

It is not the purpose of this chapter to evaluate Bush foreign policy in the round so much as just to describe some of the players and influences in it. You have to conceive of the multiple parts of the American machine or any meaningful evaluation of US policies and actions is impossible.

When Harold Macmillan was asked what themes dominated his time as prime minister of the UK he replied with the single word 'events'. Events created by non-American politicians and forces have certainly been central to the development of the Bush foreign policy. Most democratic leaders are dominated by events. Only the totalitarian ruler has the power to remould a society to his will. The genius of a democratic leader lies in responding to events effectively in their own terms, and at the same time using the opportunities they inevitably bring to move the society along the path the democratic leader thinks it should take.

The transfixing event for Bush, of course, was the terror attacks on the United States on September 11, 2001. The difference between the pre-9/11 Bush and the post-9/11 Bush is evident in the first and second inaugural speeches, one delivered at the start of his first term, the other at the start of his second.

Before the 2000 election some of Bush's foreign policy spokesmen had deprecated nation-building and humanitarian military interventions. Bush himself had talked of pursuing a 'modest' foreign policy in which Washington did not try to tell other nations what to do. In the first inaugural address, delivered by Bush on January 20, 2001, foreign policy barely gets a mention. Bush, deep in his guise as a 'compassionate conservative', talks mainly about compassion and justice and opportunity at home. Terrorism is not mentioned, not once. There is a sentence about strong defences, a sentence about weapons of mass destruction, and the following general statement: 'The enemies of liberty and our country should make no mistake: America remains engaged in the world by history and by choice, shaping a balance of power that favors freedom. We will defend our allies and our interests. We will show purpose without arrogance.'

The second inaugural is Moses hurling thunderbolts down the mountain, infused with a searing vision of the threat of terror and the American mission to spread democracy and human rights around the world.

Bush said: 'After the shipwreck of communism came years of relative quiet, years of peace, years of sabbatical – and then came a day of fire ... We are led, by events and by commonsense, to one conclusion: The survival of liberty in our land increasingly depends on the success of liberty in other lands. The best hope for peace in our world is the expansion of freedom in all the world.'

Like rolling thunder, the calls for peace and human rights exploded through the speech: 'Across the generations we have proclaimed the imperative of self-government, because no one is fit to be a master, and no one deserves to be a slave ... Eventually, the call of freedom comes to every mind and every soul ... All who live in tyranny and hopelessness can know: the United States cannot ignore your oppressors. When you stand for your liberty, we will stand with you.'

Collectively, the world scratched its head and wondered what the speech meant. How 'forward-leaning', to use a favourite American expression, was Bush going to be about all this? As it turned out the answer was 'not all that forward-leaning'. The US would encourage democracy, human rights and freedom, but it certainly wasn't planning to impose it anywhere new. Whatever the speech heralded, it certainly did not herald a series of new Iraqs.

To understand how Bush got from inaugural one to inaugural two and to try to have some ability to predict future Bush foreign policy, it is necessary to have a sense of some of the different actors in his foreign policy and how their beliefs and personalities interacted with events.

It is not so easy to define the Bush administration ideologically. It is certainly not a simple case of suave, hard-headed realists advocating restraint against wild-eyed neoconservatives determined to impose US electoral law, Hollywood movies and co-ed college sports on the whole world.

Accepting that all systems of classification are inherently messy and contain a good deal of overlap and imprecision, I would nonetheless offer five primary, identifiable, policy types of consequence in the Bush administration: the muscular nationalists, the neoconservatives, the modest realists, the foreign policy machine men (and women) and the Pentagon uniforms.

So who was who in the zoo?

Vice President Dick Cheney and Defense Secretary Donald Rumsfeld were the chief muscular nationalists. Another important member of their group is John Bolton, who was under secretary of state in the first George W Bush administration and went on to become ambassador to the United Nations in the second. It is quite wrong to describe these men as neoconservatives. They generally were uncomfortable with humanitarian military interventions and were strongly averse to nation-building. Rumsfeld was completely obsessed with his techno-centric vision of a 'transformed' military which would be newer, lighter, more mobile, more hi-tech. If the US had kept confronting conventional state enemies in clean battles his vision would have had much to commend it. It was very poorly adapted to peacekeeping or counter-insurgency. Undoubtedly, the post-war mess in Iraq owed something to Rumsfeld's hi-tech vision for the military not matching the medium-tech needs on the ground. That military, many muscular nationalists thought, should be warriors, not peacekeepers. Let the US make the dinner, others can clean the dishes, was one oft-heard formulation. The problem was that no one else was volunteering for the peacekeeping role, and once the US had conquered a nation like Iraq it per force assumed absolute political responsibility for it. That meant peacekeeping and nation-building aplenty, ready or not.

Rumsfeld and Cheney were particularly close, having worked together as far back as the Nixon administration. Cheney, himself a former defense secretary, with a reputation for sagacity and hardheadedness, added gravitas to Bush's ticket in 2000 and became immensely influential with the president. In the first Gulf war in 1991, Cheney, as defense secretary, had seemed so calm and reassuring. Later, partly out of a desire never to be seen trying to upstage his boss, he kept such a low profile that he was portrayed as a sinister, shadowy figure. A lot of Washingtonians believed he had come to feel the first Gulf war was unfinished business – that Saddam Hussein should have been pushed from power.

The neoconservatives, on the other hand, generally approve humanitarian intervention, though like all Republicans they are inclined to oppose anything the former president, Bill Clinton, did. The neocons were found mainly in the civilian side of the Pentagon. Their most prominent figures were Paul Wolfowitz, and the former under secretary of defense, Doug Feith. They both left office at the start of the second administration. But their spirit lived on, mainly through the fallout of the actions to which they had helped commit the administration, and the influence of a group of extraordinarily articulate journalists and commentators – chief among them the brilliant Bill Kristol and Charles Krauthammer. The neocons in think-tanks and journalism are gifted controversialists and have huge influence among Republicans.

The term neoconservative deserves some explanation. It first described a group of liberal Democrats who were also liberal anticommunists. They opposed dictatorships everywhere and believed in democracy everywhere. But they became increasingly uneasy at the anti-Americanism of the anti-Vietnam war movement and the anti-anticommunism, which led many liberals to spend more energy denouncing anti-communists than analysing and combatting communism itself. The neocons were generally transfixed by the threat of the Soviet Union. They shared a strong literary inheritance and were bookish and cerebral in style. They believed in America's mission to export democracy around the world. They are willing to use force for humanitarian ends. In the 1960s and 70s they became, most of them, Republican.

Many of them were Jewish. The US Jewish community is traditionally a bastion of support for liberal Democrats. Often in the analysis of neocons a rather nasty stress is put on their support for Israel as America's ally and the only democracy in that part of the world, as though this view were explained by their religion. It is even joked that in the term neocon, con stands for conservative and neo stands for Jewish. At first the term had a slightly exotic glamour but later it became an abuse term to denote an action that was wild and self indulgently impractical.

The modest realists comprised Colin Powell and his deputy, Rich Armitage, and much of the State Department. Powell had spent most of his life in uniform and had the professional soldier's scepticism about the ease with which military power could produce precise political results. Because of his past service as chairman of the joint chiefs of staff, and national security advisor, and because of his warm personality and bearing, and his rise from humble origins, he became a national icon and the only member of the cabinet to have significant political capital beyond his relationship with the president.

Armitage was and is a great friend of Australia. He got on well with Downer and Howard but also had a long friendship with Kim Beazley, dating from the days when Beazley was defence minister in the 1980s and Armitage a senior Pentagon official. Christopher Meyer, the British ambassador to Washington for most of the George W Bush years, wrote of Amitage in his memoir *DC Confidential* (Weidenfeld & Nicolson, 2005) thus: 'Rich Armitage, one of the most impressive Americans I ever met, could not conceal his contempt for the bellicose civilians of the Pentagon who had never seen combat'. Meyer's assessment of Armitage as a human being is widely shared. Bald-headed, raspy-voiced, barrel-chested, Armitage loves Australia, dating from having met so many Australians during his three tours as a naval officer during the Vietnam war. One story from his distant past will suffice to give a sense of the man. By the end of the Vietnam war Armitage had left the navy. When it was clear that South Vietnam would fall to invasion by North Vietnam, Armitage was asked by the Pentagon to go back and evacuate the South Vietnamese navy. Armitage redefined South Vietnamese naval vessel to mean anything that would float, and naval personnel to mean anyone who could get on board. Without any formal authority from the Ford administration to redefine his mission that way, Armitage took well over 20 000 people to the Philippines with him, the first boat people, people who otherwise would have faced persecution under the communists, and virtually all of whom ended up living in the United States. It was an operation of extraordinary daring and bravery, and it was undertaken because Armitage is loyal to friends and allies.

Armitage was a great Asianist and held as doctrine that you should spend most time and attention on your closest allies. Thus his approach to Asia policy centred on Australia and Japan.

The uniformed people in the Pentagon, the senior military, tended to share Powell's caution about the use of military force. Many of them indeed felt a good deal of personal loyalty to Powell and Armitage. A number were uncomfortable with Rumsfeld's new vision of the military, and wanted, if they did deploy militarily, to do so in overwhelming numbers for a short, well-defined mission.

And finally there were the machine men and women. The two most important of these were Condoleeza Rice, national security advisor in the first George W Bush administration and secretary of state in the second, and Bob Zoellick, US trade representative in the first and deputy secretary of state in the second. And the third was Stephen Hadley, who was deputy national security advisor under Rice and then national security advisor in Bush's second term. Rice and Zoellick were committed Republicans. They had ideological convictions. They were in favour of freedom and against tyranny. But their temperament was inclined towards running a machine, covering the bases, solving a problem with more work rather than more inspiration. They were details people, workaholics, both good athletes who had the stamina for endless hours of grinding effort. In a sense, they were instinctive multilateralists, not so much ideologically but because multilateralism is the machine you work when you're a foreign affairs officer. Rice had been a Sovietologist and Democrat who thought Jimmy Carter was too soft on the Soviets. Zoellick had been brought into the big time by the former secretary of state, James Baker.

I had the immense good fortune to know or interview or meet in small conferences almost all the players mentioned above. Some, through their long involvement in Asia-Pacific issues, I have known for many years. They were an enormously formidable group of people, immensely experienced and, person-for-person, way better than their counterparts in the Clinton administration. I have no doubt of their high competence, high integrity and goodness of heart. But somehow they were unbalanced. Howard was surprised if not shocked at how the US principals would keep advocating their divergent positions even after a decision was allegedly made. Bob Woodward in his book *Plan of Attack* (Simon & Schuster, 2004) recounts that Cheney and Powell were barely civil to each other as Iraq unfolded. But there were enmities from the earliest days. Before the first administration was formed, Rumsfeld had a meeting with Armitage, who was being considered for the deputy secretary of defense post.

I have to tell you there's a less than 50 per cent chance you'll be given the job, Rumsfeld told Armitage, or words to that effect. 'You're wrong', Armitage replied. 'There's a zero per cent chance I'll take the job.

Many felt Rice should have been more assertive as national security advisor in banging heads together and reaching agreed positions and sticking to them. Others, in Rice's defence, say that a national security advisor can only do that effectively when a president exerts his own authority clearly and frequently. This is especially so when dealing with such powerful, experienced and formidable figures as Cheney, Powell and Rumsfeld. While Bush was willing to exert his authority occasionally, his non-interfering, chairman-of-the-board style was predicated on everyone getting on with their job without too much interference from the boss.

The rancour and disunity among the Bush national security team in the first term must be reckoned a big negative against Bush and a collective failure for all of the highly talented people involved.

The disagreements had acute, perhaps disastrous, operational consequences. Rumsfeld ignored State Department planning for post-war Iraq. Jay Garner, the US's first administrator in Iraq, told Robert Hill, the former Australian defence minister, in Baghdad just after the war that the US would only be there for six or seven weeks, which shows he was astoundingly out of touch with the reality he was dealing with. Just before the war, Powell was busy protecting his base in Washington when he should have been in Ankara or Istanbul in person, charming and cajoling the Turks into cooperating with the Americans and letting them enter Iraq from the north. Instead the Turkish parliament decided by just a couple of votes not to let the Americans have access from the north.

Of course, beyond the team mentioned above there were many other players in Bush foreign policy. There were his domestic political advisers, chief among them Karl Rove, who knew after 9/11 that the war on terror and the war in Iraq would define the Bush presidency. There were all the shifting power plays of Congress, with its powerful committee chairmen, all the different NGOs, the businesses and business lobbies, the press and everyone else who contributes to making foreign policy in a great democracy.

Then came 9/11 and the 'day of fire'. The muscular nationalists wanted to hit back at America's enemies. The neoconservatives wanted to fight the cause of freedom, sure that tyranny was succouring terror. Everybody felt that the US would now tolerate a much lower risk threshold of a rogue state giving weapons of mass destruction technology to terrorists. Characteristically the administration took on the giant project of injecting democracy into the Middle East, believing the region's existing political culture was profoundly dysfunctional and getting worse. The modest realists were grave, willing to act if sure of their facts, but cautious, wanting to show to the world a face of grace under pressure. The machine men and women just worked the problems.

Afghanistan, which had looked hard, proved too easy. The neocons and the muscular nationalists were vindicated. See what a little decisive force could achieve. September 11, 2001 had changed the risk calculus. What if Saddam gave weapons of mass destruction to the terrorists?

And the rest, as they say, is history.

In the second administration most of the neocons left, but their heritage lived on, not least in the president's own rhetoric and in his giant project of trying to bring democracy to the Middle East. The muscular nationalists were still in place, but after the shock and scandal of Abu Ghraib, the prison in which Iraqis were abused by American soldiers, in a prison with far too many poorly trained US National Guardsmen in attendance, Rumsfeld's star was in at least partial eclipse.

The machine men and women came to the fore – Rice, Zoellick and Hadley. Rice became a powerful secretary of state because she was so close to the president. Her word was his bond. Zoellick may have lacked Armitage's outsize personality and rambunctious style but he was smart as hell and travelled the world assiduously. Hadley was self-effacing and completely loyal to Rice.

And while it responded to events, the administration responded also to the enduring, deep impulses of American foreign policy. In the first days of the first administration, the deepest impulse seemed to be to do the reverse of whatever Clinton had done. The ABC policy – Anything But Clinton. But, then, distinguishing yourself from your predecessor is an old practice in both Australia and the US. Bush's rhetoric on supporting democracy in the second inaugural address seems revolutionary but it is really just a more eloquent and heartfelt version of Clinton's project to 'enlarge democracy', or a godchild of Ronald Reagan's call to Soviet leader Mikhail Gorbachev to 'tear down that wall', or his earlier call to 'let Poland be Poland'. These ideas go back to Woodrow Wilson and so-called Wilsonian idealism. They go back, too, beyond that to the idea of America as mankind's 'last best hope'. They go back indeed to the founding ideas of America.

All that is bundled into the idea of American exceptionalism, which is not the proposition that America is above the rules, but rather that because America has been given such bounty it has special responsibilities. And while most non-Americans are loathe to admit it, this notion is true. The American alliance system is the nearest thing our planet has to a global security system, one which keeps the peace and seeks the peace. No other nation, no other association of nations, provides an international good anywhere near this in importance or effectiveness.

Bush mediated all these giant personalities, institutional influences and deep impulses of history in the midst of deadly new attacks on America, and he did so with a Texan accent the world found strange and with that insistent religiosity which is so much of so many modern American presidents – certainly it was there in Clinton.

It is indeed a great mistake to underestimate Bush himself in any analysis of US behaviour. In mid-2002, nine months before the military operation against Saddam Hussein, there was great debate not only over whether this should happen but whether it would happen. A close friend of mine, a Democrat but an astute observer of national security politics, told me he was confident the US would invade Iraq because Bush himself was a hawk on Iraq and he made the final decisions. Bush had a relatively hands-off management style, and he didn't intellectualise or hold rolling seminars on issues the way Clinton did, but he was smart and decisive when he wanted to be and he was also very clear that he was the president and he made the final call.

Indeed people tend to underestimate Bush's historic ambitions. I lunched in Washington in 2005 with one of Bush's close friends. He told me that history would regard Bush as either a very good or a very bad president. Bush was not going to muddle along in the middle, on autopilot. Bush saw himself as a 'transformative' president. He knew that presidential power lasted for a very limited time. He had seen power ebb away from his father as the possibility, and then the likelihood, of electoral defeat grew. Bush was determined to make a difference while he had the chance.

Iraq remains the defining project of the Bush presidency. No one would have dreamed it. Much of history now hangs on it.

Chapter 6

IN THE NEOCONS' LAIR: A SEASON IN WASHINGTON, AN ENCOUNTER WITH WOLFOWITZ

The Washington evening is perfect – balmy, still, but for some reason without that humidity that is often a killer in the capital of the free world in July. On the parade ground at the Marine Barracks, in DC's southeast quadrant, the nation's finest strut their stuff. Sergeant O'Leary, big, bluff and bedazzling in his red marine jacket, warms the crowd up first.

'There are three types of applause', he shouts. 'The first is golf applause – good shot, Tiger, that sort of thing. You will not commit any golf applause tonight. The same goes for polite theatre applause. Only marine applause is acceptable. You jump out of your uniform and turn a double backwards somersault. You will commit marine applause!'

On the parade ground, surrounded by the Marine Barracks founded in 1801, which was rudely burnt down by the British in 1812 but subsequently rebuilt, marines, immaculate in crisp, starched uniforms, march in formation. Marine bands play a selection of stirring anthems – Battle Hymn of the Republic, among others – and a unit drills with their five kilogram rifles in eerie silence as the spotlights and floodlights play and dance around them.

It is the heart of Washington, this display of US strength and pride. For Washington pulsates with power. It is the modern imperial Rome, greater than London at the height of empire. Down the long corridors of the Pentagon, across the elegant facades and gardens of the White House, through the many-roomed mansion of the State Department, out beyond the towering dome of the Capitol building, along the anonymous office blocks of K Street that house the lobbyists and think-tanks – this is the centre of the known universe, the most formidable agglomeration of pure power we have ever known.

The 300 million people of the US account for somewhere between a quarter and a third of the global economy. The US defence budget is as great as the next 12 defence budgets combined. Great power, of course, begets great opposition, and being powerful doesn't mean you always get what you want.

For several months in 2004 and 2005 I was a visiting fellow at a Washington think-tank and tried to take the pulse of the world's first hyper-power.

I discovered a Washington full of paradox. I spent the Christmas of 2004 in Washington and was astonished that among these welcoming and generous people no one ever wished me Happy Christmas. Half the world seems to believe the Americans are embarked on a great anti-Muslim crusade. Yet all through the Christmas period I was repeatedly brought up short by everybody wishing me 'happy holidays'. At my apartment building there were even notices distributed about the proper disposal of 'holiday trees'. I couldn't figure it out until I realised eventually that there's a sort of new law of political correctness that you don't mention Christmas in case you offend a non-Christian. These are surely the most punctiliously sensitive crusaders in the history of human warfare.

In the first George W Bush administration, elected in 2000, inaugurated in 2001 and replaced by the second George W Bush administration in 2005, one name more than any other was associated with the decisive use of US power, especially with the operation in Iraq. That name was Paul Wolfowitz. He was deputy secretary of defense until, in 2005, taking up the position of President of the World Bank.

As the single most important intellectual influence advocating the invasion of Iraq, Paul Wolfowitz was demonised by many of the critics of the Bush administration. Wolfowitz was regarded as the arch-priest of the neoconservatives. As we have seen in the preceding chapter, neocon became a kind of general abuse term, especially directed at Jewish policy makers and opinion leaders.

Wolfowitz undoubtedly is a neoconservative, meaning a new conservative, that is, a former Democrat who became disillusioned with the anti-Americanism of much of the Democratic left and shifted over to Republicanism, initially on foreign policy, later generally adopting a broader identification with Republican values. He is also a complex and fascinating intellectual whose media portrayal never seemed to quite capture the man.

I went to see Wolfowitz in his office in the Pentagon during one of the worst months for the US in Iraq, in April 2004. The city of Fallujah was under siege, the rebel Shia cleric Moqtada al-Sadr was grandly receiving envoys for negotiation, the US position in Iraq looked grim. But there was always a core of faith in the Bush administration – determination more than optimism, though irreducible optimism was a part of it – that the US would prevail in Iraq. And in Wolfowitz's office, I found myself sitting in Optimism Central.

Despite his unique profile, Wolfowitz is representative of a certain type in post-World War II US history – a national security policy professional who identified with one side of politics and rose to ever higher positions when it was in office, occupying academic positions in the out years.

He was the under secretary of defense (the number three position) during the first Gulf war in 1991 and reportedly favoured going on to get rid of Saddam Hussein after Kuwait was liberated. Before that he was the US ambassador to Indonesia, where he was a great success. Indonesians were surprised that he later gained such a reputation as a hawk, for he had been such an engaging figure in Jakarta, reaching out to every mainstream shade of Indonesian and specifically Muslim opinion. Within the limits of American policy he always pushed for greater openness in

Indonesia and other southeast Asian nations. He remained good friends with Anwar Ibrahim, the former deputy prime minister of Malaysia who spent a term in jail. He was also associated with ousting Ferdinand Marcos from the Philippines. Before serving in Jakarta, Wolfowitz had been the assistant secretary of state for East Asia and the Pacific.

He was a committed Republican and when Clinton was in office occupied high-powered academic positions before joining Bush's campaign as one of its key foreign policy advisers. Originally a mathematician, he is prodigiously brainy. He was the model for a minor character, Phil Gorman, the most brilliant student of a legendary professor, in Saul Bellow's last novel, *Ravelstein*.

In his memoirs, published before George W Bush became president, Colin Powell writes respectfully of Wolfowitz as 'tough-minded', but also at one point kids Dick Cheney, then the defense secretary, that his civilian staff, of whom Wolfowitz was the most senior, 'are all right-wing nuts like you'.

Whatever else he is, Wolfowitz is certainly no nut.

Way back in September 2002, in the lead-up to the Iraq war, I asked Wolfowitz in an interview whether Saddam Hussein had chemical and biological weapons. His response was carefully nuanced: 'Part of the problem is you can't get precise answers to some of these questions. There have been numerous cases, some involving Iraq, where major cases (of weapons of mass destruction) have been discovered years after they've taken place, and no doubt some are never discovered. Combine that capability with the possibility of anonymous delivery (of WMDs) via terrorists, and there are cases where you really can't afford to wait until the threat is about to hit you.'

Both elements of that answer are crucial to understanding Wolfowitz. The first is that the WMD question is not absolutely certain, but the second is the risk of doing nothing. This is a central theme of the neocons – that action has its risks, but so does inaction.

In that interview, Wolfowitz, who has visited Australia many times, also lavished praise on the performance of Australian troops in Afghanistan and Australia's cooperation with the US in the war on terror. He said: 'Australia has a special status among US allies'. He went on: 'Australia is a country that truly shares our values and has been forthcoming when there are problems and hard things need to be done. I want to say thanks for what Australia has done. It's been a real stand-up performance right down to the ground level, where your troops perform outstandingly. I want to assure you that it's much appreciated here in the Defense Department.'

Later, after the Bali bombings in October 2002 had killed 88 Australians among the total 202 fatalities, Wolfowitz returned to these themes, when he told me, not long after attending the Washington Cathedral service commemorating the Australian dead: 'The theme was that Australians stand by their mates and the feeling in Washington is very strong that we are mates with the Australians. I want to express my own condolences for the Australian victims of Bali and tell you that these feelings are widely shared throughout the US by the Government and the people.' Then Wolfowitz made a crucial judgment on the strategic culture of Australia, on the character of its people: 'Bali was horrendous, just horrendous, but if the motivation of the terrorists was to intimidate Australians from participating in the war on terror, from everything I can see they've had the opposite effect.'

This is a fundamental judgment that the Bush administration has made about Australia. Australia as a nation refuses to be intimidated. When it believes the fight is necessary and just, it stays in the fight.

Wolfowitz believed from early on that the attacks on the US of September 11, 2001 had profoundly changed the strategic environment, an assessment this book shares.

When the attack on the Pentagon came, Wolfowitz had just finished a meeting with members of Congress. They had been considering what nasty surprises the US might experience from terrorists, rogue states and WMDs. Wolfowitz was in his office when his staff told him to turn on the TV because a plane had crashed into the World Trade Center in New York.

'Then I heard this very loud but muffled rumble and the building shook like an earthquake', he told me. '(Defense Secretary) Rumsfeld realised quicker than me what was going on and went straight to the scene and was actually helping out carrying stretchers until his security people got to him and told him to leave.'

Wolfowitz was told a bomb had exploded and he had to evacuate. He went out the front, where a large crowd had gathered: 'It was impossible to make a cell phone call but I got to my security people and then got back into the building. There was a fair bit of adrenalin pumping, but it didn't really sink in fully what had happened. We didn't have a whole lot of time to think about what had happened. We concentrated on what we should do next. There were a couple of flights, one or two in the Pacific, that seemed anomalous. People were very concerned at that point about anything that seemed anomalous.'

Oddly, in September 2002, just before the Bali bombing, he told me he hoped the US and its allies would be able to effectively think through what the changes meant without enduring another mass attack. A few weeks later came the Bali bombs.

In any event, back to Optimism Central, Wolfowitz's office, in 2004. Wolfowitz was not giving many press interviews at that time. Perhaps his profile had just got too big. Perhaps he thought his enemies had so besmirched him, and he was so often misrepresented in the press, that he felt the utility of such interviews was limited. Perhaps he was just too damn busy.

To get to the deputy's office in the Pentagon you traverse what seem like kilometres of corridors, many with military paintings. The paintings right outside Wolfowitz's office were done by Dwight Eisenhower. The Pentagon is the most powerful building in the world. It hums 24 hours a day, every day of the year. Its 24 000 staff make it the single biggest government office building anywhere. It stood, co-equal with New York's World Trade Center, as the supreme symbol of the US for Osama bin Laden to attack but, unlike the World Trade Center, it survived the attack and very soon began hitting back.

In any event, Wolfowitz was not the least apologetic about Iraq or cast into gloom by the way the mission was unfolding there: 'You can have endless debates about how imminent the (Iraq) threat was and the president never said it was imminent. The whole point was to deal with it before it became imminent. That's all important but it's in the past. The future is creating a country in the heart of the Arab world that has an independent judiciary, that respects minority rights, that respects the rights of women, that observes democratic practices. That's going to have an influence. It's not a domino effect – that's an absurd comparison. But it will have a broad influence in the Middle East in the way I believe Japan had a great influence on east Asia, and subsequently Taiwan, Singapore and Hong Kong had a broad influence on China. It's very important to demonstrate to the Arabs that given the right circumstances they can achieve what the rest of us have done. It's unbelievably condescending to believe that the only way Iraq can be stable is to be ruled by a tyrant like Saddam.'

As Wolfowitz is outlining his passionate rationale for action in Iraq, his voice is soft and somewhat foggy, his manner professorial. He really truly passionately believes, very much as Bush expresses it in his second inaugural address, that all human beings, including Arabs, desire and deserve freedom. Much of Wolfowitz's professional life was spent involved with east Asia. He frequently recalls how widely it was held that societies like South Korea and Taiwan would never have democracy, and Japan never have 'real' democracy, because of their Confucian inheritance. Confucianism, with its stress on hierarchy and fixed social relations, was inimical to the rude exchanges of democracy, so it was said. The Confucian mandarin, with his long cultivated fingernails, could never be a hands-on businessman, and so on. A couple of short decades later and Confucianism was used with equal facility to explain the success of these societies in democracy and capitalism.

I ask Wolfowitz what a success in Iraq will look like: 'I think it is basically an Iraq that can fend for itself, with a lot of help from other people. There are multiple parts of that, but the two most important are governance and security'.

He naturally distinguishes different types of insurgent within Iraq and is savage in his view of the former Baath Party activists: 'To dignify these people as resistance or insurgents – these are not labels they deserve. These are the former killers and torturers and rapists who kept Saddam in power for 35 years and helped him kill 700 000 Iraqis. He didn't do it single-handedly. They include foreign terrorist collaborators and they include – especially among the foreigners but also among the Iraqis – people who are prepared to fight to the death. These groups may have somewhat different strategic objectives. The al-Qaeda associates like Abu Musab al-Zarkawi actually would prefer not to be labelled Saddamists, but their main goal is to defeat us and prevent a new Iraq from emerging. In that they work together very well.'

While I am in Washington everyone is comparing Iraq with Vietnam, and Wolfowitz with the defense secretary of that time, Robert McNamara, who, like Wolfowitz, also went on to head the World Bank, and who regretted his role in Vietnam and wrote a bitter book denouncing US policy there. Wolfowitz has never come across to me as bitter. He seems much more deeply rooted in his intellectual, ideological, strategic and even moral convictions than McNamara ever was, and he utterly rejects the Vietnam comparison.

Instead he has another analogy: 'I remember after the fall of (dictator Nicolae) Caucescu in Romania in 1989, being struck by the statistic that 20 or 25 per cent of the Romanian population were on the payroll of the secret police. I thought, here's a country that has no hope of making it. Well, they're now about to join NATO. It's not the perfect democracy. A lot of that poison is still in the Romanian system, but it's leaching out. Iraq has an even bigger problem and its poison has to leach out too.'

Wolfowitz hailed the Afghanistan constitution, and the Iraqi interim constitution as it then was, as two great achievements that will become seminal documents in the history of the Middle East. It's easy to scoff at such grandiloquence but it is also true that no one knows how the Middle East is going to work out. Wolfowitz embodies one of the key intellectual strengths of the neocons – they always have a vision and they always have a plan.

Certainly on Afghanistan he also explicitly extolled the idealism of what the US is trying to do: 'We want to do much more in Afghanistan than just hunt and kill terrorists. We want to show the Afghan people there is a much better life to be had following those universal values (for which the US, and by implication Australia, stand).'

Nor will Wolfowitz accept in the slightest degree that there is anything anti-Islam about US policies: 'One of the prime goals of al-Qaeda is to create the biggest possible split between Muslims and the rest of us, and the prime target in that is moderate Muslims who they want to push to the sides of society.'

Wolfowitz makes the point, which oddly perhaps you never see from anyone else, that even before Iraq the US had on numerous occasions spent the lives of its soldiers, and its national treasure, to defend Muslims: 'Look at our record, in the liberation of Kuwait, then in Operation Provide Comfort which protected the Kurds against Saddam Hussein, in Somalia, in Bosnia, in Kosovo and then in Afghanistan – that's six times US soldiers went into harm's way to protect Muslims. We didn't do it because they were Muslims but it's a pretty good record in protecting moderate Muslims.'

As always, in our discussion that day in his office, Wolfowitz was keen to emphasise Australia's role and the benefits to the US, to the international coalition, and to the Iraqis themselves, of having Australian soldiers there: 'I think (Australia's troop commitment) is very important. It's very important that everybody do (keep their troops in Iraq) especially after Madrid (terrorist bombings). Australia is such a key player in the original coalition. It's one of the few countries that had troops there in the very beginning. None of us are perfect democracies, but those of us who are the older democracies – and you Australians are one of the oldest democracies in the world – have important standards and values to set for the new ones. Since this is very much about values, I think Australia's commitment matters a lot.'

Wolfowitz, like all the neocons, reacts furiously, within the confines of his mild and considered manner, to the idea that there is something impractical in what he has championed. He does believe in the moral impulse to spread human rights and democracy, but he also believes that the old dispensation in the Middle East was unsustainable, that he and the Bush administration generally are acting to confront a real-world crisis, not something invented by their ideology. It is the so-called realists, the neocons argue, who are impractical, forever retreating into passivity and doing nothing as threats grow greater and greater.

However, in both strategic and moral terms, it is a key part of Wolfowitz's case to stress the consequences of leaving Saddam in power, the uniqueness of Saddam's situation, both his deception over WMDs, his defiance of UN Security Council resolutions which embodied the terms of the peace which allowed him to stay in office after 1991, and the extraordinary barbarity of his rule. Thus, even if the Iraq operation had not by its cost alone prohibited the idea of a series of US-led wars against other tyrants, Saddam was sui generis and the Iraq operation unlikely to be repeated.

Wolfowitz warmed to the theme of Saddam's uniqueness: 'In the last 100 years there were actually very few dictators who cut out people's tongues, who tortured children in order to make their parents talk, who raped women and sent videos of the rapes to the relatives in order to intimidate them. It was an unbelievable regime of terror. You hear people say the world is full of bad guys and Saddam Hussein was just another bad guy. Then you know they really don't know Saddam Hussein at all. To paraphrase that famous vice-presidential debate: I knew (the Philippines') Ferdinand Marcos and Ferdinand Marcos was no Saddam Hussein. I knew (Indonesia's) Suharto and Suharto was no Saddam Hussein. If Marcos and Suharto had been prepared to kill people the way Saddam Hussein was, they would have stayed in power a lot longer.'

With Wolfowitz's departure from the Pentagon the neocons lost some influence. But Bush himself seems to have imbibed much of their democratic evangelistic impulse. In truth, there is always an element of spreading democracy and defending human rights in the foreign policy of any American president. It's hard-wired into the American political culture, which is not to say it will always dominate.

Wolfowitz and his ideas have already influenced the world greatly. The ambition to change the course of history and the nature of the political culture of the Middle East is characteristically American in its scope and daring. In the end, though, statesmen are judged by practical results. The patient either gets better, stays sick or dies – judgment is not deferred forever. History's judgment on Wolfowitz, as on Bush and to some extent Howard, will be determined by Iraq. The best ideas, and the best intentions, certainly do not guarantee success.

Back at the Marine Barracks the evening climaxes with a magnificent silent drill routine. The marines are breathtaking as they twirl, throw, catch and march with their heavy rifles, bayonets fixed, without a single verbal command. Towards the end a single rifle twirls in the air, the glistening bayonet flashing under the spotlights. But the marine misses his catch and the rifle falls to the ground. The drill sergeant, silent all the while, stares at the offending weapon as though to erase it by the force of his gaze.

In a scene of perfection, it's the flaw of humanity.

Chapter 7

SEXING UP THE INTELLIGENCE RELATIONSHIP: WASHINGTON OPENS THE GOLDEN DOOR, CANBERRA WALKS THROUGH

In July of 2004 US President George W Bush sent a one-page presidential directive to the US Defense Department and the Central Intelligence Agency. It instructed them to upgrade intelligence cooperation and access for the Australians. Its purpose was to alter, by presidential directive, US national disclosure policy.

From this day forward Australians were to have access to virtually everything in the American intelligence system concerning international terrorism and joint military operations. Material previously classified as 'No Forg', meaning to be seen by no foreign eyes, would henceforth be available to Australians.

This information, and the information throughout this chapter, comes from a series of dozens of conversations with Australian and US politicians and officials intimately concerned with the intelligence relationship.

Intelligence sharing and cooperation lie at the very heart of the Australia-US alliance and specifically the military relationship. This operates at many levels: at the grand strategic level, also at the big operational level and down to the most minute tactical level. It pervades our national military posture. It is in itself a vast force-multiplier for the Australian Defence Force and it is central to Australia's overall defence capabilities. And it applies whether we are doing big things a long way from home or small things right in our back yard. As one Australian put it to me: 'For us to protect our precious but very limited military assets we need to pull down information from the whole global US intelligence network.'

In the long history of the alliance the intelligence cooperation has never been as close as it became under Howard and Bush. This new intelligence intimacy was driven by the Iraq war, by the war on terror and by the relationship between John Howard and George Bush, and their respective governments. If these new relationships are fully embedded into an operational culture on both sides of the Pacific they will represent a long-term institutional payoff from the Bush-Howard relationship.

The institutional forces involved were so great, and the pull of inertia so strong, that to achieve this kind of operational cooperation required not only a political decision at the highest level but frequent intervention from the political leaders as the process went on. Bush and Howard discussed intelligence cooperation at almost all their face-to-face meetings.

So did their defence and foreign ministers. The process was driven under the umbrella of the annual Australia-US ministerial meetings, which involve the foreign and defence ministers from both countries (AUSMIN). The AUSMIN process authorised earlier this decade a comprehensive review of inter-operability between the Australian and US militaries. A central part of this review was intelligence cooperation. Successive AUSMIN meetings took a series of decisions to give life to the closer intelligence relationship.

Howard also raised it in talks with US Defense Secretary Donald Rumsfeld in 2004 and 2005. At the implementation level there have been difficulties, not surprisingly. The further down a US agency you go, the less likely they are to be comfortable about changing established practice, especially if they are not accustomed to dealing with Australians routinely.

In an interview for this book Howard said he did not believe the new level of intelligence cooperation would have come into being without the newly close relationship of his government and the Bush administration. He also believed this intelligence cooperation to be of great benefit to Australia: 'You just don't know how valuable something like that can be. It's one of the things that if you can have it you'd be a fool not to embrace it.'

Howard's conversations with Rumsfeld grew partly out of resistance in some parts of the US intelligence machine to the unprecedented access to be given to the Australians.

Howard said: 'I pushed it with Rumsfeld. He appeared to be responsive. I'm a cautious interlocutor on this because in the American system there are always cross-pressures. One of the things which amazes me about the American system is the silo effect (where different agencies pursue policy and practice more or less in isolation from each other). I read a biography of Keynes – the Skidelsky biography. Keynes was struck when he went to Washington in 1941 by two things – the silo effect and how legalistic the whole system is. Nothing's changed since then.'

In this context the legalistic nature of the system which Howard is referring to is the reluctance of some US intelligence officers to change the meaning of no foreign eyes to exempt Australians. After all, some US intelligence operatives are reported to have reacted, 'the law's the law, and a mere presidential directive doesn't change that', although of course the presidential directive is meant to guide the interpretation of the law.

Part of the extraordinary new intelligence closeness involved increased Australian access to US information systems themselves. This is new and uncharted territory in intelligence cooperation. The normal way is that the Americans collect vast amounts of information and then give Canberra material which is relevant to its known interests, or which Canberra asks for, or which they think Canberra might find useful. The new idea is that Australians would be directly plugged into the American system and take what they want, within limits and agreed protocols.

The most obvious application for this kind of intimate cooperation is in military operations. Now, Australian forces in the Middle East, in Iraq or Afghanistan or elsewhere, get direct battle space information from the central American surveillance and intelligence systems. There's no question of asking for the information. The Australians have automatic access to it. Of course Australia-US defence intelligence cooperation has a long history, and the Americans would always want to give a close ally like Australia militarily useful information in a conflict. But the speed and comprehensiveness of the Australians having their own access is priceless. It also makes our forces extremely attractive for other coalition partners to work with.

The former defence minister, Robert Hill, told me: 'In recent years we have obtained unprecedented access to US intelligence and tactical planning. That has been of great value to Australia in terms of enhancing our national security. This is access to the greatest repository of information that exists. It's another sign of the close relationship between the US and Australia.'

I interviewed Donald Rumsfeld in Adelaide when he was there for the 2005 AUSMIN meeting. He would neither confirm nor deny the existence of the written presidential directive, although its existence and content have been confirmed to me by numerous authoritative sources. But Rumsfeld did confirm the substance of the directive, when he said of closer intelligence cooperation that the president 'has directed it' Rumsfeld went on: 'He is determined we find ways to cooperate with Australia in intelligence sharing at a new level, and we are doing so.'

Access to American systems is, however, a much broader concept than just military operations. The Australian ambition will be to push for the widest possible application of the concept.

The other area in which the presidential directive instructed that Australians were to be given complete access is counter-terrorism. The old model of intelligence was that all the little bits of information would be collected by the separate agencies who would then report it up the chain and it would be analysed at the top and at that point a decision taken on any action that might be needed. The new environment, especially terrorism, drives much faster horizontal exchanges. An agency might pick up something which requires an Australian Federal Police response instantly, or a communication with POLRI, the Indonesian police. These situations require fast decision making and effective lines of communication.

The third area which the Howard government has tried to get the Americans to move on is in intelligence concerning the proliferation of weapons of mass destruction. Canberra regards WMD proliferation as being one of the key strategic challenges facing Australia.

Howard, and the other Australian cabinet ministers, are concerned about the possibility of WMDs passing into terrorist hands. Howard told me he is constantly worried about the possibility of nuclear terrorism: 'I worry about that. I think it is at the back of everyone's mind. There's a fair bit of the stuff (nuclear weapons material) unaccounted for.'

The professional judgment of Australia's agencies is that it is unlikely that terrorists will come into possession of a nuclear weapon. But the consequence of their doing so would be so catastrophic that even the small chance has to be relentlessly tracked down and ruthlessly minimised.

It is more likely that terrorists would get chemical, biological or radiological materials. During the build-up to the Iraq war, the former US deputy secretary of state, Rich Armitage, told me that the possibility of Saddam Hussein passing WMDs (not nukes, because the Americans didn't believe he had nukes) to terrorists was 'at the top of our concerns'.

Canberra demonstrated its bona fides on WMDs to Washington not only by joining the Iraq war, but by being one of the first countries to join the Proliferation Security Initiative (PSI), which was designed to stop, by interception if necessary, North Korea from selling nuclear weapons material to anyone else. Eventually some 60-odd countries signed on to PSI. Thus it is a remarkably successful exercise in multilateralism. But it is not United Nations multilateralism. Thus it was helpful to the Bush administration to have a respectable democracy like Australia, which has over many decades a strong record in combatting nuclear proliferation, sign up quickly to the PSI.

The US agencies, under political direction, do share more or less everything they do and say and think about North Korea with Australian agencies, because they recognise how deeply Australia's interests are involved on the Korean peninsula and in north Asian security more generally.

However, it is more difficult for the Americans to give the Australians the level of access the Australians would like on all WMD issues. This is in part because the US is bound by its obligations under the Nuclear Non-Proliferation Treaty not to disclose certain types of information to non-nuclear states.

The more general ambition of the Canberra mandarins is to have the spirit of the presidential directive of June 2004 infuse the whole of the intelligence relationship. This requires a fundamental change of culture. At the moment, quite understandably, American agencies write material on the assumption that only Americans will see it. Then, if there's a good reason, a senior relevant person will show some or all of it to the Australians. What the most ambitious Australians want is a situation where the assumption is that properly cleared and trustworthy Australian agencies get to see anything unless there is some very good reason why not. When you stop and think about it, that is a breathtaking ambition for a US ally to harbour.

Certainly great trust exists at many operational levels of intelligence between Australians and Americans. At one stage in 2005 the three main analytical sections of the coalition's Combined Intelligence Operations Centre in Iraq were headed by Australians from military intelligence, two uniformed men and one civilian from the Department of Defence.

Sometimes the smallness of the Australian system is a benefit. Having people inside every coalition system operating in Iraq can mean that decision makers in Canberra can in some respects get information and assessments more quickly from Iraq than their counterparts in the US do, or if not more quickly at least in a less adulterated and pre-cooked form.

Signals intelligence, which ranges from eavesdropping on telephone calls to detecting the hidden presence of submarines to knowing instantly that a missile has been launched, is much more readily amenable to automatic sharing than is human intelligence.

The building of trust from the Iraq operation has led to a great increase in the volume and quality of human intelligence which the Americans now provide the Australians. A number of Australian intelligence agencies have people on exchange with US intelligence agencies, the most exceptionally sensitive sorts of exchanges it is possible to do. In Australia, the Defence Intelligence Group consists of the Defence Intelligence Organisation (DIO), the Defence Signals Directorate (DSD) and the Defence Imagery and Geospatial Organisation (DIGO). DIO deals with defence-related assessments and provides intelligence analysis to support the Australian Defence Force in operations, DSD deals with signals intelligence and DIGO is about interpreting satellite imagery. They all at different times have people stationed with their US counterparts, some as liaison officers and some as line officers doing real jobs. Australians have served at the US National Security Agency and at the US Defense Intelligence Agency and numerous others amongst the forest of US intelligence bodies. Similarly, Australians serve in the UK Defence Intelligence Staff.

The other Australian intelligence agencies are the Office of National Assessments (ONA), the Australian Secret Intelligence Service (ASIS) and the Australian Security Intelligence Organisation (ASIO). ONA does not collect intelligence but it makes the main strategic assessments. When it is putting together a national assessment of another nation it draws in the Department of Foreign Affairs and Trade as well as Defence expertise, normally represented through DIO. ASIS is the Australian overseas espionage body, while ASIO is concerned with domestic security.

The whole Australian intelligence community is coordinated by the Foreign Intelligence Coordination Committee, which is chaired by the director-general of ONA.

It is much harder for agencies concerned a good deal with human intelligence to send exchange personnel to the US than it is for the signals intelligence people. One of the issues for the

Americans is allowing a foreigner, any foreigner, full access to their communications systems. It has been worked out for the Australians in the signals intelligence areas on the basis that they have access but don't go browsing. No foreigner is attached to CIA headquarters.

In some ways, in the assessment area, the Australian relationship with the UK is even more intimate than it is with the US. This is exceptional but reflects, of course, Australian history. The Australian intelligence establishment, like the SAS, was closely modelled on the British version and has retained much of that institutional culture. The relationship is so intimate in fact that each Wednesday when the British Joint Intelligence Committee meets in London, the ONA liaison officer attached to the Australian High Commission in London is in attendance. The only other dedicated ONA liaison officer is in Washington, and he doesn't attend the analogous Washington meeting. The intelligence liaison function in other world capitals is carried out either by a senior professional diplomat or by a declared ASIS agent. ASIS agents generally work under diplomatic cover. Some are declared to the host government so that they can undertake liaison tasks.

Australia's intelligence cooperation with the UK is as intimate, but not as wide-ranging, as Canberra's cooperation with Washington. This is a singular state of affairs, seldom remarked on presumably because so few people know about it. The only formal security alliance which links the UK and Australia is the Five Power Defence Arrangements (FPDA), which combines Australia, the UK, New Zealand, Malaysia and Singapore for the purposes of providing for the defence of Singapore and peninsular Malaysia. The FPDA is not reciprocal – Singapore and Malaysia do not commit, for example, to providing for the security of Australia and New Zealand. Yet Tony Blair has called Australia the UK's closest ally in Asia. Certainly the UK and Australia behave like allies. The UK sent its own special forces and other military resources to help Australia in East Timor. There is a deep intimacy and trust between the UK and Australia in both military and intelligence matters.

How can this be when it is not underpinned by a formal security treaty? The answer is in three parts, each of which provides a greater clue to the real workings of the world than any number of formal international agreements, United Nations charters, published documents or any of the paraphernalia normally considered to be the basis of international relations.

The first is that the alliance system which unites Australia and the UK is the American alliance system. The American alliance system is a classic hub-and-spokes network. The spokes relate to the hub more than to each other. This is especially so in Asia where Japan and South Korea are both vitally important allies of the US but for historical reasons could not be allies of each other, so the US has a bilateral alliance with each. However, the US alliance system is superbly flexible. In some parts of the world, such as Europe, it is a multilateral alliance, through the North Atlantic Treaty Organisation (NATO). The US alliance relationship with NATO allies is both multilateral and bilateral. For those nations who don't want too close a connection with the US, they can use NATO as a kind of buffer or mediating institution, and they need only sign on to things which NATO signs on to collectively. But for the UK, which is much more comfortable in its relationship with the US, it can pursue a close bilateral alliance relationship.

It can be useful to see the US alliance system as a de facto multilateral, quasi-global security system. It would be inadequate to call it these days the Western alliance as it contains members which are not Western nations. You could call it an alliance of democracies, although there are plenty of democracies which are not members, and some members (not many) which are not really democracies. But whatever ideological label you give it, this is the central security organisation of the globe.

And it is a powerful factor integrating the security policies of Australia and the UK.

It is the contention of this book, borne out by the evidence of this chapter, that Australia is the second most intimate ally of the United States after the UK. This was confirmed in the US 2006

Quadrennial Defense Review, in which the US stated that it highly valued its 'unique' relationships with the UK and Australia, whose troops stood with those of the US in Iraq and Afghanistan and many other theatres. This is a remarkable position for Australia to have reached. There is no doubt that the UK overall is a more important nation in the global system than Australia. The UK has three times Australia's population and is the fourth largest economy in the world, whereas Australia is the 13th largest (these figures come from the Department of Foreign Affairs and Trade but are based on World Bank figures). The UK spends proportionately a much greater share of its national wealth on its military than Australia does. The UK is a permanent member of the United Nations Security Council, a member of the Group of Eight leading industrial countries, and a member of the European Union. All of these are diplomatic cards to play which make the UK more important to the US than it would otherwise be.

In saying that, it would be quite wrong to diminish Australia's own importance. Australia too has its cards to play, among them its position in the Asia-Pacific, its membership of the Asia-Pacific Economic Cooperation forum, its rich economy and its highly competent military. But getting a psychological sense of where it stands in the world, neither overestimating nor underestimating their position, is difficult for Australians. If the US is the sole super power, the UK is a great power and Australia is a leading middle power, but a middle power with great strengths (not least its alliance with the US) which make it a considerable player in global issues.

But for the purposes of this chapter it is clear that the security relationship which both the UK and Australia have with the US is a big factor in the continuing military, intelligence and security relationship they have with each other.

The second explanation for the Australian closeness to the UK is simple history. This is much more than just the fact that Australia was once a colony of the UK, or even that it still shares a monarch with the UK. It is rather that key Australian security institutions, from the SAS through much of the military to the intelligence organisations, were either modelled on or in some cases founded by the British. These Australian institutions have maintained very close relations with their British counterparts. There is nothing servile about this. Both the UK and Australian institutions find their cooperation with each other highly useful.

The other aspect that emerges from history is the sense of shared values. The UK and Australia are both liberal democracies whose unconscious grammar of international relations is very similar. The Australia-US alliance is based on shared values and shared interests, so is the Australia-UK relationship.

The third factor which explains the closeness of the Australia-UK relationship is the extraordinarily important and little known UKUSA arrangements. These emerged, as did so much in Australia-US-UK military and intelligence cooperation, directly from World War II. They are perhaps the most important, and most secret, agreements to which Australia is party. They concern signals intelligence but they underpin everything else.

UKUSA stands for United Kingdom and United States of America. However, the arrangements were also signed by Australia, Canada and New Zealand. They cover signals intelligence cooperation. During World War II signals intelligence, (sigint), especially the code breakers of Bletchley, were exceptionally important for the ultimate allied victory. After World War II the UK decided to reorganise the signals intelligence establishments of Australia, Canada and New Zealand. This led to a series of agreements between the sigint leaders of the US, UK, Australia, Canada and New Zealand in 1947 and 1948. This became UKUSA and it is perhaps the single most important intelligence agreement ever reached, and perhaps the most important security agreement after World War II.

The basic story of UKUSA is on the public record but very little known. Under UKUSA, the five nations concerned divide the world into a series of regions. Each nation has responsibility for sigint interception in a different part of the world. Canada focuses on

Russia for example. Australia's main responsibility for sigint collection under UKUSA is southeast Asia and parts of the South Pacific, as well as the eastern portions of the Indian Ocean.

Today, the collection is done primarily through listening satellites. This is what the giant US-Australia joint facility at Pine Gap is all about. Pine Gap has two main functions. One is to receive and distribute all the various satellite sigint inputs for Australia's part of the world. The second is to monitor with great precision and immediacy any missile launch in Australia's region.

All the information Australia gets through Pine Gap is automatically relayed to Australian military installations in Sydney and Melbourne and it is all also automatically relayed to the United States. So too is the sigint information from the other US allies, particularly the UKUSA participants. Thus the US is the recipient of a colossal amount of information every day from all over the world. Australia keeps and processes for itself everything it collects in its own region but it also gets from the US a vast range of information from other parts of the world on subjects in which it is agreed that Australia has a legitimate interest.

In subsequent decades after World War II other allied nations joined the UKUSA arrangements, such as Germany and Japan. Japan originally focused its sigint efforts on Russia and North Korea but now devotes most of its sigint resources to China. However, in the UKUSA context, there is a very clear distinction in status, and range of information shared, between the original UKUSA members and those joining later. Thus a quite active term in intelligence is 'five eyes only', meaning information to be shared only among the US, UK, Australia, Canada and New Zealand.

New Zealand's position is anomalous. In 1986 it left ANZUS over its refusal to allow the visit to its ports of US nuclear-armed or nuclear-powered ships. As a result it was cut out of most US-centric intelligence arrangements. But it stayed in the UKUSA arrangements. Thus New Zealand keeps the sigint material it collects itself but it also gets a range of other sigint material. However, it gets very little US human intelligence product or assessments. Similarly it gets nothing concerning military operations except in those very rare circumstances where it is participating, as in Afghanistan. But New Zealand is still an ally of Australia's and still has liaison officers in some Australian agencies. Thus the New Zealand and US liaison officers have to be housed in separate sections in Australian agencies and given separate briefings and there are tight restrictions on what Australia can share with New Zealand. This has led to an active new category, 'four eyes only' material, meaning everyone but New Zealand. However, Australia's recent elevated intelligence status and the absence of Canada from the Iraq conflict, has led to the development of a 'three eyes only' category, that is, material that is only for the Yanks, the Brits and the Aussies.

Canada has been quite unhappy about Australia's new status, because it threatens Canada's own relative standing. The UK, on the other hand, had its intelligence access upgraded by the US president at the same time as Australia did, in something of a joint operation, which again demonstrates the intimacy of the three-way relationship. Somewhat remarkably, the Bush administration did not consult congressional leaders, even at the level of the highly trusted congressional intelligence committees, about the Australian and UK intelligence upgrades.

As well as collecting information through satellites, Australia, like other nations, has a substantial range of other sigint capabilities. It has P3 Orion planes with all manner of listening and interception devices constantly flying around southeast Asia hoovering up information. Many of our naval ships have sigint boxes on them. The whole UKUSA sigint system is like a giant global vacuum cleaner sucking up vast amounts of information. Much of the information, the overwhelming majority, is of course useless. Interpreting it and sifting it is a huge challenge. Much is managed by a system of keywords.

Signals intelligence is absolutely central to modern military capacity. To know precisely when an adversary's ship has left port, or plane taken off or missile been fired, is an inestimable advantage in any military conflict. Thus, Australia's intelligence relationship with the US is a huge force multiplier for its defence forces. And any potential adversary knows it.

Even in the war on terror sigint is crucial in many ways. Sophisticated terrorists may well have learnt not to use satellite phones but there are thousands of other ways sigint can yield information vital to counter-terrorism. Of course there is a constant cat-and-mouse battle between the intelligence collectors and the would-be intelligence evaders. But the sigint capacity which the US commands, of which Australia is a vital part, is a huge resource for both nations.

Australia and the US have had close intelligence sharing for decades but it has never been as close as it is now. For it to advance still further, beyond the three areas of counter-terrorism, military operations and weapons of mass destruction proliferation, would probably require further presidential intervention. But the reverse is also true: as the new intelligence intimacy becomes embedded in an ever greater number of ever more established procedures, for it to suddenly decline would probably require some substantial decline at the political level of the countries' relationship.

The intelligence sharing between the US and Australia looks as though it's here to stay.

Chapter 8

IRAQ: A GENERAL'S STORY

Jim Molan is a great big, rough-hewn Aussie soldier. Tall, broad-shouldered, lean, with sandy hair and a freckled face, he is the epitome of the digger. He'll tell you straight – he found being under fire exhilarating, not that he was ever blind to the fear or the danger, or the human cost.

Major-General Molan of the Australian Army may have commanded more troops than any other Australian since World War II. It depends a bit on what you call command.

From April 2004 to April 2005 Molan was assigned to the headquarters of the Multinational Force in Iraq as deputy chief of staff for operations. They commonly call this position chief of operations or, in the military jargon, 'Three'.

When the Three position was offered to Australia, the then chief of the Australian Defence Force, General Peter Cosgrove, discussed it with Molan and they both had the same reaction – let's jump at the chance.

'Cos and I said they won't really give us this, but the offer's on paper', Molan recalls months later.

The position was one of extraordinary power and consequence. It encompassed responsibility for all military operations, other than immediate self-defence, for the coalition forces, which then numbered about 140 000, and the Iraq Security Force, which then numbered around 130 000. As well as military operations, Molan would be responsible for civil actions by the military. Molan was not, in an absolute sense, commander of the force. When Molan first arrived in Baghdad that was US General Ricardo Sanchez, who was later replaced by General George Casey. But Molan was in effect the chief operating officer, the day-to-day commander. With a force under him of some 270 000 souls, including more than 130 000 Americans, the balance drawn from dozens of coalition nations plus Iraq itself, it must rank as one of the most significant land commands ever held by an Australian.

Initially, Molan was not altogether welcome, just as he had predicted. No one gets a position like the one Molan occupied as an act of tokenism. This is a point Colin Powell makes in his memoirs, *A Soldier's Story* (Random House, 1995), concerning his appointment as US national security advisor and then chairman of the joint chiefs of staff. These positions are just too important for any president to appoint a black man simply for the racial politics, Powell argues. So he earned his promotions on merit. At the same time he pays tribute to the Republican administrations that were willing to appoint a black man on merit to the top of the US military and national security establishments.

Molan would find that he, too, had to earn his position. In time he would come to supervise the bitter fighting in Fallujah, Najaf and Samarra, he would be many times under fire himself, he would organise the first Iraqi election. In the view of John Negroponte, at the time US ambassador to Iraq and later US national director of intelligence, Molan 'made history and helped reshape the Middle East', as Negroponte wrote in a letter to Howard.

But at first Molan was prevented from filling the position he had been formally offered.

'I fronted up to Sanchez and said I'm your chief of operations and he said "No you're not".'

Sanchez had, like many senior American soldiers, been focused in his career on NATO and the Atlantic relationship and had no personal knowledge or experience of Australians. He certainly wasn't anti-Australian but he had no inclination to take chances in critical appointments. He was a competent commander completely absorbed by the Abu Ghraib prison scandal, and by making his relationship with Paul Bremer, the head of the Coalition Provisional Authority, work. Sanchez just wasn't interested in having Molan in the post. It was nothing personal.

'There are two positions in Iraq that are always going to be held by Americans', Sanchez told Molan bluntly, 'director of intelligence and director of operations.' It's almost impossible to overrule a commander in the field like Sanchez on a matter like that. So Sanchez told Molan to go and fix the country's infrastructure instead.

Molan spent five months on this and it was superb preparation for when he did eventually take over as chief of operations. When he first arrived the insurgency was less generally murderous than it became but it was hitting Iraq's infrastructure, both its oil supplies and its electricity generation and distribution. The insurgents were threatening Iraq's oil exports and were at times disrupting basic services like sewerage and water to Baghdad. The insurgents desperately wanted to be able to cut off Baghdad's electricity supply altogether. This would have been a devastating victory for the insurgents and called into question the coalition's authority and competence at the most basic level. Molan attacked the problem with ferocious energy. He flew in US C17 aircraft from California to bring in repair towers for the electricity network. He set up dedicated repair teams and protected them with security details. He later convinced the new Iraqi government to create a specialist security force whose only mission was to protect strategic infrastructure.

Not everything he tried worked. He used helicopters to protect trains, as well as putting armour on the trains. Sometimes the trains would carry their own bridge repair capability because blowing up bridges was a favourite tactic of the insurgents. As Molan would subsequently tell a newspaper interviewer, he set up new monitoring, security, repair, ministerial liaison, contracting and command organisations.

He did a good job and the Americans recognised it. A series of critical personnel changes gave Molan his chance to finally take the chief of operations job. Sanchez was replaced by George Casey, a general with much broader experience, and Negroponte replaced Bremer. The coalition forces ceased to be an occupying force and became a force authorised under United Nations Security Council Resolution 1546, assisting the interim Iraqi government of Iyad Allawi. And Molan became chief of operations.

'That in a war, so incredibly important to the US, they're prepared to give a key position to a coalition partner, that's where the rubber hits the road in the US-Australian relationship, it's what inter-operability is all about', Molan later told me.

It's worth pondering a second on US motives. Washington, and particularly Casey, knew Molan was a good man. But giving such senior positions to coalition partners implies a conscious desire by the US to involve its allies in the most intimate way in coalition operations. It also greatly assists coalition partners in mastering inter-operability with US forces. In other words, by treating them well, the US makes its allies into better, more effective allies.

I heard Molan's story at length in his bush home, out the back of Queanbeyan near Canberra. It is a beautiful, characteristically Australian house, set at the top of a small ridge and overlooking a gum forest. The back part of the house is all glass, in the modern Australian way, opening onto an eaves-covered terrace, inviting the light in, giving you the sense of living inside and out simultaneously. It is a rambling house in the Australian tradition, with lots of different rooms, a large but Spartan office for Molan to work in, a formal entertaining room at the front. But, again in the Australian manner, we sit at the kitchen table drinking coffee, a refill provided by Molan's undergraduate daughter, and I'm forced to reflect on the incredible contrasts of a soldier's life – the bucolic peace of Queanbeyan, the fierce fighting of Iraq.

Molan was often under fire. As he later recalled in a newspaper interview, on the night before the January 20 election, Molan and his staff were watching, in their ultra high-tech headquarters, live video of a small group of insurgents preparing to fire 127 mm rockets. They couldn't work out precisely where the insurgents were, nor what their targets would be. They were working with the greatest urgency and speed to track the insurgents down when they saw the rockets launched. Just a few seconds later the rockets hit the room next to where Molan was working. In an incredible piece of luck, the rockets didn't detonate, or they would probably have killed Molan. Even without detonating, they killed two Americans in the room they hit.

He was often fired on when driving around Baghdad or other parts of Iraq. Houses next to his were hit, with casualties. Once, flying from Baghdad to Mosul, he was dozing in a low-flying Blackhawk helicopter when he opened his eyes to see a 23 mm anti-aircraft gun blinking at the chopper, just as the gun was about to be fired. The gun was mounted on a civilian vehicle, just near a major highway oddly enough choked with American military vehicles. The insurgents fired a three or four round burst at Molan's chopper. Luckily the side gunner had seen it too and yelled out to the helicopter pilot. The pilot took radical evasive action by tipping the chopper on its side for a split second and diving virtually to ground level, then scooting off at barely tree-skimming height. Fly any higher and you attract shoulder-launched missiles.

Between 10 and 30 feet up and moving as fast as you can is generally the safest way to travel in Iraq, but as this experience shows, no way is safe. Friends and associates of Molan's were killed in Iraq. His personal security guard included four Australian SAS soldiers and a slightly larger number of US soldiers. They had plenty of work.

For all that, he does not regard his assignment in Iraq as among either the most dangerous or the most brave. He reserves that distinction for the ordinary American soldiers who manned checkpoints: 'The microcosm of the US forces that I saw was the checkpoints. There were tens of thousands of young people on checkpoints. To be on a checkpoint is a terrifying experience', Molan told me.

'The aim of a checkpoint is simple, to check a civilian's credentials and let them pass. But in Iraq you check their credentials and they blow up. Anyone who approaches can kill you. I was involved in maybe 15 attacks, rocket-propelled grenades, mortars, hostile fire etc. It comes and goes so fast, it's all over quickly. But a guy on a checkpoint for 12 hours is incredible. And for many US soldiers it's 12 hours a time, day after day, month after month.'

One of the constant tensions in Iraq, from the days of General Tommy Franks and the first US civilian administrator, Jay Garner, was that between the American military and the American civilians. This improved under Negroponte, in part because his five top diplomats were themselves Vietnam veterans and had an appreciation of US military culture. Negroponte and Casey, in Molan's observation, brought a new unity to what the Americans were doing.

Molan didn't get switched into his new role because of agitation from Canberra. Even in his infrastructure role he had been making a big contribution and no other member of the coalition had the moral authority to tell the Americans who to appoint to what posts.

'By then I knew the country, knew the people, knew the fight', Molan recalled.

His predecessor as chief of operations, US Major-General Tom Miller, a special forces veteran, had spent 15 months in the job. As Molan would do, he had worked 20 hours a day, seven days a week, and was well past exhaustion point. Nonetheless, Molan's appointment to replace him caused a stir: 'Many of the Americans were quite astounded that I had the job. It was the toughest headquarters I'd ever been in because the issues were so important. There was no such thing as an Australian level of competence and command. There was a world level of competence and command that was invariably defined by the enemy. On any day I'd have to fight off three other American generals trying to do my job. This is human nature. If you're slow or soft or incompetent people will come in over the top of you.'

Part of his job was shielding Casey from some of the gripes of his generals in the field, because that is what a deputy does.

Taken altogether, it was as near to a 24-hour-a-day job as you could get: 'I executed all the big plans and managed the day-to-day rubbish. If there was a fight somewhere and we needed more troops I'd decide who went.' Molan had six divisions under him, four headed by Americans, one by a Brit and one by a Pole. 'It was a mark of the maturity of General Casey that he was prepared to accept me. He could have had any general in the US army'. It is more or less inconceivable that any non-American other than an Australian or a Brit would have been accepted in that position. Molan's formal responsibilities came under three main heads. He had responsibility for strategic communications, which means all aspects of information. With modern round-the-clock television news this is critical both for support on the homefront and for actual operations on the battlefield. Molan says the policy was to stick to the truth but try to move information quickly and effectively. He also had responsibility for manoeuvre of all the coalition and Iraqi forces. One of the few cultural sticking points between him and his American comrades was that he refused to change the way he spelt manoeuvre. And the third was civil/military operations. He had 315 people on his direct staff, including three US one-star brigadiers and 23 US colonels.

For an Australian deployed with US troops there are always issues of whose rules of engagement to follow and who ultimately has authority. The Australian normally remains under nominal Australian command and can only himself follow Australian rules of engagement, and this applied to Molan. But he can be under operational American command. Molan explains his situation: 'My authority came from General Casey, so I applied US rules of engagement on behalf of General Casey. I still couldn't do anything illegal under international law or illegal under Australian law. But the situation never arose because the US rules of engagement come directly from the laws of armed conflict.'

Molan was a central player in the second battle for Fallujah, the one at the end of 2004 in which the Americans decisively routed the insurgents from the city. Some months earlier there had been a US try at Fallujah but the Americans had backed off because of the danger of civilian casualties. Fallujah was a bloody and controversial encounter. Molan remains not only unapologetic about Fallujah but proud of what the troops did and of the operation overall.

Molan's pretty daughter has kindly made us our second cup of coffee. He is reflective, but his mind and his argument are direct and straight, as befits a soldier. He operates on straight lines. It's an orderly mind, well organised. It cuts to the central purpose. It's a general's mind.

'We prepared for Fallujah over four months and I believe the operation will stand the test of time. We conducted Fallujah both to protect the Iraqi people and to protect the Iraqi political process from attack. Fallujah was a safe haven for straight-out terrorists, not insurgents. There were 19 IED factories in a city of 300 000 (an IED is an improvised explosive device, they have been devastating as roadside booby traps in Iraq). There were six car bomb factories. There were torture chambers, TV stations, the Islamic command centre.'

Molan believes the battle of Fallujah was strategically necessary: 'We couldn't have done the Iraqi election if we hadn't done Fallujah. We had to reduce the capacity of the enemy to produce car bombs. It was entirely legal. The laws of armed conflict do not prevent savage fighting. We went into Fallujah with 42 pre-conditions. There were 140 mosques in this city, 66 were fortified and used to store weaponry. In the first fight, in April 2004, the people of Fallujah fought and the coalition backed out. In the second fight, in November 2004, the people had gone. They had had five months of being subjected to bizarre sharia law, jihadist rule, torture, abuse.

'Some 10 000 US marines and 3000 Iraqis fought through the city. The Americans lost 80 or 90 killed and 500 wounded. The responsible use of military force by the Americans cost marine lives. We could have flattened the city in a night and killed everyone there (and lost no marines) but that would have been wrong.

'The marines said we can't allow people to come back the second time until we clear it out because there are still stay-behind groups of enemy. But later 200 000 Iraqis went back. I was critically involved in planning that operation. Prime Minister Howard said when I was appointed that I was going to Iraq to plan operations, find and destroy insurgents, and protect the Iraqi people and the coalition force. That's what Fallujah was all about.'

Yet important as that battle was, it was only the precursor of what Molan regards as the most important achievement of his time in Iraq – the Iraqi national election in January 2005.

'The election was certainly the highlight', he says. 'There is a strategy to defeat the insurgency and that involves attacking it along four lines. They are: diplomatic/political; information; military; and economic/reconstruction. The main game is always political.'

Molan left Iraq feeling cautiously optimistic: 'The majority of Iraqis now have a say in the future of their country. The jihadists don't even make an appeal to the majority of Iraqis. All they want to do is kill Shias, kill Americans and take the country back to the 14th century. Politics is the main game. The military's role is to protect the political process and protect the Iraqi people against the murderers. The terrorists only have to be right once a day to have an effect, we have to be right all the time.'

In the couple of months before the election there were 500 attacks a week. In the week before the election there were 860 attacks. Yet on election day itself the insurgents did not penetrate one of the 5200 polling stations.

'The people who defended the polling sites were all Iraqis, with coalition forces nearby as back-up. The Iraqi security forces performed magnificently on that day. We were all blown away by them.'

Molan has certainly commanded more American troops than any other living Australian. His experience, and the views he has formed as a result, are therefore important. They come from a unique vantage point. They are also rather unorthodox in the Australian context.

I remember attending a great strategic gabfest in Canberra once and chatting to a senior New Zealand official during a coffee break. New Zealand can no longer afford the high-end military capabilities, he said, but by God we still produce good soldiers: 'You Aussies always think one Australian soldier is worth two Americans, well we know one Kiwi soldier is worth three Americans'.

Even at the time, this sounded to me dangerously like bombast. After talking to Molan at length, it seems just ridiculous. There is no doubting the quality of Australian soldiers, or indeed of New Zealand soldiers either. And it is a common refrain through the Australian security establishment that soldier-for-soldier Australians are as good as anyone and generally better than the Yanks. But in truth this is a complacent and untested proposition because we never take on the same sorts of tasks as the Americans do, the SAS excepted. Molan has a wholly original and distinctly bracing view of the question.

'I spent an intense period of time in the midst of the US military organisation', he said. 'What I saw was an extraordinary military, with naturally lots of foibles. I saw commanders from General John Abizaid down who had every right to be arrogant but weren't arrogant. I saw commanders who took a force optimised for conventional war and adapted it to a counter-insurgency force.'

Here is Molan's critical judgment: 'I took with me to Iraq all the stereotypes of how good we were compared with the Americans. None of my stereotypes survived. For example, the morality of the US force is as high as you could get. General Casey on a number of occasions restricted the use of weapons which were totally legal but whose use would have caused tensions in the coalition.'

Examples of such weapons were cluster bombs, claymore mines and CS gas or teargas. Cluster bombs leave the plane as a single bomb but then separate into more than a hundred grenade-like explosives, detonating just above the ground. They are devastating to troops in open ground but not all of the ordnance always goes off and this can be very dangerous for civilians coming back later on. There was never a question of using cluster bombs in Molan's time in Iraq. The US would not in any event use them after major conventional operations had finished.

Claymore mines are put out to defend a perimeter. But the military deploying them keeps control of them and detonates them individually by an electronic signal when it believes an enemy is in their vicinity. When they are finished the military takes them back up off the ground so they are not left behind to cause damage to civilians years later. But, unlike the US, a number of coalition nations, including Australia, had signed onto the convention outlawing landmines, so the US did not use them.

CS gas or teargas was not banned altogether but the authority to use it was held very high in the chain of command. This is because while CS gas is not a chemical weapon as such, it could have that connotation, and given the past use of chemical weapons by Saddam Hussein, Casey did not want to use anything that remotely resembled chemical weapons.

Molan continued: 'I met some extraordinary (US) reservists expressing their commitment through the lens of the 9/11 terror attacks, and others through what they could do for the Iraqis.

'The American army is competent to a level unachieved by any other force. The Americans know how to fight. They fight more legally and with less mistakes than any other force. The American divisional commanders are without doubt the best in the world. Most of them have got a couple of conflicts under their belts. They train with everything they need and their training produces excellence. Also, the machinery does have an effect in counter-insurgency.'

In Molan's headquarters, for example, there were 80 operators receiving battlefield information, from video to radio intercepts and all the range of intelligence sources, from all across Iraq. Molan believes the international media underestimates the human qualities of the American troops: 'This idea that the Americans don't relate to the people in the street is a myth. There is a feeling among the uninformed that the British did it better. But the intensity of the fight in Basra (where the British were based) was not comparable to that in the central Sunni area (where the Americans had responsibility). When the British came up outside Fallujah to Forward Operating Base Dogwood, they didn't wear their soft berets then.'

I ask Molan how he felt about the scandal of Abu Ghraib, which more than anything damaged US prestige in the Arab world and around the whole world: 'There was a lack of supervision. They didn't apply the adult supervision needed to those silly kids. The question was asked of Sanchez and it was determined that he didn't have a case to answer. Detainee operations is one of the most critical operations. The shame that my American friends felt was palpable. People felt ashamed of what their fellow soldiers had done.

'But overall I found the US force a highly principled force that was well led. People expect perfection from military operations, just as they expect perfection on day one of a response to natural disasters. But in the real world it doesn't happen.'

Molan has had in every sense a high-powered military career. He graduated from the Royal Military College at Duntroon in December 1971, well before the Vietnam war had ended, although Australia's substantial commitment had finished by then. He expected, like the generations of diggers before him, to see a lot of combat, including a lot of close combat. That's not exactly the way it turned out, though he was to serve in nations which saw plenty of violence: Papua New Guinea, Indonesia, East Timor, the Solomon Islands and of course Iraq.

He did two spells in Indonesia, first as the army attaché at the embassy and then as the defence attaché, the most senior military position in the embassy. Australian governments of both political persuasions have for decades thought there was great value in having a working defence relationship with Indonesia. Cosgrove claimed publicly that this relationship saved lives in East Timor, because so many of the Australian commanders knew their Indonesian counterparts and could talk to them, so that in the tense days when the Australian-led INTERFET (International Force in East Timor) was being deployed and the Indonesian military was withdrawing, trust could be established and misunderstandings, which could have been fatal, avoided. There was also the hope, never very profound, that some of the political values of the Australian military – acceptance of civilian political authority, respect for human lives – would rub off on the Indonesians.

The public also understood pretty well one of the quieter purposes of the military relationship – to gain intelligence for Australia on Indonesia's military. But really there was always a much deeper purpose to Australian military diplomacy in Indonesia, and that was to establish in Indonesian minds the competence and deadly capacity of the Australian Defence Force. Not to put too fine a point on it, this was designed to convince the Indonesians that Australia would be a good enemy to avoid. An endless series of Indonesian military visitors was invited to Australia and they were always shown the best we had to offer, never told about our logistics problems or our recruitment and retention difficulties. The subliminal message was simple – don't tangle with these folks because they have a lot of firepower and they are very good soldiers.

In his very person and bearing, Molan was part of this message. Oddly, Indonesia also provided some of the most dangerous moments in Molan's life. He was posted there in the tumultuous period of the fall of the long-time president and dictator, Suharto. He went out each day with the Indonesian military to observe the huge, seething, roiling demonstrations in Jakarta. As a 195 cm (6 ft 4 in in the old language) blond Westerner he made a pretty good target and at several of the demonstrations mysterious snipers fired into the crowd and sometimes into the military. Later, Molan was in East Timor as part of the Australian embassy's efforts in the worst days of violence preceding the deployment of INTERFET. On one ferocious night he had to speak on the phone to Howard to tell Howard that he believed the Indonesian military would not itself take violent action against the Australian forces which formed the bulk of the United Nations-sanctioned peacekeeping force. It was a critical call and a lot rested on Molan's judgment.

That is the nature of a successful soldier's life. His judgments carry the weight of life and death. The Australian army moulded Molan into an effective military leader. The US recognised this in giving him such a crucial job in Iraq. It also recognised it explicitly in Negroponte's letter to Howard.

US Defense Secretary Donald Rumsfeld awarded Molan the US Legion of Merit. Molan's appointment and performance symbolise Australian-US military inter-operability. It is almost impossible to imagine the US having a higher level of confidence in an ally than that it would put the lives of tens of thousands of its servicemen and women effectively in the hands of the ally's general. Of course it's a two-way street. Molan then brings the lessons of that command experience back to the Australian army. Molan himself becomes an enhanced national resource for Australia.

It would be churlish beyond measure to regard Molan's deployment as anything other than a success. And yet there are aspects of it that are disquieting. First, there is the question of Australia's commitment to Iraq under Howard. At what was presumed to be the sharp end of the war in Iraq, the initial fighting stage, Canberra committed forces totalling 2000 Australians from the three services. Of these the most directly involved were the SAS and, as we have seen (chapter 3), they did magnificent work. But after the conventional war-fighting was finished it turned out that the peacekeeping and reconstruction phase was much more difficult than had been expected and more difficult than the conventional war. Yet Australia's commitment to this task has been moderate. We have furnished leaders like Molan, and a few others, some of whose experiences will be examined later in this book, but on the ground we have never furnished more than a few hundred soldiers, generally in a relatively peaceful part of the country. That is not to underestimate the risks these soldiers face, the difficulty of what they have done or the quality of their contribution. The Australian soldiers have been superb and have fulfilled every task asked of them. But it would have been well within Australia's military resources to take responsibility for security in a whole area of Iraq and to provide everything necessary to sustain security there. That is what Australia did in Vietnam.

Canberra's contribution has not matched its rhetoric. We have spent billions of dollars prosecuting the war on terror and the Howard government certainly took the view that Iraq was a central front in the war on terror, yet it never really wanted to make a sustained, big contribution. The Americans were appreciative of Australia coming in at the initial combat phase when almost no one else did, they were appreciative of the small numbers of Australian troops the government kept in Iraq in the face of some domestic opposition, they were highly appreciative of the political support the Howard government gave to the US effort in Iraq and they were appreciative of the contribution of individuals like Molan, but they also certainly noted the gap between Australia's rhetoric and the scale of the troop commitment.

Some other, seldom asked, questions arise from Australia's deployments in Iraq.

When Molan graduated from Duntroon in 1971 he looked back on the relatively recent experience of Australian soldiers in Korea, the Malayan emergency, confrontation between Malaysia and Indonesia, and of course more recently Vietnam. All had involved close combat. But since then the Australian Defence Force, with the exception of the SAS, has not been much involved in close combat, unlike the Americans, who have been in close combat after close combat – in the first Iraq war in 1991, in Somalia, in Afghanistan and in Iraq most recently.

Modern war has changed. As Molan discovered, even 'war among the people' is ferocious and deadly. Enemies who don't represent a state, who don't wear a uniform, who don't fight in military formations, can possess the most deadly and sophisticated weapons: armour-piercing missiles, rocket-propelled grenades, surface-to-air missiles, explosive devices of vast destructive power, and perhaps eventually weapons of mass destruction. If Australia is to face a more deadly challenge in its own region it could quite possibly have a lot of the elements of extremely violent close combat which have been witnessed in Iraq, and we would be under-prepared. Modern war, even if it does not involve states, is as deadly and violent as anything we've known.

There is another aspect in which our deployments are perplexing When in the last throes of the Jimmy Carter presidency the Americans tried to mount a rescue mission of their diplomats held hostage in Iran in 1979 they failed, in part because their separate services were unable to work seamlessly in a joint operation. Australians have performed superbly in their recent deployments, which have been predominantly single-service deployments into low-threat environments (the SAS excepted because it has worked in high-threat environments). But we have not undertaken truly joint operations in higher threat environments and we ought to be aware that we are inexperienced and untested in such circumstances.

In the war on terror, the soldier knows, and needs to know, the moral and political purposes of what he is doing. In a speech he prepared for a military audience Molan reflected on the nature of the enemy he faced in Iraq: 'In considering what we might learn from Iraq, we need to keep in the front of our minds that the enemy in this struggle are indeed evil. Attacks by the enemy in Iraq are indiscriminate, murderous and intimidatory, with, of course, absolutely no accountability. The themes that occur to me after one year of the closest scrutiny of my enemy was the constant misuse of religious shrines, mosques and medical facilities such as hospitals and ambulances, a willingness to use terror and intimidation, and no thought of offering a constructive alternative for the Iraqi people. This is what we must train against as generals and as private soldiers.

'For all the faults of the coalition I see no moral equivalency between the coalition force in Iraq and our enemy. One only needs to read anything that (al-Qaeda leader) Abu Musab al-Zarkawi writes, and to look at the daily actions of all anti-Iraqi groups, to see that transgressions of the laws of armed conflict are institutionalised within those groups in Iraq. Transgressions of the laws of armed conflict, even merely allegations, are comparatively few on the coalition side and are neither condoned nor institutionalised.'

Finally, Molan reflected on just what is at stake in Iraq: 'War in Iraq is about the biggest issues that mankind can address. Amongst them are concepts of freedom, religion, the role of the individual in society, the place of nations in the world, and on a daily basis, life and death. Warfare in Iraq remains violent in the extreme, and close and sustained combat is the norm that must be expected and prepared for.'

Chapter 9

THE AUSTRALIAN DEFENCE FORCE: REDESIGNED FOR GLOBAL POWER

Consider this image. An Australian force of 2000 soldiers moving through the sea on vast amphibious ships. It is protected by destroyers armed with the most sophisticated point missile defence systems in the world. It is also protected by Joint Strike Fighters – by far the most advanced war planes in the Asia-Pacific, refueling when necessary in-flight in the sky above the embarked force. Submarines also accompany the convoy, providing further protection from assault on the sea.

But look, one of the submarines is taking a different route. It has a small contingent of SAS troopers on board who are going to land secretly at night and prepare the way for the larger Australian force. The big force on the big amphibious ships contains both attack and transport helicopters and huge, powerful Abrams tanks for close protection of the troops once they have landed.

This convoy dominates, controls utterly, the sea through which it travels. Unmanned aerial vehicles are patrolling above the landing point, scooping up the most minute intelligence. Above them US satellites are taking constant photos, not only of the convoy's destination but of every military movement in the region that could be relevant. That information is passed straight on to the Australians. Satellites, spy planes, ground stations and all the rest of the paraphernalia of signals intelligence are capturing vast quantities of electronic data, intercepting phone calls, fax messages, emails and much else, and sifting through it to find information relevant to the Australian expeditionary force. Any speck of useful data is passed on to the political leadership in Canberra, the defence force chiefs and the commander of the expeditionary force itself.

Where is this Australian task force heading? Is it going to restore order to a catastrophically failed state in the South Pacific? Is it going to render assistance to a friendly state in the war on terror? Is it operating as part of a US-led coalition? Is it, in some slightly different formation, racing to assist the victims of a natural disaster?

It's a powerful, formidable Australian force. At the moment, it's all imaginary. At the time of writing, Australia does not yet possess the Abrams tanks, the Joint Strike Fighters, the huge amphibious ships or the air warfare destroyers. The Australian Defence Force (ADF) has other assets which are also formidable. But all this new equipment, due to come online in the next few years, will transform Australia's capabilities.

This ongoing transformation follows a slow revolution in Australia's defence doctrine and philosophy. In defence, as much as anywhere, the Howard government has enacted a slow, quiet but profoundly important revolution in Australian life. The accepted doctrine of decades has been ditched. A new doctrine has taken its place. And a new defence force is taking shape to give expression to it. It's been an incremental, careful, gently sold, deliberate and comprehensive transformation.

When, at the end of 2005, Howard was making a defence announcement he made an accompanying statement, largely ignored by the press, which reveals a central part of his political strategy in defence and foreign affairs. He said: 'I am always very wary of grand pronouncements of doctrines as I think they can sort of create a false and wasteful argument.'

That is a perfect statement of the true Howard doctrine not only in defence but also foreign policy. Avoid the grand rhetoric or sweeping gesture. Just follow your path step by step, always ready to adjust, justifying each step to the electorate on its merits. And as a result you'll find you've travelled much further, and taken more of the public with you, than if, Paul Keating-like, you invite them to sign up for a grand adventure.

In this, Howard seems to be much in sync with the Australian people, who are profoundly allergic to ideology, radicalism, unrealistic visions or politics as poetry. Their chief request of governments is to get the trains to run on time. This very Anglo-Saxon preference for the empirical over the theoretical, for concrete and often mundane policy discussion over grand design and symbolic gesture, makes Howard in some ways of less interest to the commentator class. Commentators are drawn to sweeping plans and ambitious visions. So quite apart from ideological hostility to Howard there is often a kind of methodological prejudice against him as well.

Howard's way can tend to leave analysts in the position of the Israeli defence industry, which often has to reverse-engineer bits of defence equipment. Reverse-engineering is when you capture the plane and then your boffins try to work out how it works without the benefit of design manuals. In some ways Howard gives you the specific day-to-day policy and lets you work out the grand design for yourself.

But this should not obscure what a profound revolution Howard has brought about in defence policy and practice. In this his partner has been the almost equally unlikely revolutionary, the long-time, former, defence minister, Robert Hill.

The foreign minister, Alexander Downer, has been the key figure, apart from Howard himself, in the overall direction of government foreign policy. Part of Downer's success in the second half of Howard's government came from being so close to Howard. People knew that what Downer said went for the government. But Hill was Howard's key partner in transforming defence.

The advent of Brendan Nelson as defence minister in early 2006 led to much speculation that he might change direction. But in conversations for this book, and in public comments, Nelson made it clear he intends to continue the Howard/Hill approach.

Hill was a most unlikely politician, certainly an unlikely warmaker and progenitor of military build-up. A slim, thoughtful, softly spoken, very gentle person from the small 'l' liberal faction of his party, he has a degree in Asian studies, an adopted Asian daughter, a wife who has expressed her distress at mandatory detention of refugees and a well-earned reputation for liberalism. None of Howard's earlier defence ministers – Ian McLachlan, John Moore, Peter Reith – was in the job long enough to leave a substantial mark. Hill was the first to give the impression of really getting his head around the portfolio, and his forensic, industrious approach to managing the job helped give defence coherence. The criticisms of Hill tended to centre around not communicating enough with his cabinet colleagues and not communicating the government's defence vision with sufficient vigour to the public. But as we've seen, Howard is not so keen on vision anyway. Nonetheless, Hill's successor in the portfolio, Brendan Nelson, is much more of a natural political communicator than Hill was.

But for all that, in defence it's the results that count.

The Howard government's defence policies have described a fascinating arc. They began with cautious acceptance of the old Labor policies. These were the legacy of Kim Beazley as defence minister and the doctrine, proclaimed under him, that the Australian Defence Force existed for the narrow continental defence of Australia (DOA) and would be structured for that purpose, which would also afford them sufficient flexibility to occasionally take part in US-led coalition operations elsewhere.

The Howard government was jolted out of its acceptance of this paradigm by the East Timor experience, in which it became obvious that Australia did not have enough soldiers. Then its thinking was further revolutionised by the terror attacks on the US of September 11, 2001, and the Bali bombings a year later. As a result today Canberra has abandoned DOA, at least in its narrow conception, and now has a doctrine of structuring its forces for the defence of Australia and Australia's interests. Australia's interests are global and the defence force is now designed, within the limits of its overall size, to take on missions at the government's discretion almost anywhere in the world. Thus Australia's forces are designed to defend the Australian continent, to participate in regional operations in the South Pacific and east Asia, and to participate in coalition operations further afield. Coalition operations primarily mean US-led coalitions.

The Defence Update issued by Howard and Hill at the end of 2005 identified three primary strategic challenges for Australia – the war on terror, the proliferation of weapons of mass destruction and the danger of failed states. It is these challenges that Australia's defence forces are increasingly designed to meet.

Throughout Australian history, since even before federation, there has always been a certain tension between the continental defence approach and the collective security approach. Continental defence is just what it implies – merely being physically able to deny the continent to an invader. The collective security approach relies on being part of an international system – not the United Nations but an alliance system. This was originally with the United Kingdom, in its empire and its Commonwealth, and since 1951 with the United States. (Of course security involves much more than alliances but the alliances have been central.) This is neither a sycophantic nor a passive view of security. It recognises that Australia maximises its independence by having mutual security arrangements which allow it to contribute to the international order, and which also help to guarantee its own security.

Despite his dislike of dogma and grand pronouncements, Howard has on occasion made his disdain for DOA clear. In early 2005 he told parliament: 'In a world more interconnected than ever before, Australia must maintain a global perspective on the security threats we face in the 21st century. Australia's ability to hold such a perspective – naturally influenced by regional interests and responsibilities – is a measure of our strategic maturity as a nation.'

When Kim Beazley was defence minister, the continental tradition, the DOA approach, was formalised into doctrine and practice following a report by the former defence bureaucrat, Paul Dibb, in

1986 and a White Paper in 1987. The DOA doctrine held that the defence forces would be structured purely to defend the Australian continent. The key to this was denial to any enemy of the sea-air gap to Australia's north. Thus all emphasis was placed on the navy and air force. The army was left to wither, for the primary role envisaged for the army was merely to mop up those few straggling invaders who got through Australia's aeroplanes and submarines to the north.

This unnatural and frankly weird doctrine led to many bizarre results. No Australian government of either persuasion ever spent anything like the money envisaged to bring even the limited ambitions of DOA to fruition. Thus Canberra became more dependent than ever on American logistics and intelligence and technology even at the same time as it was beating its chest and proclaiming its self-reliance.

Similarly, the army was starved of resources and given insane tasks to perform. At one stage the special forces were reduced to counting trucks as they rumbled along the roads near the Kimberleys because for some reason the mythical invader was always expected to follow that route. Canberra's thinking became rigid in the extreme. In one exercise, the splendid former special forces officer Brigadier Jim Wallace was given the task of heading the enemy. He proposed that instead of invading across the Arafura Sea, as Australian doctrine declared that any invader would, he should send his force in on tourist visas in civilian clothes on Qantas flights to Sydney and Melbourne, where they could begin attacking vital infrastructure. This strategic creativity on Wallace's part – the sort of creativity that any actual enemy might show – was deeply frowned upon in Canberra.

DOA led to absurd restrictions being placed on Australian soldiers. The special forces had problems getting resources for any language training because under DOA they weren't meant to be going overseas.

One of the many problems with DOA was that it ignored Australia's strategic culture. Australia had always deployed the army overseas in coalition operations – from the Boxer rebellion and the Boer war through Korea and Vietnam to Sinai and Somalia and Cambodia and later East Timor and the rest. But under DOA the army got no resources so they were sent overseas with inadequate equipment.

But history has a way of exploding irrational doctrines. The wake-up call was East Timor.

At its height Australia's troop commitment in East Timor was only 5000 soldiers, in the history of combat hardly a massive force. Yet DOA had seen the army run down so badly that Australia could only just barely make the commitment. It could not provide all the logistics, for which American help was essential. And it desperately needed the New Zealand and other nations' troops who took part.

Australia's strategic planners should have realised the crippling nature of DOA earlier. When the first Fiji coup took place in May 1987, both Beazley and the then foreign minister, Gareth Evans, wanted to explore the military options for restoring the elected government to office. That may in any circumstance have been a very problematic proposition, but it was entirely irrelevant because Australia had absolutely no way of transporting the troops there and mounting any kind of operation. DOA meant the government had no options.

Another motive for the Hawke and Keating governments sticking so close to DOA, despite its evident failures, was that it served Labor mythology so well. In the Labor myth it is forever 1942, Australia's main defence is the 'moat of blue water' to the north and a brave John Curtin is bringing back the troops, against the wishes of Australia's treacherous allies, for the defence of Australia. Of course in reality even when Curtin brought the troops home he didn't keep them behind the moat but sent them to New Guinea to fight, and later elsewhere. And most of the Curtin myth overall is based on pretty fruity history at best. But the myth served the Labor Right well, because it allowed them to steer the Labor Left away from outright pacifism and to maintain some defence spending, rather than abolishing almost all modern defence capabilities in the mode of New Zealand.

In any event, slowly, slowly, slowly after Timor, the Howard government changed all that, dispensed with the myth, not by arguing with it or denouncing it but simply by ignoring it, and dispensed with the doctrine that flowed from it.

In late 2005 the Howard government announced that it was going to expand the size of the army and harden and network the army. This was a defining moment in the rejection of DOA. But it had been preceded by a series of equipment and force structure decisions, each of which had been bitterly opposed by the DOA brigade. Nothing has so long and tenacious a life as an established defence doctrine because careers have been built around it and legacies established. For a time in the early years of this decade it was as though the Australian defence debate were being run by a group of French pre-World War II strategists still committed to the Maginot Line, the defensive fortifications which were to make France invulnerable and which were simply bypassed by Hitler.

One of the most important, and symbolic, decisions was the purchase of 59 Abrams main battle tanks from the US in 2004. A fierce bureaucratic and semi-public campaign was waged against the tank by the DOA brigade because with the tank the army is deployable in many more circumstances. and the DOA folks don't really like such a widely deployable Australian army. Also, every dollar that is spent on a soldier, or a soldier's equipment such as a tank, is a dollar not spent on aeroplanes and submarines. In many ways the battle of the tank was the turning point for the revolution in the Australian Defence Force, for without a tank the Australian army would have declined into a kind of superior gendarmerie. The essential characteristic of the modern battlefield is that technology has collapsed all the traditional boundaries. Australia's elderly Leopard tanks, which the Abrams are replacing, were deathtraps on tracks. But the Abrams is a superb and tough vehicle. Australia has been lucky that the lack of a usable tank has not embarrassed it in the past. On the Solomon Islands it was the merest good fortune that the forces of the rebel/gangster Harold Keke did not have armour-piercing weaponry. In East Timor the Australians arrived to find Indonesian soldiers with rocket-propelled grenades which could have destroyed any Australian vehicle. Thankfully the Indonesian soldiers went home and did not give their RPGs to the militias who did mount sporadic opposition to the Australians. With the porous borders that characterise every troublespot today, and with the international black market in lethal weapons, the Australian army must assume that every future enemy will have armour-piercing weapons.

In Burma there are warlords with tanks. In Somalia Australian peacekeepers found they were confronted by Mohammed Aideed's irregulars in converted Toyotas, with armour bolted to them and with cannons on top, which were more lethal than their light-armoured vehicles. Future conflict is going to happen where the people are, almost certainly in cities. Almost all of the southeast Asian population lives within 200 kilometres of the coast. There are countless scenarios in which a tank could be critical. A tank, especially a top-of-the-line-one such as the Abrams, gives you three things: force protection, superior networking and, above all, choice and discrimination in response.

As the late Democratic Labor Party senator, Vince Gair, used to say: if you must be a dog, make sure you're an Alsatian. If you're going to operate a tank, make sure it's heavy, tough and formidable. Some British tanks in Iraq took 14 and 15 hits and were still operating and their crews still protected. Modern tanks don't operate in isolation but in concert with infantry, air support and other units. The tank also has the power to be a critical networking link between what the soldier sees and what a plane might need to do in response. With its sensors and communications capacities it is priceless.

The tank also allows an army to respond humanely and proportionately. If Australian soldiers are getting shot up in a future conflict in an urban setting, they could respond by immediately calling down air strikes which might destroy a city block. The tank gives you the option to absorb a strike, work out where it came from, and target a precise response.

The Defence White Paper of 2000 called on the army to have the capacity to deploy a brigade and a battalion, offshore, simultaneously. The tank's most common modern use is to protect forces in an urban environment. If Australian forces are to be deployed, they will need to be protected.

Much is made of the size and weight of the Abrams. In fact it's not much heavier than the alternatives. But being big and tough is a great advantage. No modern military moves tanks in any numbers by air. They are moved by rail and sea, where size is less important.

The purchase of the tank had nothing to do with the military imagining the great tank battles of the past. These are rare in modern conflict, which is likely to occur more frequently in urban environments. Immense, detailed study went into every aspect of the tank purchase. The Defence Science and Technology Organisation (DSTO) undertook an extensive study of the tank and its deployability and found virtually no country in the region where it could not be deployed. The DSTO study involved endless geo-thermal imaging, calculations of mean weights, bridge capabilities and the like. Similarly the Defence Intelligence Organisation looked deeply at regional tank capabilities. Every significant regional military has tanks. Tanks are not becoming less relevant. They do of course give an Australian government many more security options. Tanks could plausibly be used in Australia, in the region or a long way away, which are exactly the options the Howard government wants for its military.

The tanks are the leading edge of the broader concept of hardening and networking the army, designed to make it 'hit harder and be harder to hit'. The chief of the army, General Peter Leahy, championed this program, which the government has, after more furious internal bureaucratic wrangling, fully endorsed. Leahy has said it is his ambition that every soldier should travel to battle in an armour-protected vehicle and every soldier should be a node in a communications network that uses satellites, aeroplanes, manned and unmanned, and other assets to provide real time, battle space information to both soldier and commander.

There will need to be a strong investment in each individual soldier, who is required to make split-second life and death decisions as well as operate extremely complex equipment. A modern infantry force may be required to transition from conventional war-fighting to counter-insurgency to peacekeeping to civic rebuilding within the space of a day. Australia needs combined arms teams that are highly capable, that can deploy quickly and look after themselves against deadly enemies, many of whom may be non-state actors. The poorly trained US National Guardsmen of the notorious Abu Ghraib prison in Iraq indicate we may be entering the era of the 'strategic private', the private whose individual actions can influence the strategic outcome.

Under DOA it didn't matter if capabilities were 'hollow' as they were never going to be used. The emphasis was entirely on the hi-tech platforms. You could have 70 F-18s but only half that number of pilots because you knew they were never going to be used in anger. You could have battalions that were short of equipment and personnel because the only ones you'd ever conceivably consider sending into harm's way would be the SAS. Many of Australia's capabilities were symbolic. The enemy was allegedly deterred by these symbols, many of which were not kept in a ready state.

A similar campaign to that waged against the tanks was waged against the air warfare destroyers (AWDs) and the amphibious ships, in part because one of the main roles of these ships is to protect and transport soldiers, which does not fit with the DOA paradigm of defending only the northern sea-air gap.

In truth the AWDs will be of immense use to Australia. The Howard government has said it wants three of them, which is a credible minimum. They will be able to protect an entire area from missile and air attack. They will be a vital communication-and-force-projection node. They will allow Australia not only to deny the sea to an enemy but to actively control any area of the sea it chooses.

Part of the criticism of the AWDs, as of the Abrams tanks, is that they are too big, as if the Australian navy should content itself with small surface ships in which it can puddle around the coastal waters. But there is a worldwide trend for modern navies to build bigger ships because they are so much more versatile and capable.

Modern ships are more reliable than the vessels they replace. This allows multi-crewing, so you can keep the ship at sea longer. The AWDs will be able to protect themselves, protect any ships with them in a naval task force and protect any associated land force. They give the government lots of options. Naturally the DOA purists hate them.

Big ships like the AWDs and the amphibious ships are also priceless in natural disasters, or in the sort of emergency rehabilitation work needed after a major military strike. As well as being formidable war-fighting machines, they are floating hospitals, water-purifiers, mess tents, whatever.

Over the years Hill became more and more explicit in his rejection of the old DOA doctrine and his embrace of a new, broader outlook – namely defence of Australia and Australia's interests. In an interview for this book Hill explained that Australia's strategic circumstances and needs were different from those of European nations and therefore needed different policy responses: 'After the Cold War many armies wanted to get lighter and more mobile. But people were thinking of Europe's armies. But the threats to soldiers were becoming greater, so to protect your army you actually need more. We needed a slightly heavier army.'

I asked Hill to clear up the confusion between DOA and the contemporary outlook of the government. He replied: 'I don't ever say defence of Australia these days but defence of Australia and Australia's interests. It's not the DOA they (Dibb and others under Beazley) developed, based on defending Australia behind the moat to our north etc. That's why they oppose the AWDs, because you wouldn't deploy.'

Hill pointed out that in defence of Australia's interests its forces were deployed to Afghanistan (far away), Iraq (far away) and the Solomon Islands (nearby).

Howard and Hill clearly believe that in line with Australia's strategic culture and history, Australia must contribute in a dynamic fashion to an international security order that embodies its values and provides for its security.

'The global role we see is not a matter of doctrine', Hill told me. 'It's a recognition that globalisation and the war on terror have reinforced the global aspect of security to us. The alliance dimension is that we will be better able to contribute to coalition operations in the future. Some have said that Iraq will be the last. I don't believe that. I believe coalitions are the way of the future. Some will be United Nations coalitions. Some will be coalitions of the willing. If Australia is more willing to contribute to coalition needs its allies will be more willing to contribute to its security needs. A lot of trying to build up the land force and make sure it's protected is dictated by the world we live in, where everyone's got very destructive capabilities.'

Howard has certainly not created a national security state in terms of either the size, the role or the budget of Australia's defence forces. Australia still only spends 1.9 per cent of its GNP on defence, compared with 5 per cent by Singapore and 3.9 per cent by China, 3.7 per cent by the US and 2.4 per cent by the UK. (All these figures come from the Australian Strategic Policy Institute.) As recently as the 1980s Canberra devoted 2.6 per cent of the national wealth to defence. But because of the rapidly growing economy the Howard government has been able to increase the defence budget each year without increasing the percentage of the national wealth which goes to defence.

The government guaranteed that each year until 2015 the defence budget would get a real increase of 3 per cent. In fact to maintain its capabilities, certainly to maintain anything like its relative position in the Asia-Pacific, at least that much of an increase will be needed year on year for many years to come.

So Howard has not created a militaristic state. But he has transformed Australia's strategic doctrine and outlook and changed substantially its force structure. In doing all this he has in fact taken us back to something more akin to Australia's traditional strategic culture – a very Howard revolution.

Chapter 10

HOWARD'S LOVE AFFAIR WITH THE SOLDIERS

There was a moment shortly after he was appointed to lead the International Force in East Timor – INTERFET – in 1999 when General Peter Cosgrove was asked a question along the lines of how his soldiers would cope with the deadly militias that were wreaking havoc and committing murder among the people of East Timor.

A correct, even assertive, military answer would have been something like: I'm sure the Australian military will carry out its job effectively.

Cosgrove's answer was much more electrifying than that. It was along the lines of: these militias have shown themselves to be pretty good at murdering women and children, let's see how they go against Australian soldiers.

The military boffins call this strategic communications – communications which can have a strategic effect. The pride, the quiet self-confidence, the sense of service and decency involved in invoking 'women and children', the slightly old-fashioned nature of the words – it was as near perfect as you could get.

That day Cosgrove disclosed himself to be a public relations genius, a natural.

Of course it was more important that he was also a supremely competent soldier, that he could undertake the mission in East Timor effectively. To combine that bedrock military competence with his natural flair for public relations created a dynamic mixture.

That Cosgrove became such a folk hero in Australia, the Kylie Minogue sex symbol of the khaki set, notwithstanding that he resembled a large egg with a tonsure of thinning hair surrounding his bald pate, is a tribute to him and a reflection of the Australian personality. Big, bluff, hearty, straightforward, Cosgrove emerged from East Timor as a national icon.

But for the purposes of this chapter, the important point about the emergence of Cosgrove is that it accelerated the march of the Australian Defence Force (ADF), and especially the army, back to the centre of national life.

In its way this is an extraordinary development. Every Australian country town, and many of the town centres in the older suburbs of our big cities, have their war memorials with the long lists of those local diggers who died in World War I, and often the shorter lists for World War II, the Korean War and Vietnam. By the 1960s and 70s these war memorials were objects of irony, at least in elite culture. The Australian habit of fighting 'other people's wars' was routinely deprecated by the symbol-wielding classes. Eric Bogle's popular folksong *And The Band Played Waltzing Matilda* saw the Anzac commitment as wholly futile. While a powerful song in some ways, the age turned against its sentiment. Never has a prophetic line from a song 'some day no one will be there at all', in reference to Anzac Day marches, been more spectacularly wrong. Anzac Day celebrations have become the true national day. They are immensely popular with the young and each year huge numbers make the pilgrimage to Gallipoli in Turkey.

Howard has both shaped and taken advantage of this dynamic, and Cosgrove has been an important component of it.

Part of it has been independent of Howard, but part of it has been Howard's deliberate doing. The Howard government in office has been a counter-puncher, reacting to challenges and opportunities. It is part of Howard's political skill to use divergent events, and the opportunities they offer, to promote an underlying philosophy. In foreign and defence policy, the Howard government has been shaped by a series of specific events and its responses to them – the 1997 east Asian economic crisis, the rise and fall of Pauline Hanson and everything she represented, the 1999 intervention in East Timor, the terror attacks on the USA on September 11, 2001, the Bali bombings in which 88 Australians were killed in October, 2002, and the military deployments in Afghanistan and Iraq.

In the first half of his prime ministership Howard was an uncertain and frequently clumsy, even reluctant, participant in much of international life. The first few years, as argued elsewhere in this book, were ugly in terms of Australian foreign policy, especially in southeast Asia. But the Howard government got better as it went along. The East Timor deployment, and then the war on terror, led Howard to become a national security prime minister. Where he had been all at sea in the mediation of national identity and regional architecture in the early years, he developed an ever surer touch on national security, which became a source of great strength to him and his government.

Allying himself to the armed forces, pressing them into the service of his political aims, has been a key to Howard's enduring success. In suggesting this I am not saying that Howard improperly or undemocratically used the defence forces against his opponents, but rather that the higher salience of national security unleashed profound social dynamics which were overwhelmingly to Howard's benefit. Identifying himself with the military, especially the army, was a central element of this.

All democratic politicians search for non-political sources of authority to validate their relationship with the public. The public is cynical about politicians. So the politicians look for something or someone the public is not cynical about and try to get close to that, if possible to receive a blessing from the non-political figure or institution. For the politician to be seen as the defender of a revered institution is the very heaven.

Thus, without trivialising Howard's security policies, or his relationship to the military, there is something of a parallel in the way he has approached the Australian cricket team. No one who knows Howard even slightly could doubt the authenticity of his interest in cricket. For as long as I've known Howard – about three decades – a brief conversation about the cricket or football has accompanied our every encounter. But similarly from his earliest days as a politician Howard also understood that this was a private passion which could have immense public benefit for him. In the 1980s Howard was not a natural populist politician in the Bob Hawke mode. Cricket was one of the few avenues down which he could travel to a popular, non-political connection with ordinary people. It's the sort of thing that can't very easily be faked. Howard loves nothing better than to spend hours sitting at the Boxing Day test each year. While Don Bradman was alive Howard routinely described him as 'the greatest living Australian'.

The parallel in Howard's relationship to the military is obvious. Howard has a genuine interest in Australian military history. He is a devotee of the great Australian World War I general, John Monash, and can tell you the subtle differences between the different Monash biographies.

Howard is of course deeply conscious of all the ramifications of his relationship with the soldiers, and specifically of Cosgrove's role in bringing the army back into the focus of national attention. In an interview for this book, Howard told me: 'I think it's a good development (the new popularity of the military). It's obviously a product of the breadth of things they've had to do and they've done them all very well. I've certainly been a very strong supporter of the military, at every point sticking up for them. It's a combination of all those things. And Cosgrove's personality had a bit to do with it. Quite a bit. His leadership role in Timor – people were very proud of the Timor intervention. They felt it was done well militarily, that it was done in a humane way. They felt we'd done the right thing. It attracted an extremely wide coalition of support, from the very conservative right to the left.'

Even Howard's language in that quote is marvellously revealing – he's a 'supporter' of the military, he 'sticks up' for the military. This wonderfully Australian, bread-and-butter language shows

Howard at almost perfect pitch, connecting himself to the most powerfully popular institution in Australia.

One of the great contrasts of the Iraq war with the Vietnam war is the way the public, in both Australia and the US, have stuck with the soldiers. In 1972, Duncan Lewis, then a very new soldier in the Australian army, was spat on in Canberra's Garema Place. Such an event is unthinkable today. Lewis went on to become a general, to head the Australian special forces and, at the time of writing, was deputy secretary of the Department of Prime Minister and Cabinet (PM&C).

Howard, and civil society more generally, have sought to harness the new authority and prestige of the military, especially, it seems, the SAS. A former SAS leader, Michael Jeffrey, was appointed governor-general. Lewis was first appointed to PM&C to run its powerful national security division, but was quickly promoted. In his place at the head of the PM&C national security division, another former SAS man was appointed. Yet another military man, General Maurie McNarn, replaced a civilian, Frank Lewincamp, as head of the Defence Intelligence Organisation.

And then when Cyclone Larry devastated northern Queensland, Cosgrove was appointed from retirement to coordinate the initially troubled relief efforts.

This is a great contrast to the 1970s, when judges were regarded as the embodiment of civic wisdom and to bring credibility to an organisation you often appointed a judge to head it, as when Edward Woodward became head of the Australian Security Intelligence Organisation in 1976. Perhaps 30 years before that churchmen had great authority – think Spencer Tracy in the film *Boys Town*. But when a churchman, Peter Hollingworth, was appointed governor-general it was a disaster and the office had to be rescued by a soldier.

The pre-eminent symbol of all this, of course, is Anzac Day, although the Australian War Memorial in Canberra offers evidence as well. It is really the only man-made place in Australia which gives an authentic sense of being a sacred space. There is nothing postmodern or ironic about its treatment of Australia's soldiers, and demonstrators and graffiti never disfigure it. But Anzac Day's growing popularity, especially but not only among the young, is prodigious. Its near-universal presence in the Australian mind is extraordinary. There is hardly a publishing house which does not try to produce an Anzac Day book of some kind each year. One of the sad ironies of all this is that of all politicians Labor's Kim Beazley, with his deep knowledge and love of Australian military history, would have been well placed as prime minister to establish his own deep connection with the military in the public's mind. But these things are much easier to do from government than from opposition.

Beazley did however make a striking contribution to the intellectual reconsideration of Anzac Day. The Left in Australian politics have the greatest difficulty coming to grips with the popular esteem of Anzac Day. Unless you oppose it root and branch, which in Australia is a recipe for instant unpopularity, how can you fashion Anzac Day into a Left-wing narrative? It was a coalition operation in a distant land. It was undertaken with one of our great and powerful friends. The terrifying events of the landing emphasise every traditional martial virtue of courage, stoicism and, of course, mateship. No matter which way you slice it, it was predominantly a masculine business.

In the 1960s and 70s for a time the Left tried to mock it, but no longer. Left-wing commentators often promote two ideas about Australia and warfare which are both profoundly wrong: one, that all war is futile, and two, that Australia has a history of fighting other people's wars. There is a modern arrogance in the implicit idea that no Australians before the last couple of decades, and certainly none before World War II, ever thought seriously about Australian security, about our national strategic circumstances. Take World War I, of which Anzac Day has become the most poignant reminder for Australians. As well as being a morally just cause, given that Germany invaded Belgium and France, it was in our vital national interest that Britain and her allies prevail in World War I.

In a 2005 paper to Sydney's Lowy Institute, a paper which should have received much wider attention, Beazley directly attacked the Left's interpretation of the Anzac landings. He said: 'It is impossible to imagine a world in which Australians did not go ashore that morning at Gallipoli. But there was nothing inevitable about it. They were there because of strategic decisions taken by Australian political leaders. The Gallipoli legend of today minimises these decisions. It suggests that Australians found themselves on the Turkish shore that day because their political leaders were too unimaginative, too supine, too emotionally tied to Britain to see that this was someone else's war in which Australia had no part. This is a travesty of the truth ... Australians as a people thought carefully about their security before 1914. As the strategic challenge from Germany grew from the 1880s, they recognised that Britain would be less and less able to continue guaranteeing Australian security. And they realised that as Britain started looking for allies in Europe and Asia, its interests would sometimes diverge from Australia's. We started to see ourselves, not as a mere strategic appendage of empire, but as an active partner in imperial security. As such we had our own unique interests and perspectives, and our own responsibilities. We cannot understand the decisions of 1914, and we cannot understand Gallipoli, if we do not understand that Australia had compelling, direct and distinctively Australian strategic reasons to play its part in helping to ensure that British power was not eclipsed. We needed British power to help defend us from what we saw, rather presciently as it turned out, as direct threats closer to home.'

Thus, according to Beazley, Australians were not fighting other people's wars but contributing to an international security order, under mortal threat, which provided for their own national security against real, emerging threats.

Nor can the proposition that all war is futile be sustained. Otherwise it was futile to resist the Nazis, or to resist Japanese aggression in the Pacific.

It is revealing of modern Australian politics that Beazley made the case with close historical analysis but Howard benefited from the broad social sentiment, which understands these arguments at an instinctive rather than intellectual level.

East Timor can be seen as the specific, local Australian factor, and the war on terror as the global factor, which have helped propel the military back to the centre of national life. Many other dynamics are at work as well – the disrepute of so many other national institutions, such as the Christian churches, the search for some spark of spirituality among young people, the contrast of the soldier's heroism with the sense of being at least a little jaded by the hedonism of modern life, the concerted and shrewd public relations efforts of the military themselves.

Similarly, while the specific Australian experience is distinctive, it mirrors trends in other societies, especially the US. In the Summer 2005 issue of the US journal *The National Interest*, two American authors, Kurt Campbell and Michael O'Hanlon, explored the desperate straits the US Democrats have got themselves into regarding the national security debate.

They point out the rather startling fact that the most loyal voter demographic for George W Bush in the USA was not southern whites or mid-west evangelicals but soldiers and their families. They reveal fascinating figures from a *Military Times* survey from 2004. This survey showed George Bush as the preferred presidential candidate among active-duty military personnel by a staggering ratio of 73 to 18. Among contemporary military leaders, more than 60 per cent identified themselves as Republicans, while fewer than 10 per cent identified themselves as Democrats. Overall, of all military personnel, 59 per cent described themselves as Republicans, 20 per cent as independents and 13 per cent as Democrats. Among veterans the figures were slightly less lop-sided but the Republicans still had a huge advantage of 46 to 22 among those described as 'civilian leaders', and among the whole veteran population 37 per cent to 31 per cent. In the US a huge 18 per cent of the population has some military experience and 57 per cent of those voted for Bush in 2004 as opposed to 41 per cent for his challenger, John Kerry, whereas the former president, Bill Clinton, had evenly split the military veteran vote against George Bush snr in 1992.

These statistics are rather startling, given that on the kindest interpretation possible the Iraq venture was equivocal and suffered from very poor planning of the post-combat phase – poor planning which in no small measure contributed to the loss of life of American soldiers. They underline the main thesis of Campbell and O'Hanlon – that the American military culture has become in effect a Republican culture, that the Democrats no longer even seriously contest it. Given the enormous US military-related industrial base, this is a vast segment of society for a major political party to be so disadvantaged with. The fact that the soldiers liked the president, and the president liked the soldiers, communicated itself clearly enough to the broader electorate, and in the age of terror, when national security is uppermost in so many voters' minds, this has significant, broad social and political consequences.

Campbell and O'Hanlon acknowledged that there were many causes of this beyond the Democrats' control, chief among them the natural advantages of an incumbent in a time of war. But, both Democrats themselves (Campbell was a senior Pentagon figure in the Clinton administration), they did not exempt the Democrats from criticism for failing to mount a much stronger effort to fight the Republicans for possession of this turf. They cited a telling piece of anecdotal evidence. When it briefly looked as though Kerry had a chance of winning the presidency, there was intense speculation as to who his secretary of state might be. High-profile candidates such as Richard Holbrooke and Senator Joe Biden were both publicly close to the Kerry campaign. Yet there was almost no speculation over who Kerry's secretary of defense, perhaps the most powerful cabinet position in America, might be. At a time of war, there was no interest in who would head the Pentagon for the Democrats, a telling absence, a dog that didn't bark.

Now it would be wrong to transpose all this to Australia. The US military, the veterans' community, and the defence industries are a much larger proportion of American society than are the military, veterans and the defence industry in Australia. Given the huge American commitments in Korea, Vietnam and now Iraq, and the tradition of National Guard service, the proportion of Americans who have directly experienced military service is much higher than the proportion of Australians who have seen military service. Nonetheless, something of what Campbell and O'Hanlon describe has happened in Australia too.

There is little doubt that Howard is popular with the soldiers, who, as he says, he 'always sticks up for', and of whom he is a great 'supporter'. Howard takes every opportunity to reinforce this, in both the popular mind and the military mind. He is always on hand to farewell the troops, to welcome them home, to pin on a medal, to take a salute. He has promised them guaranteed real budget increases as far as the horizon. He appoints them to every senior position he reasonably can.

By the way, this may not be purely political calculation on Howard's part. A former British cabinet minister in the Blair government, who had for a time served in a junior defence portfolio, told me that even in the UK the increasing tendency was to look to the military. The military, he told me, has a can do attitude whereas the civil service has a can't do attitude. The military's primary objective is to engage the enemy and destroy it. The civil service's primary objective is to follow process. This is doubtless a grossly unfair stereotype, but it is the considered view of a man, with no personal military experience himself, who had administered several big civilian portfolios, and also had a defence portfolio, and knew which group of people he preferred to deal with. The same trend is evident in the US, where the relief operation for the residents of New Orleans after Hurricane Katrina improved markedly once the military became centrally involved.

So certainly in the US, the UK and Australia the military's prestige is very high. An important part of Howard's success has been his ability to harness that prestige for himself and his government. It is likely, however, that this is not a deeply rooted partisan relationship, that is to say, a Labor government could also quite possibly establish such a relationship for itself, especially if it kept up a reasonably high tempo of military deployments and continued substantial funding for defence. Such a development would be devastating for the Liberals in opposition because they are seen as the naturally more pro-defence party, so their loss of such a constituency would be even more threatening than it is to Labor.

Nonetheless it is threatening enough to Labor while Howard remains prime minister. For essentially these are games which can only be played in government, and Howard has played them brilliantly.

Chapter 11

DEFENCE COOPERATION WITH THE UNITED STATES

There is one country where Australia keeps about half a battalion of defence personnel permanently stationed and is likely to do so as far into the future as one can imagine. Guess which country that is. At any one time there are between 350 and 400 Australian defence personnel on assignment in the US. It is in its way a staggering number. It is an indication of the depth and the breadth of the military-to-military relationship between the US and Australia. There is no other country in the world where Australia has so many defence people permanently stationed, outside the active war or peacekeeping zones of Iraq, Afghanistan or the Solomon Islands, and those deployments, though they may linger for years, are not permanent. The US deployments are as near to permanent as Australia gets. They are unique.

Nonetheless, although the numbers are smaller, a somewhat similar level of military and intelligence intimacy exists between Australia and the United Kingdom, as we shall see later in this chapter. In the research for this book I was constantly surprised by the depth and intimacy of Australia's military relationship with the UK, and of the importance of the three-way Australia-US-UK relationship, with lingering though much less significant intimacy with Canada and New Zealand.

No one could be more in favour of the closest possible association with our friends in Asia than I am, but it is clear that the high levels of cultural and political similarity, the shared values and shared backgrounds, of the Anglo countries contribute to a unique military and intelligence intimacy.

The Australian defence personnel in the US are not of course grouped together in a single command. They are spread across the United States, across military and commercial organisations. The figure of 350 to 400 is not normally published. It is derived in two ways. In late 2005 I asked the Defence Department in Canberra how many people we had in the US. Defence was cooperative about the request but it took them some time to answer for the simple reason that they did not know. Each section knew which people it had sent abroad and where, but no one had compiled the figure centrally. Eventually, Defence came back with a figure of about 350. Independently, a very senior person in Defence told me the figure was 400.

Part of the variation is explained by the fact that Australian defence personnel are coming and going from the US all the time. Apart from the soldiers and others on long-term deployment, there are myriad Australians there doing defence business, at seminars, on short courses, attending consultations, evaluating equipment etc.

What is unknown to the public is the way the scope and intensity of this process of sending the Australian military to the US has increased at a huge rate in recent years. It is really only since the Vietnam war that Australia has made a habit of sending soldiers and others to the US on a long-term basis. It began in 1966 with the army posting Australian instructors, working in many different fields of infantry soldiering, to Fort Benning in the US as instructors. But it has greatly accelerated under Howard and Bush, driven by Iraq, the war on terror and the political closeness of the two governments.

The Australians in the United States come from the army, navy and air force. There is a substantial Australian military intelligence component in the US. Australian Defence civilians also come from the Strategic section of Defence, from the Capability Development Group, from the Defence Materiel Organisation, and the Defence

Science and Technology Organisation. Australians are posted to the US army, navy, air force, marines and special forces, the Pentagon, as well as commercial organisations and industrial and scientific research centres, and of course there is a goodly number at the Australian embassy in Washington. Apart from military operations, Australian personnel are involved in training and instruction, liaison and staff duties, medical, engineering and maintenance, communications, logistics, finance and administration, project management and scientific research and policy development.

There have been Australians posted to US Pacific Command (PACOM) for many years. But now there are also Australians posted to US Central Command (CENTCOM), which has responsibility for the Middle East, US Joint Forces Command and US Strategic Command. Because of our involvement with satellites and ground stations, Australia has had a long involvement with the US Space Command as well, but Space Command is now part of Strategic Command.

It is a minor revolution to have Australian officers appointed more or less permanently to these commands. The Australians in these commands do two different types of work. Some are liaison officers. They are well worth having. A number of other liaison officers from other countries are at some of these commands, and formal consultations, and the passage of formal communications, involve these liaison officers. But often the more interesting positions are held by the Australians who do line jobs at these commands. These might range across any number of military disciplines. Quite openly and above board, these Australians not only carry out their assigned tasks within the American commands but they are a priceless further line of communication between the Australian and American militaries. If they are high-quality people in high-quality jobs, as they generally are, they offer a distinctive separate line of communication between the Australian and American militaries. They also allow Canberra to inject an element of Australian thinking into the US system at the planning and design stage, especially of what might become joint operations.

It is important not to overestimate or underestimate these positions. They are not acting as spies or fifth columnists. In such a vast system as the US, any influence the Australians may bring to bear is incremental and just one particle in a vast galaxy of interests and institutions. But they do play a role, often commensurate with their ability. The fact that they're allowed to play such an intimate role is a direct result of the high level of trust the two militaries have for each other.

This has very practical applications. The Australians involved see a great deal of sensitive military information, not just active intelligence but core information about US weapons systems, battle plans and the like. The Americans accept the Australian security clearances for such officers. This indicates a high level of confidence.

Naturally this is a two-way street. Numerous Americans are deployed in Australia and the Australians too accept the Americans and their security clearances.

The sensitivity of the material to which Australians have access is evident even from the official explanation of US Strategic Command of its purposes. Its official mission statement says it is to 'provide the nation with global deterrence capabilities and synchronised Department of Defense effects to combat adversary weapons of mass destruction worldwide. Enable decisive global kinetic and non-kinetic combat effects through the application and advocacy of integrated intelligence, surveillance and reconnaissance; space and global strike operations; information operations; integrated missile defence and robust command and control.' (A word on jargon: kinetic means when you hit something, non-kinetic means when you have an effect on it without actually hitting it.)

An area of intense growth in recent years has been deployments of exchange personnel to third countries. In significant terms this only happens with the US and the UK, although in principle Australia will do it with Canada and New Zealand and has on occasion in the past done it with Canada and New Zealand.

Again, this demonstrates what a high level of intimacy and confidence exists among the militaries of the original UKUSA five Anglo countries. For it is a big step to send your military off to battle under the colours of another country, and this is what we are talking about.

Australian soldiers often spend a year or two in a US unit and some Americans do the same in Australia. As was explored in chapter 8 on the army's General Jim Molan, and will be explored in chapters 15 and 21 on the navy's Commodore Steve Gilmore and the air force's Air Commodore Mark Binskin, respectively, and as was mentioned in chapter 3 on Colonel Rowan Tink of the SAS and Afghanistan, many who rise to senior positions in the Australian Defence Force have done stints on exchange in the US. The Chief of the Defence Force, Air Mashall Angus Houston, himself spent a period based in Utah in the early 1980s flying helicopters with the US air force.

While they are on exchange in the US, the Australians are treated as Americans. They are responsible to their American commanders and they follow American orders. However, they are also bound by Australian rules of engagement, which are slightly different from those of the US. Australia, for example, has signed a treaty banning the use of land mines. The US has not. Similarly, there is a slightly greater range of prohibited targets and munitions for an Australian conducting operations from the air. The Americans know this and accommodate it, although all the veterans of such exchanges I spoke to said it was never an issue in practice.

At the same time as they follow the orders of their American commanders, the Australians on exchange with US forces are nominally under the command of the Australian army, air force or navy attachés in the Australian embassy in Washington. If they are with an American unit which is deployed to a third country, such as one in the Middle East, the request for them to participate comes back to the chief of the defence force in Canberra to approve on a case-by-case basis. Twenty years ago such approval was rare and I have spoken to Australian SAS veterans who were intensely frustrated when on exchange with their British counterparts they were not allowed to deploy into third countries. So when their British units went into action, the Australians had to stay home. Now, the situation is reversed. The assumption is that approval for such deployments will generally be given unless there is some overriding reason why not.

Thus there were Australians who went into Iraq as part of American units, and there were Americans flying combat missions in Australian F-18s as part of the air combat commitment Australia made to the Iraq campaign. Again, military trust and confidence simply does not come any higher than this. Australia and the US have been allies for a long time but this is not the way things were routinely done 20 years ago.

Thus the intimacy of the cooperation happens in the field, with the forces working together, it happens at the highest political level, with the governments committing to joint objectives, it happens at the most sensitive levels of the various US commands, with Australians integrated into the American decision-making processes.

This operational intimacy also flows directly out of decisions taken by the political leadership. Howard's willingness to join Bush in some highly controversial ventures is of substantial political use to the Americans and as a result they want to cement it, and repay it, by involving Australia as much as possible and sharing whatever benefit comes out of it. Similarly, the Australians want to reap any operational or intelligence benefit to be had for their own forces as a result. The most important case of Australia joining the US in a controversial venture was Iraq, where only three nations did substantial work at the combat phase – the Americans, the British and the Australians. However, there are other examples. Australia is a participant in the US missile defence effort. Australia's contribution is small at this stage, participating in research and development. Australia's military leaders believe this is a good investment for Australia. It keeps Australia closely in touch with developing

US technology. No one envisages Australia ever constructing a national missile defence for itself, but theatre missile defence, in which deployed troops or a naval convoy defends itself against missile attack, is already a reality. Given the proliferation of missiles in the Asia-Pacific region this is a development of acute relevance to Australia.

Similarly, Australia was one of the first nations to commit to the Proliferation Security Initiative (PSI), designed to prevent North Korea from proliferating weapons of mass destruction or the ingredients from which to make them, by intercepting suspect North Korean vessels if necessary. The PSI fits closely with Australia's own national policy, which sees WMD proliferation as one of the greatest strategic challenges to Australia's national interest. But when it was first announced the PSI was controversial because it simply goes around the United Nations, so Canberra's early commitment was of extra political use to Washington in selling the PSI internationally.

Other Australian commitments are less controversial. The Howard government took a $100-million equity position in the development of the F-35 Joint Strike Fighter. It is thus presumed that the JSF will in due course be the main aeroplane in the Australian air force. The Australian government could still back away from such a decision but is unlikely to. The equity position makes sure it is closely involved in the development of the project.

Then of course there are the other pillars of defence cooperation – the hosting of the joint facilities, which are essentially communications bases for intelligence purposes, and the holding of regular joint exercises. Australia hosts some of the biggest bilateral joint exercises the US has with anyone. There are several reasons for this. The US's biggest alliance, NATO, is a multilateral alliance involving many nations. With New Zealand dropped from ANZUS since 1986 (over its refusal to allow the visit to its ports of US nuclear armed or powered ships), Australia is one of the most significant bilateral defence partners the US has. The other quality which Australia offers is space. The Australian forces, like the

Americans, are trained in the tradition of manoeuvre. The vast open spaces of northern Australia especially are perfect for large-scale military exercises.

The very fact, too, of New Zealand's exclusion gives the US another motive for emphasising what Australia gains in technology and military expertise through the ANZUS alliance. In an interview for this book Howard said he favoured keeping the name ANZUS even though New Zealand is not any longer a part of the alliance. Said Howard: 'Let's not rename it because one day you might get a New Zealend government with enough commonsense to come back. But I wouldn't bet your inheritance on it.'

When he was New Zealand's deputy prime minister and foreign minister, Don McKinnon once told me he thought the New Zealand policy of banning visits by US ships which were nuclear armed or nuclear powered was baseless, and that a New Zealand government inquiry had established beyond doubt that there were no health risks of any kind from a visit by a nuclear powered ship (US ships no longer carry nuclear weapons). However, McKinnon told me, the politics of changing the policy were just beyond the then National government in Wellington.

Howard confirms that shortly after winning the 1996 election he had a similar conversation with New Zealand's then prime minister, Jim Bolger.

'He (Bolger) felt it was all too difficult,' Howard said.

There is no doubt that the extensive joint exercises Australia does with the US contribute a significant part of the professional capability of the Australian forces. According to Christopher Hubbard in his book *Australian and US Military Cooperation* (Ashgate, 2005), in 2003 there were 19 separate joint exercises between the US and Australian forces. Among other things, these joint exercises allow the Americans to feel comfortable with Australian officers in command of large coalition operations.

At times it is impossible to keep track of all the different elements of defence cooperation between the US and Australia – apart from high-profile activities such as deployments in Iraq and

Afghanistan. The Australian army, for example, participates in the ABCA (America, Britain, Canada, Australia) program, under which the armies of those countries try to standardise their equipment and practices. There are similar programs for the other services At the 2004 AUSMIN meeting the two countries' defence and foreign ministers agreed to develop a Joint Combined Training Centre, a concept still being worked out as this book was written. At the 2005 AUSMIN meeting the two nations announced a regular program of visits by US strategic bombers – B-52, B-1 and B-2 aircraft. The ministers said this would provide opportunities for enhanced joint training with the Australian military, mainly to be undertaken in northern Australia.

This vast, day-by-day defence cooperation between Australia and the US has been going on for a long time. But it has increased substantially in scale and intensity under the reigns of Howard and Bush. While it may not always remain at the level of intensity brought on by Iraq and Afghanistan and the war on terror, Howard and Bush's successors are likely to find that the broad outlines of the arrangement are agreeable politically and of value to both militaries.

Chapter 12

AUSTRALIA'S STANDING IN AMERICA

In 2002 I flew into the United States through San Francisco. Whenever I can I come into the west coast through San Francisco. It is so much lovelier a city than its ugly, misshapen sibling down the coast, Los Angeles. Two things struck me on that trip. One was the familiar yet always slightly unsettling sensation of the absolute vastness of America, the sheer stupendous magnitude and variety of the American adventure. The other was the quite astounding popularity of Australia.

Everywhere I went in the beguiling city by the bay I seemed to come up against images of Australia. Part of it is sport, of course. There on the front page of the *San Francisco Chronicle* was a picture of Lleyton Hewitt, shortly before he won the Wimbledon final, under the blaring headline 'Awesome Aussie'. At the restaurant that night pride of place on the menu went to something called 'Aussie surf 'n' turf'. This strangely labelled delicacy was apparently a steak. Whether the steak was actually Australian meat or not was less important than that the restaurateur obviously thought it would benefit his sales if he identified the dish as Australian. Later I would see a similar theme in a chain of restaurants called Outback Steakhouse.

Finally that night, back in the hotel room, I turn on the television and what do I see but a beer commercial which ends with the solemn intonation: 'Fosters – it's Australian for beer'. This seems to indicate not that there's any particularly flavoursome quality to Fosters but rather that somehow or other there's an inherent moral purpose in buying Australian. If you drink Australian beer you'll be more like an Australian.

Later on that same trip I would participate in a seminar addressed by the then national security advisor, Condoleeza Rice, who would begin by observing that she knew God was in his heaven and all was right with the world when she reflected that the two Wimbledon singles champions were an Australian man and an African-American woman (one of the Williams sisters).

My personal experience bore this out as well. In Hawaii during the Iraq war my wife and I were taken to dinner by a typical young US naval couple – he Caucasian, she of Chinese ethnic background, both officers in the navy –simply because we were Australians, and Australians were such good allies of the US. People came up to my wife and me in the restaurant to say hello when they heard our accent.

In 2004 and 2005 I had two separate stints as a visiting fellow at the Centre for Strategic and International Studies (CSIS) in Washington, DC. Although the CSIS is a security-oriented think-tank, my impression of it was that there were at least as many Democrats as Republicans in residence, and certainly at in-house seminars and the like there was plenty of criticism of the Bush administration policy and much opposition to the war in Iraq. But hardly a day went by without some American knocking on my door to say they'd heard an Australian was in residence and wanted to be welcoming and see if there was anything they could do to make my time there more worthwhile and enjoyable.

But assessments of a favourable US view of Australians don't just rest on my personal experience. In 2004 the then Australian ambassador to the United Nations, John Dauth, hosted a cocktail party at which Nicole Kidman was the guest of honour. She had starred in *The Interpreter*, the first movie to be allowed to be filmed in the UN building itself. Dauth was metaphorically stampeded in the crush to get tickets – there was a limit of 500 – and not just from every middle-aged male in New York. For Kidman was at that point the premier diva of her time.

The Australian invasion of Hollywood is of course legendary. Kidman, Cate Blanchett, Naomi Watts, Mel Gibson, Russell Crowe, Heath Ledger, Eric Bana, Hugh Jackman, Geoffrey Rush, the list goes on and on, all of them A-list stars, and there are countless lesser lights as well. Australian directors, from the generation of Peter Weir and Bruce Beresford, and cinematographers and film people of every stripe, have taken advantage of the US's exceptional openness to foreign talent.

But it's not just sport and showbiz. Michael Thawley, the former Australian ambassador to the US, who finished up in 2005, recalled that when he took up his post in 2000 there was a swathe of Australian corporate and institutional leaders in the US. Thawley said: 'Rupert Murdoch headed the largest media empire in the world, Jim Wolfensohn headed the World Bank, and Jac Nasser, Doug Daft and Geoff Bible were in charge of three of America's business icons – Ford, Coca-Cola and Philip Morris. The Lowy family and the Pratt family were already major forces in their respective industries. Macquarie Bank now has a large real estate presence and is a leader in developing infrastructure in the United States.'

Every year Thawley went to a dinner to honour an Australian businessman who had risen to the top of his field in the US. In 2005 that Australian was Andrew Liveris. Born in Darwin of a Greek immigrant family, Liveris had become chief executive officer of Dow Chemicals.

And then there are the professors, and the artists and the gallery curators and the writers and countless others. America has been a promised land for talented Australians.

So what does it all add up to in terms of Australia's standing in the US?

It all adds up to a very good name and a species of soft power – that is, a significant dollop of goodwill and a willingness to listen to an Australian with ideas.

Of course there are negatives. The mandatory detention of boat people got a lot of bad publicity in the US, so too occasionally do indigenous issues. The Cronulla race riot was widely covered. Similarly the scandals arising out of the kickbacks paid in AWB, formerly the Australian Wheat Board, contracts with Saddam Hussein's Iraq under the United Nations oil for food program were embarrassing. But none of these seems lasting in its damage. And you'd have to be an exceptionally jaundiced observer to believe the negative comes anywhere near balancing the positive.

As I argue elsewhere in this book it is naturally a challenge for a strong middle power like Australia to get the tone just right in its dealings with big powers, especially a superpower like the US. Excessive humility does not convince Americans that you're a morally superior person. If you tell them you're powerless and not worth talking to or taking seriously, they'll take you at your word. At the other end of the scale, braggadocio is equally counterproductive. If you come across as boasting about things you can't really deliver, underestimating the intellectual sophistication of your interlocutors or pretending to knowledge and expertise you don't possess because you haven't put the work in, Americans quickly lose interest.

My impression is that Australians in government, the national security bureaucracies, especially the military, business, sports, the arts and entertainment are increasingly getting the tone right. They are increasingly self-confident because they know they have something to offer.

But Australia's standing in the US is a mixture of soft power and hard power. Soft power is essentially a nation's capacity to attract and influence people, without exercising force or even necessarily money. It's especially a question of reputation. Hard power is military power and to some extent overwhelming financial power. The hard power in Australia's case is its military and economy. The Australian military deployments in Afghanistan and Iraq, and later in response to the Asian tsunami, won a lot of publicity in the US. Of course you can ridicule this notion by saying the average

American is not much aware of Australia, but so what? The average American is well disposed towards Australia, and those Americans who follow international affairs at all are particularly impressed by Australia's sustained high economic growth and by its military deployments. They are impressed that Australia makes the military deployments at all, and that its military is so competent.

America's critics see it as pushy and domineering. Americans tend to see themselves, however inaccurately, as bearing the world's most difficult burdens, especially in security, mostly alone. They are profoundly appreciative of those who are willing to share the burden.

This is not a party political issue in the US. The Noam Chomsky far Left no doubt see Australian policy as an arm of evil Western imperialism, but mainstream Democrats certainly do not. Kurt Campbell, now of CSIS but a senior Pentagon official under Bill Clinton, told me in an interview that he believed the Australian-US relationship had taken a great step up under Bush and Howard and that as a Democrat he applauded that. More significantly, Senator John Kerry in running against Bush in 2004 pledged to seek greater allied support for the US effort in Iraq. Had he won the presidency, he would hardly be hostile to those nations which helped the US, the very nations he would have asked for more help had he become president. Democrats' hostility over the Iraq war was squarely aimed at the Bush administration, not at US allies. Kerry demonstrated this by supporting passage of the US-Australia Free Trade Agreement at a time when he was attacking Bush from a broadly protectionist position.

I put the question of Australia's standing in the US to Richard Haass, the head of the prestigious Council of Foreign Relations, in that body's splendidly antique New York headquarters. Haass was for a while head of policy planning at the State Department under Powell, during George W Bush's first administration. The policy planning position is generally regarded as the intellectual's position at State and has been occupied by many august luminaries. Haass was a Powell-like moderate, no neoconservative, probably more dovish than Powell, rumoured to have left State because he got sick of losing all the policy battles to the Pentagon. His response was telling. Australia, he said, was now one of the few countries that the US would consult as a priority in a crisis: 'Australia has now emerged on the shortlist of countries the US sees as a dependable ally. Australia has two things going for it – it's like-minded and it has some relevant capabilities.'

This is a big call from Haass. He also told me he didn't think the Howard government would have had any difficulty forming a close relationship with a Kerry administration, just as Tony Blair had effortlessly switched from Clinton to Bush.

The Bush administration takes an extremely positive view of Australia. Deputy Secretary of State Bob Zoellick declared just before the AUSMIN (Australia-United States Ministerial) meeting in Adelaide in November 2005, that 'the US has no closer alliance partner than Australia'. I wrote a column commenting on the line at the time and got an email from Zoellick emphasising that he had in fact chosen the words very precisely. Words like that have consequences. They get reported, as the Americans know they will, by every embassy in Australia back to head office.

What about a non-American assessment of Australia's standing, from some independent institution like the London School of Economics, say. Professor Gwyn Prins, a Brit, who holds a chair at both the LSE and Columbia University in New York, and is one of Europe's leading strategic analysts, provided me with an initially rather startling evaluation over a Turkish lunch in Sydney.

Australia, he said, is in the most globally powerful position it has ever occupied in its history and it has the most influence globally which it has ever held in its history.

Prins's professional work is centred on making strategic assessment and projection more complex, taking account of a greater number of variables. He told me his assessment of Australia's historic position was based on four considerations.

One, Australia's status as a front-rank insider in the innermost circles of the Western intelligence club, ranking only behind the US and the UK. For the true strategic professional, that is always a first-order consideration.

Two, Australia's ability, within the US alliance system, to project military force decisively in a way that few others can. That may seem outlandish, given the small size of our military. But the spectacular performance of the Australian SAS in Afghanistan and Iraq was militarily vital. We have seen in chapter 1 President Bush thanking Australia for knocking out any Iraqi capacity to attack Israel from its western desert and thus draw Israel into the Iraq war. The role of the SAS and the Australian military keeps cropping up. Oddly enough, at the beginning of the Iraq war I interviewed former Israeli prime minister, Ehud Barak, himself a special forces veteran and military hero. He singled out the Australian SAS: 'Your special forces are highly appreciated in the whole world. (Your contribution) is very important to Bush and Blair symbolically, but it is also important operationally since you supply something which is in very short supply, namely special forces. In special forces it's about quality, not quantity, and your forces are high quality.' So Barak, it would seem, makes a similar assessment to Prins.

Consideration three, Prins said, is Australia's stellar economic performance. Australia has not abolished the business cycle but it has had strong growth for a decade and a half. It undertook a great burst of economic reform in the 1980s and has continued that reform more modestly in recent years. At the same time growth and demographic vitality have been underpinned by a strong immigration program. Australia is actually one of the best equipped economies to take advantage of globalisation. A high-growth, rich economy will always interest the world. And it gives a nation a range of options for exercising power, everything from dispensing economic aid to sustained military investment. It also has a high correlation to social stability.

Consideration four, for Prins, is the very nature of Australia's defence capability, its inter-operability with US defence capability, always potentially a massive force multiplier, and its overall technological quality.

It's telling that in Prins's consideration of Australian power, the American connection is quite vital.

Most people in most countries of the world do not think that often about Australia. But the ones who study power closely come to similar conclusions to Prins.

Indeed you strike Prins-style thinking about Australia all the time. In an opinion page article in *The Wall Street Journal* just before the Canadian election in late January 2006, Mary Anastasia O'Grady listed the reasons there would be a change of government in Canada. She wrote inter alia: 'There is dismay over Canada's declining role in world affairs. It was once akin to Australia in its ability to participate in Free World alliances and peacekeeping missions. But neglect of the armed forces has badly damaged its influence.' O'Grady's column is not about Australia, that sentence is Australia's only mention, but her assumption that everyone understands that Australia is a significant military power and player on the world stage is the more telling for not needing, in her view, any elaboration or argument. It's just obvious.

Rich Armitage, the former US deputy secretary of state, rates Australian power higher than most Australians do. He told me in 2003, when he was still in office, that Australia is 'a global power' (his words, not mine) and increasingly a 'critical player on the world stage'. Australia, he said, had 'a global role and global responsibilities'. The US-Australian alliance is not limited, in Armitage's view, to the Asia-Pacific region. By 2005, when he had just left office, he was making a much bigger claim for the Howard-Bush relationship than even Howard does himself: 'At the end of the day, the relationship between President Bush and Prime Minister Howard is such that any bureaucrat in Washington knows that if push comes to shove all Howard has to do is ring the president, and if it's legal and it's moral, it'll happen.'

That is a claim no prime minister would make for himself. Armitage made the remarks in the sure knowledge that they would be reported not only in Australia but back into the American official system and on the international diplomatic network.

Armitage's words are somewhat borne out by Bob Woodward's book on the Iraq war, *Plan of Attack* (Simon & Schuster, 2004), a book written entirely from American sources, entirely for an American readership, without a thought, I should imagine, of any Australian market. The book repeatedly recounts Bush consulting Howard in the lead-up to the Iraq war, taking Howard's political difficulties into account. It tells of Howard successfully urging Bush, against Cheney's advice, to try the UN route.

Armitage, like Howard, rejected utterly the idea that al-Qaeda and similar terrorist groups make Australia a priority target because of Canberra's closeness to Washington: 'You (Australia) are not targets because you're allies of the US but because you stand against things that al-Qaeda wants to bring forward.' Armitage also stressed the breadth of support for Australia in the US: 'Australia is not a Republican-versus-Democrat issue in the US. Australia has a lot of political capital to draw on.' This was somewhat confirmed even in Bill Clinton's memoirs, in which Howard gets an honourable mention for leading the East Timor peacekeeping operation.

To its critics on the Left in Australia, the Howard government is uniquely wicked and reactionary, full of malevolence, always damaging Australia's international reputation, always on the brink of earning Australia international pariah status. But to the vast majority of people in the world who have ever heard of the Howard government, and certainly to mainstream Americans be they Democrat or Republican, the Howard government is just a straightforward centre-right government of an unusually successful and pleasant country with a strong military tradition.

Bush of course has many times heaped praise on Howard, calling him 'a man of steel' and 'a man of courage and conviction', 'my good friend', and so on. It is pretty difficult to regard these words as meaningless but you can interpret them as primarily an expression of gratitude for having an ally in Iraq.

What is more telling in a way, perhaps, are the remarks Bush made to the Republican national convention in the midst of the presidential election campaign in September 2004. In one of what must be very few ever references to Australia in a presidential nomination acceptance speech, Bush said: 'I deeply appreciate the courage and wise counsel of leaders like Prime Minister Howard'. Howard was first in the list, ahead of the British, Italian and Polish leaders, the only others Bush mentioned by name. Bush went on to lampoon his challenger, John Kerry, for having once referred to the US's allies in Iraq as a 'coalition of the coerced and bribed' (a remark Kerry came to greatly regret). Surely, Bush said, Kerry could not be referring to proud nations such as Australia and a few others he named.

The significance of all this is Bush's political calculation. In the most important and watched speech of a desperately close presidential election, in a speech doubtlessly crafted and negotiated and polished a thousand times, Bush and his advisers judged it would help him win US votes to be associated with Australia. There is no big ethnic Australian lobby in the US. It's not like being associated with the Poles or the Italians or even the Filipinos. Rather, Bush and his team decided that Australia's reputation was so bright that it helped Bush to be associated with it.

The material in this chapter is literally the tiniest tip of the biggest iceberg. You could go on collecting American references to Australia forever. What they indicate is that Australia enjoys a favourable image in the US. They also establish that the Howard government is held in reasonably high esteem by the US political class and especially by the Bush administration.

Will it slacken once Bush or Howard passes from the scene? The answer must be yes. A Kerry administration would have been dominated by Atlanticists and more Europe-centric than Bush's administration. To some extent the alliance always takes on the character of the respective leaders. But the lesson there is just that important alliances need constant political nourishment. At the same time the Howard government has tried to establish institutional structures – from the enhanced intelligence cooperation, through the Free Trade Agreement and even the commitment to an

Australian equity position in the development of the F-35 Joint Strike Fighter, which will endure. There are already a range of institutional structures in place – the annual AUSMIN talks, the annual leaders' meetings of APEC (the Asia-Pacific Economic Cooperation forum) and a tradition now of both prime ministerial visits to Washington and presidential visits to Australia (the last three presidents, Bush snr, Clinton and George W Bush have all visited Australia while in office).

Part of the American goodwill, of course, is based on misconceptions of Australia. Australians are often seen in the US as inhabiting a rugged frontier society, whereas Australia is one of the most urbanised societies on Earth. Americans often see Australians as a better version of themselves – living in a big country, a new world nation of immigrants, an egalitarian and collegial society, republican in sentiment, democratic in practice. In all such ideals, in all such stereotypes, the good and the bad, there is a deal of inaccuracy, a failure to pick up much nuance. That is just the nature of public opinion. But more Americans are visiting Australia as tourists or on business and they invariably enjoy the experience. The bottom line is that Australia possesses significant soft and hard power, which decision makers in America respect.

The great challenge to Australian policy makers is to maintain and deepen the connections between the two societies, and to take advantage of the access and opportunity which the US system offers to advance Australia's national interests and also our values, and by so doing to advance the cause of mankind.

Chapter 13

INDONESIA: HELPING WITH LEVIATHAN, OR DEPUTY SHERIFF?

When you fly into Semarang, the bustling port city and provincial capital of central Java, you realise all over again just how densely the main island of Indonesia is populated. The profusion of red roofs on approach to the airport reminds you irresistibly of the approach to Sydney. Semarang indeed is not that much smaller than Sydney in population, while on Java there are 100 million souls.

Semarang is known as a centre of radical Islam. It is also the location for the Jakarta Centre for Law Enforcement Cooperation, an odd name given that JCLEC is not located in Jakarta. Perhaps that's designed to put the terrorists off the scent.

JCLEC is a state-of-the-art counter-terrorism training and operational support facility, jointly managed by Indonesia and Australia.

The day I visit JCLEC with Australian foreign minister Alexander Downer security is very tight. We arrive on a small RAAF VIP jet with two Australian soldiers and a small party of officials on board. From the moment we alight we are accompanied by a virtual army of sleek, wiry, black pyjama-clad Indonesian security police, in dark glasses and wired for sound. At least one security man travels in each car. We are whisked away in seconds, never spending a stationary moment in the open.

JCLEC is located inside AKPOL, the Indonesian Police Academy. After we get inside the gates a troop of Indonesian policemen presents arms, a trumpet greeting is played and Downer lights some ceremonial flames. He is greeted by police Brigadier-General Paulus Purwoko, who, with his counterpart from the Australian Federal Police, is joint executive director of JCLEC.

Downer asks about a triumphant statue at the front of AKPOL. It turns out to be a likeness of an Indonesian general killed by the communists in 1965. There aren't many communists in the Australian government, Downer assures his Indonesian host. We're a very anti-communist government.

JCLEC is set on a hillside of dense tropical greenery. It has the air of an upmarket university. Some if its buildings are converted police academy buildings. Others are brand spanking new, and look it. It has state-of-the-art technology spread throughout a sizeable campus – 50 km of data cabling and 3500 sq m of indoor training space, from computers and video cameras to every form of simulation facility for training. There are six 'burn cells'– little huts that can be repeatedly burnt down and rebuilt to train fire investigators.

Much of JCLEC's focus has a grim necessity. A group of 80 Indonesians had barely completed a course on disaster victim identification (of which gruesome skill there is a worldwide shortage) when the second Bali bombings took place in October 2004. Some of the course graduates flew straight from Semarang to Bali to practise what they had just been taught.

Touring JCLEC we pass a disused Merpati Airlines jet, now used for hijacking simulations. There is a train for the same purpose, and a mock hotel. We enter one of the training buildings and come upon four beefy, friendly, open-faced American blokes. They are agents of the US Bureau of Alcohol, Tobacco, Firearms and Explosives, and they are there to teach a course on investigating arson scenes.

JCLEC is a symbol of the intimate Australian-Indonesian counter-terrorism cooperation. The presence of the Americans at JCLEC is a symbol of the Australian-US alliance, and its important role in the Australian-Indonesian relationship.

JCLEC, an Australian initiative to which the Indonesians readily agreed, grew out of the response to the first Bali bombings in 2002. The closeness between Jakarta and Canberra it symbolises is fairly recent, and as the Papuan asylum-seeker crisis of early 2006 demonstrated always somewhat fragile. A few years ago a joint project like JCLEC would have been unthinkable.

Howard's relationship with southeast Asia, more specifically with Indonesia, has described a fascinating arc. The Howard government came into office in 1996 accepting the close relationship the Keating government had built up with the Suharto government in Jakarta, including the security treaty which Keating had secretly negotiated with the Indonesians. Howard's first deputy prime minister, Tim Fischer, described Suharto as the man of the century and the Howard government's first foreign affairs White Paper hailed the security treaty with Indonesia as being of historic significance.

At the same time Howard was profoundly uneasy with aspects of Keating's approach to Asia, in particular the idea that in order to relate fully to Asia, aspects of Australia's national identity would need to be amended. Howard also felt, inaccurately in my view, that Keating had neglected some of Australia's traditional relationships, in particular with the US and the UK. This led the government to embrace for a while the clumsy slogan: 'Asia first but not Asia only'.

The real trouble for Howard in southeast Asia began with the rise of Pauline Hanson. Each country is to some extent imprisoned in its stereotypes and one stereotype of Australia in southeast Asia is racism and the White Australian policy. This is changing as more southeast Asians gain direct experience of Australia through tourism, education and immigration, and find that Australia, while it has its share of problems, is not a noticeably racist society. The problem was never that Howard embraced Hanson but that he seemed unenergetic in opposing her and slow to reject absolutely that element of racism which was an undoubted part of her semi-incoherent but complicated appeal to a small minority of the electorate.

In the whole weird Hanson eruption the Americans played absolutely no role. Whatever problems Australia was encountering in southeast Asia then were all its own making. Eventually, Hanson faded away and her policies, such as restricting Asian immigration, were not implemented.

Then came the 1997/98 east Asian economic crisis. This began with a run on the currency in Thailand and spread throughout most of southeast Asia and South Korea This was a devastating blow for southeast Asia and South Korea. Although the Howard government had somewhat de-emphasised relations with southeast Asia, it had always understood the importance of a stable Indonesia to Australia's national interest. Howard's foreign policy views were formed substantially by the Cold War. The Cold War mindset always saw Indonesian stability as critical to Australia.

Australia was one of only two countries – Japan was the other – to contribute money to all three International Monetary Fund (IMF) bail-out programs, for Thailand, Indonesia and South Korea. This book has examined the growing closeness between the Howard government and the Bush administration and the increased intimacy of the alliance between the two nations under those leaders. However, there have always been things Canberra and Washington disagree on. For example, the Howard government signed up to the convention outlawing land mines, to the International Criminal Court, the Comprehensive Test Ban Treaty and a raft of other international agreements Washington disdained.

At any one time there are always a great many things Washington and Canberra agree on, and a number of things they disagree on. Throughout the 90s Canberra opposed the US linking China's most favoured nation trade status with human rights, before that it opposed the punitive so-called Super 301 trade legislation aimed at Japan, and it always opposed the inclusion of labor and environment clauses in trade agreements, an issue that was a big deal for southeast Asia.

In the 1997/98 east Asian economic crisis Canberra and Washington diverged sharply over the severity of the IMF program imposed on Indonesia as a condition of emergency financial support. The disagreement came to a head at a meeting between Downer and the then deputy secretary of the US Treasury, Larry Summers, in the grand Treasury building in Washington on March 18, 1998. Both Downer and Summers were accompanied by a raft of officials, and while they didn't exactly have a screaming match there was blunt, difficult disagreement.

Downer thought the US was pushing the IMF to make unrealistic demands on Indonesia, demands which it couldn't fulfil and which threatened to tear Indonesia's social fabric apart. Summers, a completely orthodox economist and an abrasive personality, responded that he was concerned with the message coming out of Australia that the IMF was the problem rather than the Indonesian government. Some in Australia, Summers said, had been operating in a way that would help those who wanted to subvert the IMF program.

The argument went back and forth and was pretty willing. Downer said the substance of the IMF program was OK but sequencing was crucial. In other words not everything could be done at once. Summers asked, semi-rhetorically, what did Australia think could be done straight away. While Downer answered Summers's question, Summers went on to say that the integrity of the whole program was of the greatest importance, suggesting he wanted everything done more or less straight away and his question was rhetorical. Summers did agree that immediate food aid to Indonesia was OK, but he again stressed that if Indonesia got a message from its neighbours that there was no alternative to providing it with unconditional aid that would undermine the IMF. Summers didn't say it in so many words but he went very close in effect to accusing Australia of working against the IMF program, and therefore against the US, in Indonesia.

Downer started to become impatient with Summers. He told the American he was trying to be constructive. He was trying to explain what would and would not work in Indonesia. Australia lived right next door to Indonesia and this gave it some particular insights. Canberra broadly supported the IMF program, Downer told Summers, but Australia would pursue its own interests, not the interests of others. He bluntly told Summers that Australia did not always agree with US actions on Indonesia.

Downer told Summers that the photograph, which had become notorious, of IMF director Michel Camdessus standing over Suharto, arms crossed, as the seemingly supplicant Indonesian president signed an IMF agreement had been 'most unfortunate'.

Summers made one fairly startling statement which would have accorded with Australia's views. He said that the then treasury secretary, Robert Rubin, had told the president, Bill Clinton, that dealing with Indonesia could be the most important issue Clinton would have to deal with in the remainder of his presidency. Certainly Americans were giving Indonesia sustained attention at the highest level, but it remained the withering Australian view that the Americans never fully grasped what they were dealing with or indeed what they were doing.

The conversation finished with the usual courtesies. Its detailed content has never been revealed before. I have confirmed the substance of it with a number of participants. My purpose in recounting it here is to demonstrate that Australian cabinet ministers have no difficulty at all disagreeing with American leaders to their face. They may soft-soap the Americans a good deal when things are going OK but if Australia's interests are at stake they are invariably forthright in their representations.

This was to be even more the case in the next great Australian-Indonesian episode, East Timor.

Throughout the Hanson years most of the criticism of Howard's performance in southeast Asia came from the political left and the foreign policy class itself. When Suharto resigned in May 1998 and BJ Habibie succeeded him as president, and Indonesia committed itself to democratic processes, Howard and Downer recognised that this offered a chance to change the nature of the Indonesian-Australian relationship. It meant the governing dynamic could move from one where the political leaderships in both countries could interact pragmatically, but there was little public support for the relationship on each side, to a more normal, broadly based political interaction.

On December 21, 1998 Howard sent a fateful letter to Habibie. In it he suggested that Habibie grant greater autonomy to East Timor and consider eventually holding a referendum for independence there. To Howard's astonishment Habibie almost immediately decided to hold a referendum in 1999. Senior Indonesian figures felt they didn't want to go on paying money for East Timor's development if at the end of the day it was going to become independent anyway.

Again, the US was not a central player in all this. Certainly Canberra was not taking initiatives to please Washington. Rather the strategic calculation in Canberra was that a prolonged period of autonomy was actually Jakarta's best chance of hanging on to East Timor, which was still Canberra's preferred outcome. The Howard government also believed – and this was Canberra's central purpose – that if East Timor could be normalised through an internationally and domestically accepted autonomy package the one great irritant in the Australian-Indonesian relationship could be removed.

It is now history that while the Indonesian government did allow a free vote parts of its military also conspired to create a murderous militia movement opposed to East Timorese independence. After the vote for independence on August 30, 1999, a wave of murderous violence swept over East Timor. Australia swiftly organised a United Nations mandate to lead a coalition of the willing to act as peacekeepers in East Timor. This was done with the cooperation of the Jakarta government. This led to permanent hostility to Australia by Osama bin Laden and al-Qaeda, because removing from Muslim rule land which had once been under Muslim rule was a grievous offence in al-Qaeda ideology.

It also led to harsh anti-Australian feelings from some Indonesians, but these seemed short-lived. Straight after the exercise it looked as though Canberra's policy objectives were lost – East Timor had become independent, which was not Canberra's original preferred option, and relations with Indonesia had been poisoned. But within a few years relations recovered and the underlying policy objective seemed to work over time – the politics of the Indonesian relationship were no longer bedevilled in Australia by the East Timor issue.

However, for the purposes of considering the Australian-US alliance, two other aspects deserve examination. First, the American response. Bill Clinton, in the last days of his presidency, stood in a weak position vis-à-vis the Republican controlled Congress. He had endured bad experiences with a number of peacekeeping operations. He had little wish to entangle himself in what was for him a new problem far away in southeast Asia.

Because Australia had let its army run down under the disastrous Defence of Australia doctrine, Canberra was stretched to the limit to provide sufficient troops. It had two priorities in assembling the International Force for East Timor (INTERFET) – to recruit some southeast Asian forces so that politically it looked more acceptable, and secondly just to get enough soldiers to do the job. Howard and Downer made a plea for American 'boots on the ground', and were initially rebuffed.

This led to some criticism of the US in Australia and a questioning of Washington's commitment to the alliance. In fact, Australia similarly had not committed troops to US regional peacekeeping efforts, as in Kosovo, and there was nothing in the East Timor experience to suggest the Americans were any less committed to the basic security guarantee under ANZUS.

However, after a good deal of contact between Howard and Clinton, and a robust and frank meeting between the two at an APEC (Asia-Pacific Economic Cooperation forum) summit in New Zealand, and after some important work by Australia's friends at the Pentagon and the State Department, the Americans came powerfully on board. They still did not commit ground combat troops under Australian command, but they provided other substantial and perhaps critical support. Quite possibly Australia could not have done the job in the way it did without this support.

The Americans provided necessary logistics units which Australia did not have. The Defence of Australia doctrine was always a charade and a fraud and at its heart lay the idea that the Australian army would not deploy significantly overseas. When you have to mount an operation like East Timor in a hurry, the logistics requirements are huge. Australia did not have all the logistics required. The Americans made up the gap. A joint Australian-US military exercise was underway and military resources were able to be diverted straight from it to the Timor operation.

The Americans also provided crucial intelligence support. This does not mean revealing secrets whispered around the Indonesian cabinet table but operational intelligence – satellite, spy plane and ship-based surveillance of everything that moved in or near the Australian area of operations. Of course, Australians did a lot of this themselves, but their efforts were massively augmented by the Americans.

The Americans also provided direct military support. There were 250 US military personnel on the ground in East Timor – not combat troops but specialists doing a variety of other jobs. But the important military resources were the powerful naval cruiser with a contingent of 850 marines plus another naval ship kept in the East Timor area. The Indonesians cooperated with INTERFET, which was brilliantly led by General Peter Cosgrove, but feelings were running high and it may have been that some Indonesian units could have been tempted to cut up rough. The Indonesians knew all about the American military presence on the ground in East Timor and the marines on the US cruiser and the cruiser's own firepower. Any thought of military action by any Indonesian unit would have had to confront the possibility that the Americans would use their massive military power assembled nearby.

Finally, Australia could only carry out the operation in the first place if Indonesia agreed. The Americans put massive diplomatic pressure on the Indonesians to accede to a UN force, including public statements by Clinton and the cut-off of all US military aid. It is more than likely that this pressure was a decisive factor.

When Clinton decided to get involved, he cited standing by Australia as the key reason.

Thus, for an episode which some believe illustrates the limits of the Australian-US alliance, East Timor does precisely the reverse. It illustrates the immense strength of the alliance, even when led by two figures unsympathetic to each other such as Howard and Clinton, personally not close, politically on opposite sides of the fence. All the region saw that Howard could call the Americans to his side. It was a powerful demonstration of alliance potency.

The UK also gave important diplomatic support and important military support on the ground, including a regiment of Gurkhas plus a vital special forces detachment. East Timor was not remotely connected to British interests or responsibilities except in a general humanitarian way and through its impact on Australia. That the UK got involved is also a tribute to the enduring strength of the Australian-UK relationship.

None of this is to diminish the hugely important contributions of Australia's southeast Asian partners, such as Thailand and the Philippines. The fact that they contributed so generously and effectively underlines a theme of this book: that the US alliance and good relations with southeast Asia reinforce each other.

The final, almost farcical, element of the episode was the deputy sheriff title which Howard allowed a journalist to pin on him. Although East Timor was a confused policy episode for both Canberra and Jakarta, it resulted in an independent East Timor and the end of government human rights abuses there. It also resulted in the Australian public feeling great pride in the performance of the nation's soldiers. There was a period when Howard was inclined to talk boastfully of Australians as the UN's 'preferred peacekeepers'. He answered affirmatively a journalist's question based on a reference to Australia as the US's 'deputy sheriff'.

Quite reasonably the magazine involved trumpeted the quote. It was highly offensive throughout southeast Asia and Howard, stubborn like most strong politicians, took a few days to correct it. It cast Australia's successful East Timor intervention in the worst possible light in southeast Asia and it provoked many critical commentaries on Howard in the regional press.

But in the end it was a mistake not a policy, a stylistic slip not a substantive change. The hardheads in the region had great respect for what Australia achieved in East Timor. It is also worth noting that while it involved the US, the deputy sheriff gaffe was not in any way the US's doing. It was all Howard's own work. Otherwise all the troubles with Indonesia, and southeast Asia more generally, in Howard's first five or six years in office had nothing to do with the Americans and do not support the fashionable but wholly groundless proposition that the US alliance damages Australia's standing in southeast Asia.

After East Timor, relations between Australia and Indonesia were testy for a couple of years but Canberra kept trying to help Jakarta in Washington, and with direct aid. The Bali bombings in October 2002 threw the two nations together in a way that was completely new to the generations now in office. The bombings killed 202 people, 88 of them Australians. Apart from killing a number of Indonesians the bombings devastated Bali's economy. Megawati Sukarnoputri, then Indonesia's president, was passive and clumsy in response. But her security minister, Susilo Bambang Yudhoyono, SBY as he's universally known, was magnificent.

The Indonesians, under SBY's leadership, made a vital decision. They allowed investigators from the Australian Federal Police to come in and help them. This had two long-term results of the greatest importance. The first was to cement a pattern of Australian-Indonesian counter terrorist cooperation which has become ever more significant and led to such outcomes as the Jakarta Centre for Law Enforcement Cooperation in Semarang. The second was to set in train a process which captured the perpetrators of the Bali bombings and had them stand trial in the most transparent and detailed terrorist trials to have taken place in the Muslim world. These trials, with their exhaustive evidence and the testimony of survivors and victims' relatives, did more to convince the Indonesian public of the reality of the terrorist threat than any other imaginable process could have done. The Americans were also involved, with the FBI lending investigative assistance.

When Australia decided to join the Americans in Iraq, Howard made a trip to Jakarta to brief Megawati about the decision personally and to reassure her that a war against Saddam Hussein was not a war against Islam. It was a deft touch by Howard, showing courtesy and consideration to Megawati and delivering the right message. I spoke to many Indonesian policy makers at that time and they were unanimous in their view that Saddam did not represent Islam and Indonesia had no wish to suffer in defence of his cruel regime. So, while they formally opposed the US and Australian action, the Indonesians did not allow it to become an issue in the bilateral relationships.

On the first anniversary of the Bali bombing SBY as security minister made a magnificent speech in commemoration, a speech broadcast in Australia. He said, of all the Bali victims of all their different nationalities: 'They were our sons, our daughters, our fathers and mothers, brothers and sisters, our cousins, our best friends, our soul mates. And they were all innocents.' But SBY went further that day. He didn't neglect the hard political truths of terrorism: 'These diabolical men and their brand of evil simply have no place in our society. They belong in our darkest dungeons, locked away beneath our children's playgrounds. History will condemn them forever.' SBY's closest advisers believe this was the moment when he developed his own special relationship with the Australian public. This too is unique – an Indonesian president whose rhetoric touched a broad Australian audience.

When SBY became president in October 2004 it was a stroke of good fortune for Australia. SBY was a proud nationalist and a proud soldier, but he had no anti-American or anti-Australian hang-ups. In some ways he resembled the former Philippines president, Fidel Ramos, another technocratic soldier who got things done. SBY had done some of his military education in the US. He had a child at university in Australia. He was moderate, technocratic, instinctively pro-American, and the most pro-Australian president Indonesia had ever had.

I have had the good fortune to interview SBY a number of times. In April 2005 I met him not long after he had come back from a ceremony honouring the nine Australians killed in the helicopter crash on the Indonesian island of Nias. He had awarded posthumous medals to the nine in a ceremony with their grieving families, whom he had tried to comfort. Yudhoyono is a military man in Indonesia. His vast and sprawling and difficult nation has many types of pain, many refinements of suffering. Tragedy is an everyday companion. But SBY was greatly moved that day by his encounter with the Australian families, and cancelled a number of appointments afterwards. One of his aides told me that the nine were 'heroes' to the Indonesian nation.

When I met him that night SBY struggled to get the words just right: 'My own feelings of course we really mourn the loss and I have to respect and honour all soldiers who have lost their lives and who have showed their great courage, sacrifice and dedication for helping their brothers and sisters in Nias.'

It was a simple enough statement, but this completely unselfconscious reflex of calling Australians Indonesia's 'brothers and sisters' is a wonderful human instinct, quite distinctive in the history of Australian-Indonesian relations.

Howard and Downer have constantly hammered home a message to Washington about Yudhoyono. The message is simple: if you care about democracy and stability, counter-terrorism and economic growth, the development of moderate Islamic politics and the normalisation of the military in Indonesia and throughout southeast Asia, SBY is the very best possible president of Indonesia you could have. In other words, as well as being good for Indonesia he is good for Australia and good for the US. Therefore Washington should take yes for an answer. It should pursue the closest cooperation it can with Indonesia. It should resume an intimate military-to-military relationship and it should take any opportunity it can find to help SBY.

Jakarta, of course, is well aware that this is the message Canberra is giving to Washington. Thus the US alliance, and the access it gives to Australians in Washington, is a dimension of Australian national power which it can deploy as part of its relationship with Indonesia.

In December 2005 I had the chance to talk to SBY in his Jakarta office, not long after the Americans had lifted a ban on providing certain types of military equipment to Indonesia and engaging in certain types of military cooperation. Canberra had quietly lobbied Washington for months on this. As so often happens in the US system, the administration had been sympathetic but a couple of key congressmen had held things up.

Naturally SBY was upbeat about that particular development but he outlined a general approach to me which has been consistent through his presidency: 'I am delighted to note that the US has lifted the sanctions it imposed first since 1991 and the Dili incident in the Santa Cruz (cemetery) and again following the events in East Timor in 1999. Because of the embargo we have had a lot of difficulty in getting spare parts and maintaining operations and training for our forces. Since I became president I have had good talks with President Bush and Prime Minister Howard – I have not given them promises – but good talks on things we have to do to solve our problems peacefully and democratically.

'We are fighting hard against terrorism, not only as a global commitment but to make my nation safer. We are also trying to address the root causes of terrorism, to empower our moderate ulemma (Islamic scholars) to save our brothers and sisters from being deceived. What I'm doing is seen positively in the US. I want to strengthen, normalise and widen relations (with the US). I want to develop concepts to strengthen cooperation with the US and Australia and other friendly nations. I really enjoy the existing friendships and cooperations between the leaders. John Howard and I realise that even if we have some differences we have to stay close, we have to cooperate. In fighting terrorism we were both shocked by the October (2004) attacks in Bali. It's a wake-up call to both Indonesia and Australia to stay close.

'I'm really grateful that when Indonesia was hit by the tsunami, Mr Howard and Australian soldiers helped us in a speedy manner. Australian soldiers arrived just in time. Australia has helped financially to rehabilitate Aceh and is part of the overall reconstruction of Aceh. Both leaderships, both John Howard and I, fully realise that in facing our regional challenges and global threats we have to cooperate. We have to maintain this closeness. Of course there are still several elements here in Indonesia that are probably unhappy with the US and with Australia, especially over actions in Iraq.

'We realise that we could disagree on certain issues but we are satisfied and happy with how we work together. I don't see growing anti-US or anti-Australian feeling in Indonesia.'

Across town I had the opportunity to meet the urbane and deeply intellectual Juwono Sudarsono, Indonesia's defence minister. He rejects out of hand the proposition that Australia suffers in southeast Asia because of its alliance with the US.

'The US has somewhat delegated to Australia some aspects of defence, political and cultural cooperation with Indonesia, to reduce the over-prominence of the US in seeming to assist Indonesia. It's important for the perception problems in Congress that Australia be seen to take the lead with cooperation from the US. I think the recent ministerial dialogue between Australia and the US (AUSMIN), held in Adelaide in November 2005, mentioned that, not so much the deputy sheriff thing, much more discreet, much more measured and much more effective, low key so to speak,'

In some ways this is an extraordinary statement, for an Indonesian defence minister to be welcoming Australia into the middle of Indonesia's relationship with the US. It demonstrates just how deeply the US is enmeshed into the security arrangements of southeast Asia.

The notable thing about Australia's periodic troubles with Indonesia is that the US plays virtually no role in them, beyond urging Canberra and Jakarta to patch up their differences. That was certainly the case in the Papuan asylum seeker crisis of 2006.

Whether Canberra can establish a long-term, durable stability in its relations with Jakarta is still unclear, and one of the central questions of Australian foreign policy.

Some analysts believe that China will one day become more influential in southeast Asia than the US is. Yet both the Boxing Day 2004 tsunami and the war on terror demonstrate the limits of Chinese influence and capability. On both these issues the US and Australia, bearing in mind the constraints of Australia's size, were able to offer much more effective assistance to southeast Asia than was China.

In southeast Asia other than Indonesia the US consults Australia but is less likely to acknowledge an Australian lead. It has a long, deep history with the Philippines and it is US forces, and the CIA, which have taken the lead in helping the Philippines counter its own terrorist problem.

Singapore has a similar relationship to the US as does Australia, though naturally somewhat less intense. Singapore's foreign minister, George Yeo, has told me that Australia's alliance relationship with the US is a major asset for Australian diplomacy in the region.

Clearly, the US alliance helps Australia achieve its diplomatic, geo-political, economic, security and political objectives in southeast Asia.

In a region of prime importance to Australia it is a priceless asset.

Chapter 14

THE ASIAN GIANTS: CHINA, AGREEING TO DISAGREE; JAPAN, AUSTRALIA'S STRATEGIC PARTNER

Towards the end of 2004 and in early 2005, a rare growth was to be found in Washington, DC. It was an exotic species, seldom to be glimpsed but now it was breaking out in several parts of the US capital. It was to be spied in clumps in Arlington, at the Pentagon; on the anonymous reaches of C Street, in the State Department; and in the toney real estate of Pennsylvania Avenue, in the august halls of the White House itself.

It was perplexity, dissatisfaction even, with Canberra. During the war on terror, after the Afghanistan and Iraq commitments, this was a rare plant indeed. By the end of 2005 it had subsided into a minor weed, stubbornly refusing to be extirpated altogether, but seen much less often.

But this dissatisfaction in the State Department, annoyance in the Pentagon, impatience in the White House had a very specific cause, namely a series of signals Canberra sent out, some inadvertently, on China. It is as important to this story to realise that Canberra and Washington later moved back much closer together on China, but for a time a significant breach opened up between them.

The Howard government overall was in such good odour in Washington that the Americans never said anything in public about the China split. But they said plenty in private.

The specific signals that Canberra sent out were not only that they disagreed with US policy, which of course is a reasonable enough thing to do, but there were confused signals, suggesting that Australia's own policy was unclear. The most important was a strange gaffe made by the foreign minister, Alexander Downer, in Beijing in 2004, in which he said a military conflict between the US and China over Taiwan would not trigger the invoking of the ANZUS treaty because it would not be an attack on the US itself.

The second most important was Canberra's refusal to back the US and Japan in publicly calling on the European Union to maintain its arms embargo on China.

The third was Canberra's refusal ever to say anything publicly about China's appalling human rights record.

Another factor, which the government in Canberra had no control over but which exacerbated Americans' feelings, was that some Australian commentators had been negative about a free trade agreement (FTA) between Australia and the US but were positive about a proposed free trade agreement with the infinitely less transparent economy of China. Indeed some who claimed to be cautious about or even hostile to FTAs in principle lost this opposition altogether when China entered the equation.

There is undoubtedly a strong and often uncritical China lobby in Australia, not least among academics. Anyone who makes the huge intellectual investment required to master the Chinese language, or even the Chinese economy or politics, needs constant access to China. The Chinese government, adept at many of the arts of influence, is superb at limiting access for critics while enhancing access for supporters.

The Americans felt that Australians had been both bribed and bullied by China, and as a result were sending out signals that were often unhelpful to Washington's own diplomacy regarding China.

It's important not to exaggerate this. The Americans didn't feel that the Australians had decamped and joined China's side. Nor did they feel that Canberra was actively trying to thwart them in Asian diplomacy. Quite the reverse. As we shall see, on critical issues with Japan, which were much opposed by the Chinese, the Howard government gave strong support to US policies. On North

Korea, the State Department occasionally felt Canberra was a bit clumsy in the way it tried to inject itself into the US inter-agency arguments, but there was no real distance between the US and Australia on this. On Indonesia, Washington was not only in tune with Canberra but happy to defer to Australia's lead on most occasions. And as for the South Pacific, this was seen primarily as Australia's responsibility, which it was handling well, and the Americans were happy to help where they could, reinforcing the right messages, contributing a little aid.

But on China there was some unease, and for a time a substantial gap opened between the US and Australia. Canberra eventually took action to ease American concerns on every one of the signals listed above. But at the end of the day the US and Australia do have a slightly different view of China, mainly arising out of their differences in size and location. It does not constitute a strategic rift, and as Howard and others have made clear Australia is infinitely closer to the Americans than to the Chinese. In any conflict between the US and China, however unlikely such a conflict is, Australia would inevitably side with the Americans. That is the judgment of the Americans. And it's also the judgment of the Chinese who count – the People's Liberation Army has examined this issue closely and come to the conclusion that the Australian-US alliance is unbreakable. The much less influential Chinese foreign ministry still harbours hopes that it could peel Australia away from the Americans, but these hopes must be regarded as unrealistic.

It is worth briefly examining each of Australia's mixed signals.

The oddest by far was Downer's statement in Beijing. Early in his tenure as foreign minister, Downer made a number of gaffes and was sometimes ill-disciplined. He had a few political near-death experiences. But it is a great strength of Downer's that he learnt from such experiences. He became much more disciplined. He put a lot of work into anticipating what questions he would be asked on a given topic, having his main lines ready and sticking to them. He is a hard-working foreign minister and over the years accumulated a lot of knowledge and experience. His touch got consistently better. But every now and again a gaffe would still appear.

In August 2004, in Beijing, Downer had been prattling some nonsense about Australia and China being strategic partners, a more or less content-free term which has seldom been repeated. He was asked by a journalist a natural question. How could Australia be a strategic partner of China given our ANZUS alliance with the US, which would see us siding with the US in any conflict over Taiwan?

Taiwan, an island nation and democracy of 23 million people, is de facto independent but claimed by Beijing as a renegade province. The US and Australia both follow a one-China policy which formally recognises China's sovereignty over Taiwan but also opposes the use of force by China to compel unification. The US is pledged to protect Taiwan's security. This is one of the most sensitive security flashpoints in the region and normally any Australian minister knows never to speculate publicly about what Australia might do in the hypothetical event of a military conflict.

But Downer said: 'Well, the ANZUS treaty is a treaty which, of course, is symbolic of the Australian alliance with the US, but the ANZUS alliance is invoked in the event of one of our two countries, Australia or the US, being attacked. So some other military activity elsewhere in the world, be it in Iraq or anywhere else for that matter, does not automatically invoke the ANZUS treaty. It is important to remember that we only invoked the ANZUS treaty once, that is after the events of 9/11, because there was an attack on the territory of the US.'

As it happens, Downer's remarks were completely wrong in their own terms. Article V of the ANZUS treaty states: 'An armed attack on any one of the Parties is deemed to include an armed attack on the metropolitan territory of any of the Parties, or on the island territories under its jurisdiction in the Pacific or on its armed forces, public vessels or aircraft in the Pacific.'

If, God forbid, China and the US were ever involved in armed conflict over the Taiwan Straits it is pretty hard to see how this would not constitute an attack on US armed forces in the Pacific, thus invoking ANZUS. Of course, as with all such treaties, Australia's response would not be dictated by the wording of the treaty but by political, moral, military and geo-strategic judgments at the time. Nonetheless the fact that Downer's remarks were wrong even in their own terms added to the sense that he'd gone to a lot of needless trouble to make a gesture of obeisance to the Chinese.

And the Chinese were indeed delighted. They used the statement at every subsequent possible opportunity, especially at security conferences and the like around the region. The Americans on the other hand were flabbergasted and literally could not make out what Downer was about.

Downer is a capable and resilient politician. One unfortunate characteristic such politicians naturally adopt, however, is a reluctance to admit publicly to mistakes. This made it more difficult to interpret the Downer remark. One theory is that it was just a silly gaffe, plain and simple. There is probably a lot of truth in that. Another is that Downer was trying to chart a new position and distance Australia from the US. Downer in many subsequent interviews, including with me, absolutely and emphatically denied that this was the case.

My own theory is slightly different. Washington had in fact secretly asked Canberra to reinforce particular messages to both Beijing and Taipei. Canberra had complied by sending high-level secret delegations to both capitals. Washington wanted Beijing told that under no circumstances should it use force against Taiwan. And it wanted Taipei told that it should not try to alter the status quo unilaterally, especially by declaring formal independence from China. Indeed, if it was Taiwan which provoked a war, by declaring independence, the US security guarantee might not apply. Quite naturally there were some limits to the US security guarantee. Washington had conveyed these messages to Beijing and Taiwan itself, but it is always useful to have another voice, especially a respected power like Australia, reinforce such messages.

It's always easier to send an unpalatable message to the weaker party in a dispute than to the stronger party. My theory is that Downer was actually trying to help the US by reinforcing the message to Taipei. Of course Beijing is not the place to be sending a message to Taipei.

Without ever contradicting Downer, and without himself speculating directly on a possible conflict, Howard made it clear in subsequent days that he would expect that Australia and the US would always come to each others' aid in time of conflict. This led for a time to the Americans seeing Howard as sound on China and Downer as suspect. This led to an even broader American judgment, that while the Australian Defence Department and prime minister and cabinet were solid on China, Foreign Affairs was weak.

The case of the European Union arms embargo was in some respects even more disturbing to Washington because it involved a more deliberate act of policy by Canberra. The EU had imposed an arms embargo on China after the Tiananmen Square massacre in 1989. It was not comprehensive but it did play a role in preventing China getting many types of hi-tech weapons systems, and sub-systems or parts of systems. While the Chinese will eventually get all this stuff anyway, an effective EU and US arms embargo could help keep it 10 or 15 years behind the US at the hi-tech end of weaponry.

The Pentagon, as it made clear in a report released in early 2006, believes that China is the power most likely to be able to challenge the US militarily in the coming decades. This does not mean that China, even then, would be the US's military equal, but rather that it would be able to inflict unacceptable losses on US navy and air force units operating anywhere near the Chinese coast.

After a visit to China in late 2004 by the French president, Jacques Chirac, the Europeans made it clear they intended to lift the embargo. The Americans, publicly and privately, strongly lobbied the Europeans not to lift the embargo. It was thought that anything related to missiles would be a priority acquisition for the Chinese, as would computer-based technologies that allow for miniaturisation and precise targeting. In other words, the Chinese would want technology that would enable them to have a crack at sinking American aircraft carriers. An anonymous senior US official was widely quoted in the American press as saying: 'We are talking about the Europeans making it easier for the Chinese to kill Americans.' China was known to be energetically pursuing four methods of obtaining military hi-tech: indigenous development, intelligence efforts, purchase of Western dual-use technology and direct purchase of military technology.

The Americans tried to get the Europeans to change their minds. They wanted Japan and Australia to join them so that there could be a joint approach to the EU by the three great Pacific democracies. Japan agreed, showing a lot of courage and earning a great deal of Chinese ire in the process. Australia declined.

One of Canberra's justifications was that it did not have an arms embargo itself against China so would look hypocritical in asking the Europeans to maintain theirs. Given the minuscule nature of Australian defence exports, this was grossly disingenuous.

This was a serious policy difference between Canberra and Washington but eventually Canberra went some distance to accommodate the Americans. As one senior American official said to me at the time: 'Australia is important because it's a bellwether of how well the US coalition will hold.' Canberra publicly asked the Europeans not to sell any weapons to China which would alter the strategic balance. It scolded the EU for apparently reaching a consensus position before consulting Asia-Pacific friends such as Australia. And according to some sources it finally did engage in some private lobbying of Europeans sympathetic to the US viewpoint.

Then there was human rights. It cannot possibly be a good thing for the international system, for China itself, for the Asia-Pacific region, for America, or for Australia if the only government in the world which is prepared to speak forthrightly and in public about Chinese human rights is the American one. Yet that is close to how the situation has developed.

Since 1997 Australia has had an officials' human rights dialogue with China. Without doubting in any way the goodwill of any of the Australians involved, it is fair to note that it meets behind closed doors and never utters a word of public criticism of China. It has zero effect on human rights. It serves only one real purpose: to allow the Australian government to claim it is raising human rights with China while never doing the one thing Beijing hates, and that normal self-respect would demand: raising the issue publicly.

The degree to which Beijing has Canberra spooked is evident in the contrast with Indonesia. However much realpolitik is supposed to have influenced Australian government behaviour towards Jakarta in the 80s and 90s, human rights were always publicly on the agenda. Sensitivity to China reached the bizarre point where a full public, press and political campaign, led by the government, could be waged against Japan because it was allegedly insufficiently kind to whales, but no frontbencher of either major party would ever utter the name of a single Chinese dissident.

Human rights activists around the world, who so easily demonise the Americans, should reflect that it is the Americans far more than anyone else who consistently campaign for the rights of Chinese dissidents and the rights of Chinese generally.

However, in mid-2005 a diplomat at the Chinese consulate in Sydney, Chen Yonglin, attempted to defect. The Howard government was embarrassed and at first unsure how to handle him. The case quickly developed a high public profile and a great deal of public sympathy was aroused for Chen. The Americans took Chen more seriously than the Australians did. Australian officials briefed journalists to the effect that Chen had little intelligence value. The Americans in contrast flew him to the US to give testimony before Congress. Inside cabinet there was unease at the length of time the government took to grant Chen a protection visa. Treasurer Peter Costello spoke up inside cabinet on Chen's behalf, so did Health

Minister Tony Abbott. The Americans were delighted with how the debate unfolded inside Australia because it showed how quickly Australia's political culture could polarise around human rights issues.

Eventually the government did grant Chen a visa to stay in Australia. Beijing was not happy and protested. Howard, in a joint press conference with Bush in mid-2005, used this disagreement between Canberra and Beijing to demonstrate that Australia had a different view of human rights from China and would disagree with China on this and other issues, while of course trying to keep the overall relationship amicable.

It is common in Australian strategic analysis to conceive of deadly Chinese-US strategic competition as inevitable and that this must provoke a nightmare choice for Australia between its security relationship with the US and its booming economic relationship with China.

In a series of speeches Howard has made it clear that he does not believe conflict between the US and China is either inevitable or likely. He sees no value in declaring a position over a hypothetical problem that may never arise. This illustrates the difference between the policy maker and the intellectual. The intellectual wants to anticipate intellectual problems, to confront them and perhaps to solve them. The policy maker is happy to defer them endlessly, merely to manage them if they can't readily be solved.

In any event the proposed choice is fake at many levels. I have no doubt the interests of the alliance would always prevail. But if – and every civilised person on the planet would work to prevent this from happening – there were conflict between the US and China, China would lose the US market and probably many other markets, and its economy would be gravely affected. There could never be a simple choice between Chinese economic goodies and American strategic obligation. The calculus would always be much more complicated.

China poses another kind of problem for liberal democracies, and this is a conceptual and moral problem. China is the world's only successful dictatorship. The world has not been in the situation of dealing with a successful dictatorship for many decades. The phenomenon deserves thinking about because it challenges our view of humanity and the way societies are organised. The Cold War between the democratic West and the communists dominated international politics between 1945 and 1989. It was a moral as well as a geo-political struggle. The democratic West enjoyed the synergy of morality and practicality. Democracy was best because it most deeply accorded with man's true nature, observing his innate rights and freedoms better than any other system. But capitalism was also clearly the most productive and best economic system, and it was founded on the same virtue, freedom. Political freedom guaranteed human rights, economic freedom generated wealth and prosperity. Freedom was both a political and an economic program.

China shows you can have one without the other, whereas we used to think they were indivisible. It would be wrong to equate China with the Soviet Union. China in its modern incarnation does not threaten its neighbours militarily, nor does it fund military subversion of others.

For several decades in the first half of the 20th century a significant number of Western intellectuals believed the Soviet Union was successful. Lincoln Steffens famously declared after visiting Moscow in 1919: 'I have seen the future and it works.' The admiration of many intellectuals and artists gave the Soviet Union a degree of soft power in the West. But given that most people don't take any notice of artists and intellectuals, in some ways that soft power was less significant than China's soft power today. This soft power is not based on an idealistic desire by anyone to emulate the Chinese system. The Chinese sensibly make no universal claims for their system. Chinese economic reform and development, like most successful social movements, has been overwhelmingly empirical and pragmatic, with very little theory of any kind. And, as the whole world knows, it has produced spectacular economic growth, which allows China to deploy soft power based on business.

It is more than incidental too that the Chinese experiment has greatly improved the life of tens, if not hundreds, of millions of its citizens. So it is a successful dictatorship not merely by the measure of staying in power, but also because it delivers a good deal of what it promises to its people. This is formidable and it means that cooperating with the Chinese government is, at some level, cooperating in the betterment of the Chinese people. That is no small consideration.

Nonetheless, China remains deeply authoritarian. According to the US State Department, hundreds of thousands of Chinese languish in gulags. Many thousands were arrested in a crackdown on the religious movement Falun Gong in 1999. In recent years the ruling party has re-emphasised ideological education and stamped down on press freedom, even on internet freedom.

At the end of the Cold War many people thought the ideological struggle about politics was over. This led Francis Fukuyama to write one of the great silly essays, 'The End of History', in the distinguished US journal *The National Interest*. Fukuyama argued that everybody now accepts the supremacy of free markets and liberal democracy. Even Fukuyama saw that the Islamic world contradicted his thesis. But few have recognised that China, too, rebuts his argument.

China's market reforms began in 1978. They have been successful now for 30 years. After the Tiananmen massacre of 1989 many analysts thought the Chinese Communist Party was politically bankrupt and would lose power within a few years. Instead it has gone from strength to strength.

It was once assumed that all the east Asian tigers were on the same basic path to liberalisation. The first stage of economic takeoff occurred under rough authoritarian governments, but this economic growth produced a middle class that craved stability and a more representative political system. This happened in South Korea and Taiwan, and after a fashion in Indonesia. But it has not happened in China, where the ruling party has thought things over and decided that it does not want democracy, ever. And it looks to have a solid hold on power.

None of this is to argue that China should be demonised or treated like an enemy. Its future political course is unknowable, and there are various contradictory dynamics and contradictory scenarios. What is certain from Australia's point of view is that two of the keys to coping well with increasing Chinese power are the continued intimate strategic involvement of the US in the region, and the self-confident contribution of an economically powerful Japan.

Whereas there is some distance still between Canberra and Washington over Beijing they have been as one over Tokyo. Howard has frequently outlined the colossally important developments between Canberra and Tokyo, but the media and academic commentators are so transfixed by China that they have largely ignored what he has said. In many speeches Howard has given on Asia he has dealt with Japan before dealing with China and he has often reiterated his theme that Australia has no closer partner in Asia than Japan. Howard's approach to China is that he acknowledges the differences but concentrates on the positives, especially the trade relationship. Japan he describes as a strategic partner, with shared political values, a common alliance with the US and still a bigger economic relationship than Australia has with China.

In taking a very pro-Japan line Howard has been happy to support a lot of things that Beijing opposes. The Howard government has strongly supported Japan's bid for a permanent seat at the UN Security Council, a proposition that infuriates Beijing.

Howard himself became a good friend and strong supporter of Japan's prime minister, Junichiro Koizumi, and his much more assertive style in foreign policy. The Howard government enthusiastically backed the redesign of the US-Japanese alliance to make it a reciprocal one. Traditionally, Japan allowed the US to base forces there and the US provided for Japan's security. Japan was not under any obligation, beyond hosting the US bases, to take any measure to assist US security. But now the alliance is reciprocal and Japan can help the US. This implies, indeed requires, a more assertive Japan and a greater role for Japan's military.

Australia mid-wifed Japan's first dispatch of peacekeeping troops after World War II, to Cambodia. Then it facilitated a quite large presence of Japanese civil reconstruction troops in Iraq by sending Australian forces to provide for their security.

Japan also joined with the US in issuing a joint declaration urging Beijing not to resort to the use of force on Taiwan.

This enraged Beijing, although every aspect of this more assertive Japanese foreign and security policy was strongly opposed by Beijing, not just the moves on Taiwan. This was so much the case that Beijing allowed a series of vicious anti-Japanese demonstrations in its major cities in 2005. Government control is so intense in China, especially in its big cities, that these demonstrations can only be seen as an act of Chinese state policy. As such they were a crude and anachronistic attempt at intimidation of Japan by Beijing. And they were tremendously counter-productive. The Japanese leader China likes least, Koizumi, won a huge electoral victory.

Beijing is clumsy in dealing with democratic opinion, except through the business community. Its attempts to influence elections in Taiwan always result in the candidate it most dislikes becoming president. This is an interesting contrast to the US ability to drain support away from pro-independence forces on Taiwan by proclaiming their ambitions unrealistic. It may even be that contrary to all the stereotypes the Americans have a more sophisticated understanding of Asian politics than the Chinese.

The Canberra-Tokyo diplomatic partnership can be seen on many levels. Japan's advocacy was crucial in Australia being invited to attend the inaugural East Asia Summit in 2005, a significant advance in Australian involvement in purely east Asian political architecture. The Japanese did that in part out of long-term alliance solidarity, but also because it was in their interests to have another country with such similar political and geo-strategic outlook present, in part to balance the influence of China. Beijing was notably cool on Australia's participation. And once Australia, India and New Zealand were confirmed as members, Beijing tended to place its diplomatic emphasis back on other regional structures, rather than the East Asian Summit.

Canberra has embarked on any number of military and strategic dialogues with Tokyo. The most significant of these is the Trilateral Security Dialogue (TSD), involving the US, Japan and Australia. This has made Beijing deeply uneasy. The TSD, which derived great horsepower from Rich Armitage's championing of the process, began with the level of representation of US deputy secretary of state, Japanese vice-minister of foreign affairs and the secretary of the Australian Department of Foreign Affairs. When the second George W Bush administration replaced the first, Bob Zoellick, Armitage's replacement, didn't want to be running a deputies' dialogue and in any event didn't get on well with the Japanese. So the dialogue slipped down one bureaucratic notch. But as that would have looked too bad a way for the US to treat its allies, it was simultaneously lifted up a notch to the foreign minister level. It now runs on two tracks, one involving the bureaucrats and one involving the foreign ministers. The Chinese don't like either track.

It is a besetting mistake of strategic analysts to underestimate Japan. It remains an immensely important global power. It is the second largest economy in the world and its economy is three times as big as China's. Its alliance with the US and the bases it provides the US, especially in Okinawa, remain the very heart of American force-projection capability in Asia.

Japan's chief weakness is its demographic profile. Its population, about 128 million, has already started to decline in absolute terms. It cannot convince its people to have more children and it has a debilitating cultural hostility to embarking on a large-scale immigration program.

The enduring strength and power of the US position in Asia, especially northeast Asia, is evident in the priority both Japan and China, in their different ways, accord to the American relationship (it is also noteworthy that within the Chinese foreign ministry, Australia is dealt with in the American section).

In truth the US position in Asia is immensely strong. Asia is the most pro-US region in the world. The east Asian economic miracle is partly a result of deliberate US strategic and economic policy, pursued consistently over several decades.

The US has five formal alliances in Asia – with Japan, South Korea, Thailand, the Philippines and Australia. It has a de facto alliance with Singapore. It is developing a new, strategic relationship of the greatest long-term importance with India. No one can play the Indian card except the Indians themselves, but without crudely attempting to play the Indian card, the mere presence of India tends to balance China, politically, militarily, economically.

This web of US alliances and security relationships is really a multilateral security system in everything but name. Sometimes it is even called the Pacific alliance system. Partly because it is coordinated centrally by the US, it is superbly flexible. No other system could integrate Japan and South Korea into a single security unit. Although the alliances are all bilateral, each US ally views its alliance as a central part of its international posture, thus when the US invaded Iraq, all its Asian allies lent their political support. Although Australia was the only US ally in Asia to send troops for the initial combat phase in Iraq, all of Washington's other formal treaty allies in Asia sent troops to help in the reconstruction, a remarkable and little noticed diplomatic achievement by the United States.

It could well be that the US position gets stronger in Asia over time, partly because of demographics. By 2050, the US is likely to have a population of 500 million. There will be one American for every three Chinese, whereas now the ratio is one to four. And the American population will be the youngest Western population.

Howard for one believes the widely held view of US decline is simply wrong, and recalls the fashion for books in the 1980s predicting as surely as night follows day that Japan would eclipse the US and dominate the global economy. In an interview for this book I asked Howard if he believed the US alliance system was a long-term structure for Asia. He said: 'Yeah I do. I think apart from anything else a lot of countries see it as a counterpoint to China, don't they? Enough said. Not that I have any kind of apocalyptic view of China. As you know I'm sometimes seen as being on the optimistic side of that and perhaps I am. But I am quite sure a lot of countries simultaneously welcome the rise of China and also reinforce their relationship with the US.'

Countries such as Japan? 'Oh yes, and Singapore and even Indonesia. And that's sort of commonsense. You shouldn't have some attitude that inevitably there's going to be a dust-up between China and America.' This is a central point of doctrine for Howard – there is no reason to assume the worst in US-China relations and nothing to be gained in constantly highlighting it as a possibility.

So the next logical question is: are the US and China relating on a reasonable basis? 'I think they are now. I think maybe in a small way we played a part in that.'

Howard referred to his joint press conference with Bush in mid-2005 in which he said that Australia saw the economic rise of China as beneficial, and while he would be open about the things he disagreed with China about, nonetheless he wanted to concentrate on the things Australia and China agreed about.

However, in our interview he stressed another enduring reality: 'There's obviously no misunderstanding about our relative closeness. Of course Australia is much, much closer to the United States than it is to China. But we don't want to get into these silly positions of always having to express a preference. What is gained by that? It doesn't achieve anything.'

Howard acknowledged that there had been some differences between Washington and Canberra but made a significant assessment: 'That phase has by and large passed.'

Not that he was for a second admitting that there was serious fault on Canberra's side. He added: 'I think there was a bit of a failure (by the Americans) to understand some of the geo-political realities that we have. I don't think perhaps there was sufficient understanding of the extraordinary growth in the Chinese-Australian economic relationship.'

So Howard has ticked all his boxes for the US. He supports the US alliance system absolutely, he supports the rejuvenation of the US-Japanese alliance, he opposes the use of force by China on Taiwan, he will speak openly about his disagreements with China on human rights (although this only ever happens in general, never in a specific case, where it would really count) – all of which positions are opposed by China. However, he opposes Taiwanese independence, as does the US, and he will concentrate on things over which Australia and China can cooperate, such as the booming trade relationship. He will speak about Chinese human rights less forcefully than the United States does. No administration in Washington could realistically ask for much more.

Howard was also keen to reiterate his support for Japan: 'I've worked very hard to keep the Japanese relationship up front. Of course there is a danger that as we're experiencing this extraordinary expansion of our trade relationship with China some will get the impression that we're indifferent to some of the other relationships. Japan is still our best customer and is likely to remain so for some time. There are still three great Pacific democracies – America, Australia and Japan.

'I have a very good (relationship with Koizumi). I rang him up after he got re-elected and had a great discussion with him. I'm very supportive (of Koizumi's foreign policy). I understand there's sensitivity (in the region) about visiting the shrine (the Yasukuni Shrine which honours Japan's war dead, among them some war criminals). I don't see the point of focusing on that.'

When asked about Japan's more active participation in the US alliance, Howard responded: 'It's very desirable. I do think it's better for the region for Japan to be active. But there is still in many countries of the region, for reasons that you can understand, long memories.'

I then put it to Howard that there was every reason to be cynical about China's supposed long memory of Japanese war crimes of 60 years ago, given how many Chinese citizens have since been killed by their own governments, including the huge death toll under Chairman Mao, the citizens killed at Tiananmen Square and the rest.

Howard replied with a modest 'Oh yeah'. But I think it's fair to record that as he said it he repeatedly nodded his head in the affirmative and had a big grin on his face, followed by a laugh. He was not laughing at anyone's historical suffering of course, but merely at the restrictions on comment which prudence dictates for even a self-confident middle power.

Some things a careful prime minister cannot say on tape.

Chapter 15

COMMANDER OF THE GULF: A SAILOR'S STORY

The first time since the Vietnam war that the Royal Australian Navy fired shots in anger – not warning shots, not shots designed to get a people smuggler to stop or an illegal fishing vessel to change course, but shots designed to damage and kill – was in the 2003 Iraq war to remove Saddam Hussein. That war also resulted in an Australian naval officer leading the most senior 'at-sea' command that any Australian has held since World War II.

The American navy has always been the military institution most critical to Australian security. It has also been the arm of the US military, even more than the US Marine Corps, which has had the most intimate connections to Australia.

In the long decades of the Cold War, the Pacific Ocean was often described as an American lake. There was never any doubt which institution ruled the lake. The Commander-in-Chief of the Pacific Forces (CINPAC) as he was then called (the titles have since been changed) was invariably an admiral, and sat in Hawaii like a potentate of vast, imperial power. Going to see the CINCPAC was always a big deal and the Americans would prepare a journalist thoroughly for the honour. There would be a command briefing first, outlining the immense power and responsibilities of the CINCPAC. This briefing was often given by the civilian political adviser to the CINCPAC, and was conducted in one of the big military conference rooms, with maps and assorted, state-of-the-art audiovisual aids. Another naval officer would also talk to you. You might visit a ship or two. And then, when you were thoroughly prepared and the full majesty of the CINCPAC was seared into your brain, finally you would be ushered into the magisterial presence of the CINCPAC himself, a man invariably skilled at strategic communications with the media. Indeed his informality and military-regular-guy qualities would often appear as a perfect foil, a refreshing contrast, to the pomp of the preparation. Precisely as, no doubt, it was meant to.

CINCPAC has now been renamed as Pacific Command (PACOM) and Australia's connections with it are as deep and as broad-ranging as ever. Its area of responsibility is immense. PACOM covers half the globe. And it's our half.

But the Gulf wars, number one of 1991 to expel Saddam Hussein from Kuwait, and number two in 2003 were run by US Central Command (CENTCOM). As explored elsewhere in this book, the second Gulf war occasioned a new level of Australian involvement with CENTCOM, an involvement which is likely to continue.

No one embodies this connection more than Commodore Steve Gilmore. He was not involved in the conventional fighting of the war itself, which occurred in 2003, but in the nation-building and counter-insurgent phase in 2005. From April in 2005 to August of the same year, Gilmore was Commander Task Force 58, leading all coalition naval operations in the northern part of the Persian Gulf. He had a US commander above him, in Bahrain, and the US commander in turn had a British deputy. But Gilmore was the man in charge at sea. The coalition operations in the Gulf were divided into three sectors – northern, central and southern. Gilmore was in command of the northern sector. As this sector contained Iraq, Kuwait and the maritime border between Iraq and Iran, this was where the action was.

Not even in Vietnam had an Australian naval officer commanded such a large coalition force. It was 90 per cent American, although it always had British and Australian components as well. Before Gilmore arrived there had been a Singaporean ship. And of course there was the emerging Iraqi navy itself. There were always ships rotating in and out, but on any given day Gilmore's task force would comprise 10 or more main ships and nearly 2000 sailors. As well as the ships and their crews, he had land-based helicopters and fast attack boats, as well as Iraqi marines, under his command. Following discussions in January 2005, the Americans made a formal request for an Australian commander and his team and this was approved by the Australian government in February of that year. Gilmore brought together a team of 15 Australians, mostly drawn from Deployable Joint Force Headquarters, for a month of intensive preparations. They were in electronic communication with the US navy headquarters in Bahrain. The Australian contingent included experts in operations, intelligence, logistics, communications and maritime law.

Three Australians had been sent for a brief mission in January to Bahrain, before even the deployment was agreed by Canberra, to make sure the Australians knew everything they needed to know. Gilmore spent a week in Bahrain himself before taking his Australian contingent to his flagship, the US guided missile cruiser *USS Antietam*.

How must it have felt for these US sailors all of a sudden to be under Australian command, when the United States navy is incomparably bigger and more powerful than any navy the world has ever seen?

From the American point of view, part of the rationale for such a deployment is to keep our forces as inter-operable with theirs as possible, so that we can most easily be of mutual assistance to each other in the future. The Americans would only accept an allied commander of the highest competence to undertake such a role, because they are putting their own people's lives in his hands, but they also know that by accepting a non-American coalition commander they make that commander much more competent still for the future. In people like Molan, Gilmore, and Air Commodore Mark Binskin (whose experience we will examine in due course) the Australian Defence Force now has military leaders who have commanded big forces at high intensity in operationally sophisticated and demanding environments. The Americans also know that such deployments increase what one might regard as the American constituency within the Australian military.

I met Gilmore at Australia's Defence Department headquarters at Russell, in Canberra, where he was by then navigating a desk. A lean, wiry man, with rimless steel glasses and steel-grey hair, in the perfect white uniform of the navy, he looked crisp and perfectly turned out. Again I was struck by the incredible contrasts in a military life: the radical transitions that soldiers and sailors must make.

Gilmore talked openly about his experience, but as with the other military men I interviewed, there were clear red lines he wouldn't cross. One of his most important missions, for example, was to guard Iraq's oil terminals. These had been the subject of attempted terrorist attack in 2004. I asked Gilmore whether he had word of any specific planned terrorist attack on these terminals while he had responsibility for their security.

'We based our patrols on the presumption of threat to the oil terminals. Attacks had happened before. We continually monitored the threat intelligence', he replied.

In other words, he was not saying yes or no to my question. I asked the same question three or four times and he politely gave me the same non-answer each time, just ever so fractionally differently worded so as to appear polite. That's fair enough, but I construe this answer to mean yes, there was some specific intelligence concerning possible attacks but these attacks were thwarted or simply didn't eventuate. It must have been a nightmare, to contemplate being the commander when a devastating attack did occur. But Gilmore's not going to say that to me, either. Naturally military commanders at all levels are extremely careful when talking about operational intelligence, even if the intelligence is a few months old.

Gilmore's responsibilities were legion. His principal mission was to protect Iraq's two offshore oil terminals, through which

95 per cent of its export oil flowed, generating about 80 per cent of the country's gross domestic product. During Gilmore's time on command they typically pumped oil worth US $100 million a day.

Gilmore also had responsibility for the security of maritime commerce, to enable the free use of the sea, not least by fishing fleets. As well as terrorists, Gilmore had to battle pirates, who have been active in the Persian Gulf for hundreds of years: 'We conducted many daily patrols against pirates. We deterred a number of pirates and chased away many. We needed to engage the local maritime community.' The vast majority of the local maritime community were there for wholly legitimate purposes, just trying to make a living between wars and regime changes, pirates and contending navies. Gilmore was their friend, because he offered protection, but he also had to work hard to establish his credibility, to gain the trust and assistance of the locals.

A huge task was the integration of and transition to Iraqi security forces: 'The Iraqi navy is small but it is increasingly formidable and well led. I tried to formalise their integration. By the time we'd left I'd certified all the Iraqi patrol boats. Increasingly, they're out there replacing coalition forces.'

Gilmore also had to lay down a road map for the Iraqi navy – what pace its integration and expansion would occur at, when it should aim to reach certain levels of competence and responsibility. When Gilmore left the Gulf, Iraq had five patrol boats and was about to commission six larger ships and a range of support vessels. Integrating the Iraqi forces brought Gilmore into close contact with one of the most remarkable people he was to meet in Iraq – Captain Adel. The Iraqi Umm Qasr naval base had been flattened by coalition forces. All that was left of the old Iraqi navy were a few abandoned and obsolete patrol boats and a few river patrol inflatable boats. So the Iraqi navy had to be rebuilt from scratch. However, naval skills are specialist in their nature and the coalition had to call on former officers of Saddam's navy. In particular there was Captain Adel, who was the operational commander of the Iraqi navy while Gilmore was in charge.

Gilmore recalled Adel fondly: 'He was an ex-Saddam Hussein naval officer and I found him to be very professional, competent and motivated. He said to me once, "In the wars of the past you and I represented our governments of the day and we're doing so again now." He was also responsible for the Iraqi marines who will take over the point defence of the oil terminals (from the Americans). Captain Adel was very courageous. He had a price on his head (from the terrorists) but he kept going. I found working with the Iraqi navy very rewarding. They will need to expand their fleet to get a 24/7 capability in place.'

Gilmore was also responsible for international military maritime relations in his explosive little corner of the world – in defence parlance, theatre security cooperation.

This was trickier than it might first seem, for it involved Iraq's relations with two neighbours with whom it had been to war in the past – Kuwait and Iran. Gilmore was able to organise Operation United River Dragon, in which Iraqi and Kuwaiti forces worked together, perhaps for the first time in their history: 'It was a very small tactical event but with huge strategic consequences.'

The border with Iran was always tense: 'One of the (Iraqi) oil terminals is extremely close to the disputed Iran/Iraq maritime border. So there was visual contact all the time. They were patrolling and so were we. There was occasionally communication. It was short and polite.'

Short and polite.

Marvellous words with an almost technical military meaning – short and polite.

The Australian navy has had a long involvement in the Persian Gulf, dating from the first Gulf war. The former US deputy secretary of state, Rich Armitage, told me the willingness of Australia to contribute to patrol and interdiction operations in the Gulf after 1991, essentially to enforce sanctions against Saddam Hussein, was seen by Washington as a critical indicator that Canberra was determined to remain a full partner in coalition security operations, that it did not see its security and military interests as confined entirely to continental defence of Australia or even narrow regional operations.

In the decade after 1991, the Australian navy earned a good reputation in the Gulf. As numerous American military sources have told me, the Australian sailors had 'attitude', or to put it more politely they were willing to enforce the sanctions with a great deal of vigour. They wanted to make sure nothing illegal got through. We now know the sanctions continually degraded from the day they were imposed. By the end they were not so much leaky as porous and ineffective. But most of the smuggling went overland, not by sea. The naval blockade was effective.

Gilmore made a point that I hear from other coalition commanders, that coalition warfare, for all its coordination difficulties, provides inestimable ancillary benefits. Each nation's force brings a little bit of different knowledge to the table. Even the biggest force can learn something from the smallest force. Different forces' circumstances and equipment have given them slightly different skills, slightly different areas of special competence: 'Australians for example are very good at boarding operations. It's a skill that's been honed over the years, at home in enforcing the exclusive economic zone and in the Gulf.' Perhaps diplomacy prevented Gilmore adding that it was also a skill much in use in dealing with illegal people smugglers coming to Australia.

In any event, this was one particular skill where Australians made a special contribution: 'We look at it through a different lens and we're not bashful about putting it on the table.'

Like so many Australians at his level, Gilmore has a history of close interaction with the Americans, participating in and planning numerous joint exercises. In 1996 and 97 he spent 18 months in US Naval Doctrine Command in Virginia. He has been deeply involved in the project for Australia to acquire three air-warfare destroyers which, whether they come from the US or not, are in substantial part about inter-operability with the US: 'Part of the inter-operability challenge is to know what the US navy is pursuing equipment-wise. It all contributes to meaningful inter-operability. With the US we can be integrated into one force at high-end capability.'

That is a very high level of inter-operability.

It would have been a perfectly feasible option for Gilmore to go in and be supported by a US staff rather than taking a staff from Australia. But taking 14 other Australians with him spread the benefit of his unique command experience. The trust level in all this is remarkable. Every day Gilmore and his Australian staff were dealing with US intelligence and operational information of the highest sensitivity. The Australians all had high-level security clearances, as you'd expect. What is significant is that these were all accepted by the Americans. This level of trust and confidence isn't built quickly, it takes years to develop: 'Australian clearances are well understood and well accepted by the Americans.'

The pay-off for the Australian navy is large: 'We've got 15 people who are far better, more effective members of the Australian Defence Force. This level of command cannot be replicated in the Australian Defence Force or in peace time. We fold back the experience into our whole organisation. We systematically pass on the experience. We have a defence force lessons-learned database.'

Gilmore is the opposite of a braggart. He speaks with some precision and it is an effort for him to avoid military jargon. His mind is saturated in his calling. He is neither boastful nor modest. The pride he takes is in the force he led and the opportunity he was given. But like all good military men he looks both success and failure in the face in a matter-of-fact way: 'On my final day as I looked over my shoulder I saw two functioning oil terminals and there was an Iraqi navy well on the way to achieving their own security. I felt pride in my own team and in keeping up our reputation. All the mission sets had been progressed.'

Chapter 16

THE UNITED NATIONS: MANGLING MULTILATERALISM TOGETHER

In early 2004, when I was for a time based in the US, I was invited by a dear friend to attend a dinner in New York. It was to be a gathering mainly of senior United Nations officials and some ambassadors to the UN. It was a lovely evening, urbane, sophisticated, elegant. No city in the world, not even Paris, has quite the power to intoxicate which New York possesses. This night the city was at its intoxicating best.

Rather to my surprise I was called on to make a few remarks about Australian foreign policy. I stressed that I did not speak on behalf of the government but found myself in agreement with it on a few security matters. This was all going along OK until I made a shocking faux pas.

I commented that I agreed with the Australian government that US support for Israel was not the central problem in the Middle East. More generally, I said, Israel itself was not central to the problems of Arab and Middle East political culture. After all, how could the presence of six million Jews determine the political culture of hundreds of millions of Arabs and North Africans? The successes, and the failures, of these more numerous political cultures were surely their own doing.

Shock! Shame! Outrage!

The sophistication of the evening slipped away. Here was something truly terrible. A point of universally accepted good form was being contradicted in a most improper fashion. This conversation was not fit for polite company. It was as if I had advocated paedophilia as state policy. Clearly I had broken a taboo, gone beyond the bounds of civilised discourse. This was a scandalous remark.

The experience brought home to me one of the many paradoxes of the United Nations – the closed and insular nature of its environment, despite the seeming cosmopolitanism and sophistication of its inhabitants. Australia's policies on Israel at the UN have been causing a stir these last few years, but they are just one part of a much deeper philosophical – perhaps theological is the better term – divide over the UN, a divide within Australia itself, and a divide between nations.

I have always regarded Malcolm Muggeridge as one of the greatest and most underestimated writers of the 20th century. For some time a British intelligence agent, he was mostly a journalist. Known in Britain chiefly as a TV and radio broadcaster, known internationally mainly for his later books about Christianity, for me he was supreme as a social and political critic, an active, engaged and energetic participant in the affairs of the world, whose knowledge of his own fallibility and the fatuousness of many fashionable conceits, led him to write the most acute and satirically insightful accounts of the preoccupations of the age in which he lived. He was especially gifted at capturing the Zeitgeist, and skewering it.

He had been a correspondent in Stalin's Soviet Union in the 1930s and his account of the Russian famine was so unfashionable that he could not get a job when he returned to England. His contemporary, Walter Duranty of *The New York Times*, wrote glowingly of Stalin's achievements and won the Pulitzer Prize, which his newspaper finally had the grace to return in shame 70 years later.

Muggeridge's memoirs *The Infernal Grove* (Fontana Collins, 1975) I regard as one of the most revealing books of the 20th century. He recounts his work at the League of Nations, the ill-fated precursor of the UN, and compares the two bodies. He writes: 'When Hitler's panzers were actually roaring into Poland from the West, and Stalin's divisions lumbering in to meet them from the East, the League was in session in its new premises, discussing the codification of level-crossing signs. At the time I remember feeling a sort of relief. At least there would be no more compromised resolutions ... How wrong I was! Another Tower of Babel, more tower-like and babulous would spring up in Manhattan, to outdo the League many times over in the irrelevance of its proceedings, the ambiguity of its resolutions and the confusion of its purposes.'

Muggeridge is too subtle a thinker merely to sneer but he came to hold the UN in something like contempt. The passage of his memoirs quoted above highlights many of the continuing weaknesses of the UN – the inability to make any serious difference to any serious security problem, the fatuousness of so much that it does, the foolishness of so much that it says and its spectacular inability to make much real difference to the world.

So how should we think about the UN today? This is one of the great, fundamental divides in international policy around the world. People who work on the UN full-time in universities and the like have come to accept the UN as if its reality were the same as its lofty aspirations. While often acknowledging some faults, they tend to write about the UN with a kind of reverence, almost a religious awe. The problem is that the overlap between their writings and reality is very slim and their effect on the policies of governments marginal at best.

Then there are some, mainly in conservative think-tanks in the US, who regard the UN and all its works as inherently evil, a conspiracy to constrain US power, which they see as the chief force for good in the world.

So how should we in Australia think of the UN?

Three very mistaken and often destructive ways of thinking about the UN are as a world government, as an embodiment of international law which all must obey, or as a counterweight to the power of the United States. The UN is none of those things.

But first a little story to indicate the routine way the UN operates.

In January 2004, an Australian diplomat, Mike Smith, was unanimously elected chairman of the UN Human Rights Commission (HRC) for a year. A defender of the Howard government could easily make the case that this shows how highly Australia is esteemed in the global community and especially within the UN system itself, and so on and so forth. Given that the country Australia was replacing on the Human Rights Commission was Libya, and therefore such encomiums would have to apply equally to Colonel Gaddafi's odious regime, this is not an argument I am inclined to make.

The Human Rights Commission and its processes had become such a farce that even UN Secretary-General Kofi Annan came to call for its abolition. But it operated, especially in terms of elections, no differently from the rest of the UN. The inside story of Australia's 'triumph' is therefore revealing in a wider sense.

The truth is Australia came very close to a train wreck over the Human Rights Commission. At one point the Africa bloc at the HRC had decided to vote against Australia's candidacy. Had they done so, many would have explained their reasons as centred on Australian policy towards our Aboriginal population. This would have been a complete lie but would have caused no end of political trouble for the Howard government.

The real story of the African intrigue against Australia is utterly unedifying and lays bare the cynicism and moral corruption of the whole UN process. It all started in 2002 when the African Group at the UN decided to pick Libya – that paragon of human rights – to take up its turn as the chairman of the HRC.

The UN is organised around five regional groupings – Western Europe and Others Group (WEOG, which includes Australia), East Europe, Asia (which includes the Arab Middle East but not Israel), Africa, and the Latin American and Caribbean Group. The chairmanship of the HRC rotates among the five geographical groupings. 2004 was WEOG's turn and Australia was WEOG's nominee.

In 2002 the Africans had taken the pretty fruity, if not surreally comic, decision to nominate Libya as chairman of the HRC for 2003. Libya had recently taken welcome steps to rejoin the community of civilised nations but to nominate such a brutal military dictatorship, and a state which had sponsored and conducted international terrorism, including the Lockerbie air disaster, as well as flouting rules on pursuing nuclear weapons, would make a mockery and a farce of the HRC.

So the US took the unusual step of publicly opposing Libya's candidacy and calling for a vote, whereas normally the choice of each geographical group is accepted automatically. The Africans regarded the US action as a monstrous interference in their rights and were determined to get back at WEOG.

In the end, the US compromised and Libya was elected with 33 votes in favor, 3 opposed and 17 abstentions. Australia abstained. As part of the compromise, the US agreed not to make a speech at the vote denouncing Libya's candidacy and the Africans agreed not to oppose Australia's nomination on behalf of WEOG for the deputy chairmanship.

But a year later some Africans were determined to exact revenge on the Western group for having embarrassed them over Libya. Australia was formally nominated in September 2003, but the South African delegation, which was coordinating the African response, started a campaign saying Australia was a 'controversial' choice, would not make a good chairman and that WEOG had insulted Africa's dignity by challenging Libya's nomination.

The African ambassadors met in Geneva on December 19, 2003, and decided formally to call a vote on Australia's candidacy and that they would vote against Australia. The membership of HRC numbered about 55 and there were more African than Western nations involved. The result could have been very embarrassing for the Howard government.

At this point it started to become ugly. Plenty of threats were issued. Australian diplomats let it be known that they would campaign hard and publicly on the ridiculous contrast between

Australia and Libya on their respective human rights records. That could have been seriously embarrassing for all of Africa. It could indeed have prompted a debate on African human rights. In the numerous African caucus meetings the most dedicated opponent of Australia was Zimbabwe. This was because of Howard's prominent role in suspending Zimbabwe from the Commonwealth due to Robert Mugabe's shocking human rights record.

This was shaping up to a truly farcical outcome. Australia was to be prevented from chairing a human rights body precisely because of its principled stance against the savage human rights abuses of the Mugabe regime. A dictatorship like Libya was acceptable as a human rights champion but not a democracy like Australia.

In the end, Australia's hard ball and the intervention of both the Americans and the Europeans forced the Africans to back down: The Europeans as much as the Americans could not allow a respectable WEOG candidate such as Australia to be vetoed. And so, in the end, Australia was elected unanimously.

But it's a revealing episode. It's not just that UN elections, like all elections, always involve a good deal of wheeling and dealing, it's that UN agencies have nothing to do with their stated purposes. Also, that their governments, mostly undemocratic, do not represent their people but only the interests behind the governments themselves. Therefore there is nothing democratic even about a UN election. The notion that Robert Mugabe, in campaigning against a leader like Howard who highlighted the human rights abuses suffered by Zimbabweans, is thus acting on behalf of the Zimbabwean people is a sick joke. The HRC itself was a joke, and everything about it was feeble and hypocritical and ridiculous. There may be good realpolitik reasons for participating in such charades but no one should imagine they constitute an aspect of international law or embody any moral authority.

Under the Howard government, Australia took a more robust and independent line at the UN. But it was not independence from the US which was required but independence from the stultifying mindset, foolish political correctness and sterile processes of the UN itself.

The most important case was the Australian attitude on Israel and the Middle East. In this, Australian independence consisted of moving much closer to the US, and Australia's position materially strengthened the US position. Australia has for a long time been a strong friend of Israel. But for most of the past few decades it took an understandable, if less than wholly inspiring, refuge in abstaining from, rather than outright opposing, the plethora of anti-Israel resolutions at the UN. Some time in 2003 the Howard government decided to change all that. As much as anything the Howard government was influenced by watching the international community respond to the wave of suicide bomb terror attacks on Israel. These elicited muted international condemnation. But when Israel tried to protect itself by building a wall to keep the terrorists out, the fury of the liberal international establishment and activist class, especially at the UN, was boundless.

The UN for decades has had a deep, structural bias against Israel. To take one example, at the Human Right Commission there was always a separate agenda item devoted entirely to Israel. No other nation got an entire agenda item – not North Korea, not China, not Iran. It proved impossible to get even a single resolution passed concerning Zimbabwe's murderous practices. For more than 40 years, one quarter of the resolutions passed at the HRC were aimed at Israel. Whatever Israel's sins, no one could think that balanced.

Similarly, the UN has established a vast bureaucracy part of whose role is to campaign against Israel. Within the UN secretariat there is a whole division called the Division for Palestinian Rights, while the General Assembly has the Committee on the Exercise of the Inalienable Rights of the Palestinian People and the Special Committee to Investigate Israeli Practices Affecting the Human Rights of the Palestinian People.

It's important not to be misunderstood here. The Palestinians do suffer injustices and these injustices should be remedied. The Palestinians, like all human beings in the world, have human rights and the UN should play a role in protecting these rights. But no other nation is singled out for the relentless attack at the UN that Israel is. All this anti-Israel activity at the UN does absolutely nothing to improve the Palestinians' lot. It makes the UN singularly worthless in the Middle East because Israel is utterly hostile and distrustful of it, while the Palestinian cause is endlessly inflamed by soaring and worthless rhetoric, and taken over by the international bureaucrat class, far from the realities on the ground.

And it is in any event a distortion of what the UN is meant to be about. Most nations that Australia would regard as like-minded, such as those of western Europe, Canada and some others, traditionally find this all too hard to deal with and find solace in abstaining from most anti-Israel resolutions and activities, rather than opposing them.

Howard and the Australian foreign minister, Alexander Downer, in a very personal intervention, decided to change Australia's approach. As a result, Australia voted against referring Israel's security wall in the West Bank to the International Court of Justice. The ICJ inevitably ruled against Israel and in July 2004 the UN passed the standard anti-Israel resolution. The Department of Foreign Affairs advised the government to abstain. Howard and Downer were personally involved in this issue. Downer explicitly overruled the bureaucracy and instructed that Australia vote against the resolution. Australia was one of only six nations to do so – the US, Israel, the Marshall Islands, Palau and Micronesia being the others.

What did this vote really mean? For a start, it was intellectually consistent because Australia had voted against the ICJ referral in the first place. Further, Canberra was not just being reflexively pro-Israel. Downer had been harshly critical of part of the route taken by the Israeli security wall. Being against Israel-bashing at the UN does not mean that the Howard government endorses every policy of every Israeli government.

Australia's ambassador to the UN at the time, John Dauth, the finest and most effective diplomat we have had in that position in decades, said of Australia's vote: 'We remain of the view that the resolution unfairly isolated a single issue in a complex conflict: that it served no purpose, given the nature and content of resolutions already passed by this assembly; that it would politicise the court; and that it would distract the parties – as is happening – from the urgent need to resume negotiations.'

Howard told me of his own personal involvement in the decision on that vote, and commented: 'That's not accidental, I can assure you. I felt very strongly about the resolution about that wall. I felt that the majority position on that was untenable, given everything that was happening. It (the wall) was an act of self-defence. That's how I saw it.'

The vote was not a one-off. Nor was it a sign of subservience to the Americans. Canberra could easily have taken refuge in abstention – as did all of the US's other significant allies, including the UK – without earning the ire of Washington. So the vote must be seen as a point of Australian foreign policy independence, though not one most academic and media commentators in Australia supported.

While it was not an action taken to please the Americans, it did draw Canberra closer to Washington because it was an action in concert with the US. It reflected the Howard government coming to the same judgment on the merits of an issue as the Bush administration and then having the capacity to act.

Australia's actions had some effect. Under Dauth's ambassadorship, Australia did not lose a single election for anything at the UN. This came about in part because of much more systematic attention to Australia's natural friends in the South Pacific, who all have a vote at the UN. Without distorting its priorities, Canberra did make an effort to influence both the South Pacific, and our friends in southeast Asia. The Australian mission in New York has a lot of interaction with the UK, Canadian and New Zealand missions. Canada, itself fiercely independent, joined Australia on some resolutions.

And the UN attitude to Israel changed a bit – partly as a result of Canberra's efforts, partly as a result of the efforts of others.

Traditionally, Israel was unique in not even being allowed to join a UN regional group. Now, like Australia, it is part of WEOG. Its prime minister has been received at the UN, it has proposed a UN resolution and it will stand for a term on the Security Council. The fact that these are all unprecedented moves shows how unbalanced the UN has been. The fact that they are happening shows that change can occur.

Australia's moves annoyed the Arab League bureaucracy but cost it nothing in trade or diplomatic relations. Australian trade with the Middle East, especially the Gulf States, boomed this decade and Syria and Libya set up embassies in Canberra.

It is good that Canberra did all this and it had the effect of drawing us still closer to Washington, but it was a lot of work for marginal gains and it shows the great limitations on the UN as any kind of effective body.

Structurally the UN is a mess, but it is probably better that it stay a mess, as its messiness does not prevent it from doing the little good that it does, and it helps prevent it from doing larger harm.

The General Assembly is notionally the most democratic arm of the UN because all governments are represented equally here. But insofar as many of those governments are undemocratic the General Assembly is not a forum of global democracy but a cabal of dictatorships. Its prolix resolutions and rhetorical declarations have no effect on anything and receive very little publicity.

When he left his UN ambassadorship, Dauth argued that the General Assembly was 'defunct'. Its debates never led to action, there was never compromise or a negotiated settlement of anything in the General Assembly. It was the 'core' of the UN, and the UN was 'rotten' at its core.

The UN bureaucracy has been mired in corruption and scandals of all kinds.

The Security Council is both the strength and the weakness of the UN. Its five permanent members (P5) – the US, UK, China, Russia and France – have the veto power, so nothing can be done in the security realm against their interests. This is a weakness of the UN because it prevents action being taken and the P5 are not representative of the world today, but of the victorious powers after World War II. But it is also the strength of the UN because it prevents the UN from taking crazy actions that would start a war, and it keeps those five powers engaged.

However, the veto power is also one of the reasons that it is utterly fatuous to pretend that the UN represents a system of international law. The veto alone means that the international law does not apply to that 30 per cent or more of the world's population represented by the P5. Given that the P5 members are always willing to exercise the veto on behalf of their friends, it means that, if the UN is international law, that international law does not apply to an even greater part of the world – namely friends of the P5. When no P5 interests are engaged it is possible for the Security Council to do something, as in endorsing the Australian-led mission in East Timor. But consider the case of the Solomon Islands. Because the Solomons have diplomatic relations with Taiwan, China would have vetoed any Security Council resolution to help the Solomons. Therefore Australia did not seek a Security Council resolution to legitimise its efforts in the Solomons. But it is quite clear that had it been possible to do so, Canberra would have gone to the Security Council for endorsement. It was not possible for reasons that had nothing to do with the merits of the mission themselves.

It is increasingly unclear that the Security Council can provide even international legitimacy, much less security. The coalition operations in Iraq after the military phase fairly quickly acquired unanimous Security Council backing. This has made not much difference to their legitimacy. And the appalling tragedies of Rwanda, the Balkans and Darfur show that the UN cannot provide anybody with security.

Canberra notionally supports enlargement of the Security Council's permanent members to include Japan and India, and has even talked of Indonesia as a possible future permanent member. These gestures are taken to improve bilateral relations with the countries concerned. The Howard government's real, secret view is that Australia's interests are best served by the Security Council staying as it is. Australia's closest ally, the US, has the veto, as does another close ally and friend, the UK. While Canberra is closely aligned with Tokyo, any enlargement would inevitably include more countries than Japan and tend to dilute the influence of Australia's friends.

The real security system in the world is not provided by the UN but by the US alliance system. This is an unpalatable truth to draw attention to as it seems to privilege the US above other nations. But it is the truth nonetheless. No consequential nation is ever constrained by the UN in a serious matter of national security. Many nations are constrained by the US alliance system. In the only two cases where the Security Council notionally took serious action – the Korean war and the 1991 Iraq war to expel Saddam Hussein from Kuwait – it was merely endorsing an American action.

All through the Cold War the Soviets were constrained in their actions against Western Europe not by the UN but by the US security guarantees under NATO. China is constrained in potential military action against Taiwan not because of the UN, which given China's veto power could certainly do nothing against it under any circumstances, but by the US security guarantee for Taiwan. The same dynamic is repeated around the world.

It is almost obscenely unfashionable to speak in this manner, but it has one great virtue – it is true. A nation should always base its security policies on reality. There can on occasion be some virtue in paying lip service to illusion but one must always recognise that it remains illusion.

Yet for all that, critics of the UN must recognise three countervailing factors. Many of its specialist agencies do good work. Occasionally, when the big powers agree, it can broker helpful international agreements. And thirdly, millions of people around the world continue to invest idealism and hope in the UN. Even if that idealism and hope is misplaced and based on ignorance of what the UN is really about, it is a significant political factor and must be weighed in geo-strategic calculations.

All of this indicates that Australia should be utterly pragmatic towards the UN, supporting it where it does good, remaining involved, but not remotely constrained by its authority in any matter of serious national interest. This, in practise if not formal policy, is the approach most nations take to the UN.

In an interview for this book, Howard told me that he viewed the UN as 'a curate's egg – good in parts'. He said: 'Some of the UN's specialised agencies do great work. The High Commission for Refugees over the years has got quite a good track record, UNICEF, WHO. Its human rights manifestations are completely different. And of course it's only as strong as the collective will of those who exercise power on the Security Council. (Sometimes) they all agree to act together, or to turn a blind eye, as happened in relation to Kosovo and Rwanda. Rwanda was a disgrace. And was Darfur much better? (Many more people) died in Darfur than in Iraq since the Iraqi elections in January (2005 – the interview took place at the end of 2005) yet it (Darfur) hardly ever gets mentioned, yet it's a great tragedy. My attitude to the UN is we'll continue to be a member in good standing but we have no starry-eyed illusions. Where it can work it's a great idea but Australia's security does not lie in a starry-eyed investment of hope in the United Nations.'

Nor does Howard believe that the UN system embodies a system of international law: 'No, we are still a world of nation states and understandings, alliances, cooperation, coalitions among nation states are still the things that in the end will save the world or prevent the world from deteriorating further. That was the truth in the 1930s. It's the truth in the first years of the 21st century. It's a stunning parallel. The failure of process in the 1930s produced horrific consequences and it could still again.'

Australia's position and performance at the UN, and in multilateralism considered as part of the UN system, has grown much closer to the US position, though by no means become identical. This is not something Howard needed to do to earn favour with

Bush. He has all the favour with Bush he could possibly need. Rather it is a sign of Howard, and Downer, running a mature and self-confident government, coming to the same conclusions as Bush on a set of key issues. The new closeness in this case proceeds from a similar world view, rather than from the mechanisms of the alliance, nonetheless it draws the alliance partners that much closer together.

Chapter 17

HOWARD AND BUSH AS NATIONAL SECURITY HEADS OF GOVERNMENT

At the 2004 federal election the Australian Labor Party went to the people with a promise to create a Minister for Homeland Security. Naturally this was accompanied by a promise to create a Department of Homeland Security. It was a most unusual case of the ALP apeing an innovation of George W Bush.

Bush, like Howard, began his period in office as a domestically focused government leader, promising a more 'modest' US foreign policy after what was seen as the empty grandiloquence of his predecessor, Bill Clinton. Bush's presidency, his life and to some extent the American nation were transformed by the terror attacks on September 11, 2001. Bush became the national security president. And Americans, certainly right up through Bush's re-election campaign against John Kerry, gave him high approval ratings for his handling of the war on terror. It was after his re-election that the ratings started to decline.

Partly prodded by the report of the bipartisan congressional 9/11 commission, Bush instituted some big changes in the structure of American government and bureaucracy to deal with the war on terror. He began a reform process of the intelligence agencies to make them more aggressive in collecting human intelligence and to force them to work much more closely together, especially the Federal Bureau of Investigation and the Central Intelligence Agency. He put new chiefs in charge of the agencies and he created a new post – Director of National Intelligence–to act as a kind of intelligence czar.

His biggest change, however, was the creation of the Department of Homeland Security, which brought together 22 former agencies and departments which were seen as having a significant role in homeland security. It had a workforce of 180 000, a massive number of people to be shifting into a new department and a giant challenge of coordination.

As is always the case with such a huge bureaucratic change, the disruption was immense, the teething problems staggering. With the devastating tragedy of hurricane Katrina, and the feckless response of the first few days, it seemed to have fallen at its first hurdle. No doubt in time the Americans will make it work, but so far it is a cautionary tale of the dangers of change for change's sake.

Two political imperatives drove Bush – the need to do something to address the failings revealed by 9/11, and the desire to have a cabinet secretary's face which the public could identify with reassuring themes of homeland security. In fact it turned out the public only ever held one face accountable for homeland security, and for national security more generally, and that face belonged to the president.

In the 2004 Australian election the Liberal and National parties did not match Labor's commitment to appoint a homeland security minister. They already had one. His name was John Howard.

The evolution of Howard as a national security prime minister (embracing both homeland security and international security) has changed the shape of government in Australia. All governments everywhere have become more presidential, whether their system is nominally a parliamentary or a presidential one. This is certainly true of the UK, where Tony Blair's office runs the government and a senior personal adviser to Blair has more power than any but the most senior two or three cabinet ministers.

Partly this is a consequence of technology and the culture of 24-hour-a-day media. The big issues are brought to the public's attention with great immediacy and force and they expect their government leader, who these days is in any event always before them on the media, to have the answers.

This has been magnified a hundred times by the dynamics of the war on terror, when a government leader is seen as responsible for people's very hold on life.

Howard, although a plain personality who shrewdly markets his plainness, came to totally dominate his government while nonetheless operating an effective cabinet system. Polls have consistently given him a huge lead over any of the Opposition leaders he has faced on the question of who is better able to handle national security.

What is little understood by the broader Australian public is the substantial way in which Howard has reformed and rearranged institutional structures and the bureaucracy to support the new, dominant role for the prime minister in national security.

It is a work in progress and there is much evolution still to come.

But however substantial the reforms have been up to now, more radical ones could be on the way. Serious consideration at the highest levels of government and the Canberra mandarinate has been given to whether Australia should create a formal National Security Council along the lines of the United States. This would incorporate the powerful National Security Division of the Department of the Prime Minister and Cabinet (PM & C), as well as its International Division, and the Office of National Assessments (ONA), the peak intelligence agency, which reports directly to the prime minister. It could also draw in some other parts of the bureaucracy.

Howard takes a day-by-day interest in virtually all aspects of national security and has moved the centre of institutional and bureaucratic gravity closer and closer to his own office, so that a new prime minister who was less interested in these issues would have to rearrange the machinery again to get the power and day-to-day responsibility out of his hands. Of course a prime minister always has ultimate responsibility for all areas of government policy but much of the day-to-day responsibility now rests with bureaucrats who work directly for the prime minister. That's different from other areas of policy and outside of war time it's unique in Australian history.

For example, the role of the director-general of ONA (who reports to the PM) as the coordinator and leader of the entire intelligence community has been strengthened in several ways. The ONA conducts the formal evaluation of the other intelligence agencies. The government has also established the Foreign Intelligence Coordination Committee, which the head of ONA chairs.

Of course not everything is run or supervised by ONA. The government has also established a National Terrorism Threat Assessment Centre, which is run by the Australian Security Intelligence Organisation (ASIO), and in which there are representatives from the other intelligence agencies.

The government has given the responsibility of coordination of terrorist policy to PM & C. The National Security Division of this department was only set up in mid-2003 and it has already become a powerhouse of government policy. Its first head was Miles Jordana, who had worked as Howard's personal foreign policy adviser. Then came General Duncan Lewis, a former special forces commander. When Lewis was appointed deputy secretary of PM & C he was succeeded as national security division head by an army colonel. When the Howard government gives the job to soldiers, you know it's a serious business.

The most important institutional innovation is the National Security Committee (NSC) of the Cabinet. Howard set this up in 1996. As he told me in an interview for this book: 'There were various other combinations and permutations which met spasmodically under other governments. But from the very beginning, we had a policy commitment. We said we'd have a National Security Committee and it's always comprised the portfolios that are on it now. Earlier on we may have met with some officials. But certainly since Timor or just before we've had that core group (of officials). All our major foreign policy and defence decisions are made by that group. In some cases I'll take it (a decision) to a full cabinet but not very often. I do from time to time. Obviously the decision to go to war in Iraq, I had an NSC and then a full cabinet. The decision to take the troops to Al Muthanna (province in Iraq) I took to a full cabinet as well.'

The membership of the NSC consists of the prime minister, deputy prime minister, the treasurer, the ministers for foreign affairs and defence and the attorney-general. At the NSC, unlike the cabinet, the group of senior officials who attend sit at the main table and have equal status, participating fully in the discussions and the decision making. The officials who attend are the secretaries of the PM&C, and of the foreign affairs and defence departments, and sometimes the secretary of the attorney-general's department. Critically, the chief of the defence force, the director-general of ONA, the director-general of ASIO and the commissioner of the Australian Federal Police (AFP) also attend. Other officials and other ministers can be called in as required.

We have already seen how the extraordinary profile of the former chief of the defence force, General Peter Cosgrove, helped bring the military back to the centre of national life and also helped the Howard government. Although less important politically, the emergence of the former head of ASIO, Dennis Richardson, and the boss of the AFP, Mick Keelty, was also immensely influential in shaping public perceptions of national security.

As with Cosgrove, there was nothing improper about their emergence, but the huge moral and political authority they acquired as apolitical guardians of the public safety was of inestimable help to the government and shrewdly used by it. It also represented a significant new stage in the evolution of the public role of such officials in Australia.

The two are very different. Richardson had been chief of staff to the former Labor prime minister Bob Hawke. Under no circumstances could he be dismissed as a Coalition stooge. A small, trim man with thinnish hair and what might be called plain Irish looks, Richardson was one of the famous class of 1969 – the recruits to the diplomatic corps of that year, many of whom went on to stellar careers in the bureaucracy. They had a reputation as being tough-minded and plain-spoken, and Richardson certainly fits that mould. He has a hard, well-organised, methodical mind and a fierce, take-no-prisoners style in private argument. He is ferociously independent. Whether it was the government's idea or his, he performed two vital roles for the nation after 9/11 and then even more so after the Bali bombings. He ran ASIO well and effectively and oversaw its rapid expansion. And he brought the organisation out from the shadows. In a series of carefully thought out speeches and public presentations, and in testimony to the Senate Estimates Committee, he told the public in broad terms what ASIO was doing and told it about the nature of the terrorist threat. The Senate Estimates Committee functions a little like a US congressional hearing and its highlights are frequently recorded for television news or sometimes broadcast live. They are extensively reported in newspapers. They too contribute to the growing public status of officials like Richardson. The government showed what it thought of Richardson's performance by appointing him as Australia's ambassador to Washington, the most important and prestigious post in our diplomatic service. This appointment must also be seen in the light of the new Australian-US intelligence intimacy, explored in chapter 7.

Keelty had an even higher public profile as AFP commissioner. The AFP did magnificent work in counter-terrorism, especially in helping other agencies, mainly police, throughout southeast Asia. This began particularly in the forensic work done in response to the first Bali bombings in October 2002, which led directly to the capture, trial and conviction of the terrorists who had murdered 88 Australians (as well as 114 innocent people of other nationalities, including dozens of Indonesians). Keelty, like Cosgrove, had the inestimable benefit of wearing a uniform. Keelty was not as sharp or as sure-footed as Richardson in media appearances, and he made a few gaffes, but the AFP's formidable media machine kept him frequently in the public eye. And in a way even his gaffes served to reinforce the image of a decent man doing important work.

Even the director-general of ONA, Peter Varghese, intellectually an immensely gifted diplomat with a fine, subtle, analytical mind, who for a time served as Howard's personal foreign policy adviser, gave a couple of on-the-record interviews and appeared at Senate Estimates Committee hearings.

With the exception of the Senate processes, the government could turn this publicity off any time it wanted. But it is hugely useful, for genuine purposes of informing the public and also politically for the government, to have the chief of the defence force, the heads of ASIO and ONA and the commissioner of the AFP as important, recognised public figures, much more in the mould of senior American officials, working public opinion, the public/private institutional interface and all the bureaucratic issues of Canberra.

To support the NSC, the Howard government also set up the Secretaries Committee on National Security, with the wonderfully Sir Humphrey acronym of SCONS. This consists essentially of the departmental secretaries on the NSC itself plus a few others. It is a sign of the centrality of the PM & C department that the deputy secretary of the department responsible for the national security division also attends the SCONS meetings. Submissions to the National Security Committee of Cabinet go through SCONS. Peter Shergold, the secretary of PM & C, is the chairman of SCONS and PM & C provides the secretariat for both SCONS and cabinet's NSC.

On specifically homeland security questions there are also a substantial range of consultative and crisis-management mechanisms which the government has set up and which are mostly coordinated by PM & C. The National Counter-Terrorism Committee, which meets at least twice a year and is supported by a raft of officials, involves all the state governments as well as the federal government. The nature of terrorism means that the federal government has to coordinate possible responses across many departments, and of course many state government agencies as well. It is a huge effort of government to get all the structures in place so that threats are minimised and if there is a terrorist incident the machinery of government can respond quickly.

Not everything has been a response to terrorism. The Solomon Islands peacekeeping and reconstruction mission, and before that the East Timor mission, demonstrated the need for a whole-of-government approach, with, for example, the AFP and the military working hand-in-glove, though this was by no means without some tensions in the Solomons.

Similarly, responding to the first Bali bombings, the second Bali bombings, and the Asian tsunami all required many different government agencies to work together and to move fast.

Of all of these bodies, the NSC has been the most effective. It involves the key ministers and the key officials and it is small enough to be manageable. It meets at least once a month – more frequently than any other cabinet committee, a sure sign that the prime minister finds it effective. When there is a crisis it meets much more often than that. As we have seen in chapter 1, the foreign minister, Alexander Downer, told the US vice president, Dick Cheney, that during the combat phase in Iraq the NSC met every day. During the height of the Timor crisis it met twice a day, morning and evening. As well as taking policy decisions it can engage in active crisis-management oversight.

Bush's changes to governmental structures to cope with the war on terror were driven by political and public pressure. Partly as a result, and as is in any event the American way, they were bold and sweeping and involved new structures. This American tendency to boldness often works wonders, but in shaking up huge government structures it can produce more chaos than coordination. The delicate tissues of connectivity which already exist between agencies can easily be disrupted so that uniting agencies into one department can actually result, in the short term at least, in less coordination.

Howard's changes have occurred mostly below the radar of public awareness. They have been incremental and been adopted mostly within existing Australian structures. Thus, although transformative in their cumulative effect, they have been much less disruptive than the US changes. Of course the US system is so infinitely bigger, and its tasks correspondingly greater and more complex, that moving the US system naturally takes longer and is more difficult than moving the Australian system.

Nonetheless the differences in approach are real. Howard often operates according to the old Chinese proverb – crossing the river by feeling the stones. He has done that in national security. But the net effect is to centralise more power and control in the hands of the prime minister over all aspects of national security. Given that the public will hold the prime minister accountable for national security, this is not necessarily a bad thing, but it might not be the optimal structure if national security becomes more calm and relaxed again. However, Howard believes the war on terror is here for a long time to come. So, presumably, whether it is Howard or someone else, is the national security prime minister.

Chapter 18

TWO CASE STUDIES IN THE NEW PARTNERSHIP: THE TSUNAMI AND CLIMATE CHANGE

For much of the time that he has been US president, George W Bush has had the habit of speaking about fortnightly – sometimes a little more frequently, sometimes a little less – to the UK's Tony Blair. It is seldom, perhaps never, that Blair has rung Bush to complain about being excluded from something, especially something Australia is included in. Except once.

At the end of 2004, Blair rang Bush for exactly that purpose. He was unhappy that the US had combined with Australia, Japan and India to form a core group to coordinate assistance to southeast Asia and south Asia in response to the devastating tsunami.

On Boxing Day, 2004, a giant tsunami had crashed a wave of destruction across southeast Asia, killing tens of thousands of people in Indonesia's Aceh province, and also bringing destruction and devastation to Sri Lanka, parts of India, Thailand and Malaysia. The purpose of this short treatment is not to recount the overwhelming suffering of those hit by the tsunami (though that of course is the most important fact about it), nor, except in the most general way, the heroism of those who brought what relief they could. Its much more limited purpose is to look at how the Australian-US alliance functioned in the crisis and to see whether this holds any general lessons.

The first policy objective of both Canberra and Washington was to render effective assistance, especially to Indonesia, which had been hardest hit. The response of both capitals was swift. When the magnitude 9.0 quake struck off the coast of Sumatra, triggering the terrible destruction of the tsunami, it was mid-evening on Christmas night in Washington. Within six hours the US Agency for International Development was moving relief funds to US embassies in the region. Given the location of the disaster it was pretty natural that Washington would look to Canberra for cooperation straight away.

Canberra itself reacted with great speed. After clearing things with the Indonesian government, the Australian and American militaries both raced to Aceh to render assistance. In this type of disaster only the military has the capacity to move fast enough and do enough. Giant naval ships have giant facilities for making sea water drinkable, they have substantial medical facilities, they can transport food and people, not least the ship's crew themselves, to render emergency assistance. The then US commander of the Pacific Fleet, Admiral Thomas Fargo, based in Hawaii, was on the phone to the then chief of the Australian Defence Force (ADF), General Peter Cosgrove. The Australian military and US Pacific Command (PACOM) work so much and so intimately together that everyone knows everyone and when necessary they can cooperate swiftly and effectively.

The idea for a core group of nations to coordinate the immediate relief effort in the critical first few days came from US Under Secretary of State for Political Affairs Marc Grossman. A group of senior US officials from the State Department, the Pentagon and the National Security Council, who were not away from Washington on Christmas leave, were called back to their posts and worked almost round the clock for the next few days. Ships and resources had already been dispatched but these officials were trying to both augment and structure the response as fast as possible. As they constantly phoned each other with ideas, requests and plans, senior people in each of these agencies also repeatedly spoke to their contacts in the Australian embassy in Washington.

At that stage the ambassador was Michael Thawley, who was then coming to the end of his five years in Washington. Thawley was a professional diplomat with substantial experience also in the international division of the Department of Prime Minister and Cabinet. Immediately before coming to Washington Thawley worked in Howard's office as his personal foreign policy adviser. Thawley turned out to be an exceptionally effective Australian ambassador to the United States. He was later criticised for making representations to congressmen on behalf of AWB, but that was his job. He had several advantages which he used ruthlessly. He was representing an ally which committed to arms in a time of war. He was representing a fellow centre-right government much more sympathetic to many of Bush's positions than most European governments. He was known to be close to Howard. Everyone knew that Howard would cash any cheque that Thawley wrote. And he had been in Washington for five years, an inestimable advantage in a town where everything runs on personal connections.

Thawley became a Washington powerbroker in his own right. He not only saw whoever he wanted to on the foreign side of the shop, he also regularly met with Bush's most important domestic adviser, Karl Rove. Thawley's status was demonstrated the following March when he went to pay his farewell call at the White House. Bush received Thawley and his wife in the Oval Office but after a few minutes asked Thawley to remain, there were a few others who wanted to say goodbye to the Australian. He went out of the room and brought back Defense Secretary Don Rumsfeld and his then deputy Paul Wolfowitz, National Security Advisor Stephen Hadley, the then White House chief of staff, Andy Card, and the then chairman of the joint chiefs of staff, General Richard Myers. There are very few heads of state who would command a group like this.

Under Thawley the embassy was organised to work every relevant US agency — starting with the White House and including the Pentagon, State Department, National Security Council, Congress and many others. He also mobilised the Australian economic and commercial presence in the US, which is substantial, for relevant policy ends. As a result of all this the Australian embassy was plugged into US thinking on the tsunami core group from the first hours of the crisis. Australia was able to have an active input into the inter-agency process from the start. In Washington it's very hard to change an inter-agency consensus or compromise position, once it's been reached. But it's just at that ineffective moment when foreign governments routinely get involved. An effective embassy has to be involved at the start of the inter-agency process, in consultation, of course, with Canberra.

The core group concept was formalised in a phone call between Condoleeza Rice, then US national security advisor, and Colin Powell, then US secretary of state. Powell asked his deputy, Rich Armitage, to ring Thawley and the Japanese ambassador to get the ball rolling. Armitage rang Thawley on December 27. He told him that Powell wanted to talk to the Australian foreign minister, Alexander Downer, directly. Thawley was able to respond positively to the core group straight away. He then himself rang both Downer and Powell. The two foreign ministers then spoke directly and the in-principle commitment was made. Australia's capacity to commit fast and follow up with real action was crucial.

Thawley suggested to Canberra that they furnish a senior person, in the Australian capital, to be the ongoing contact person for the core group. Doug Chester, a deputy secretary of the Department of Foreign Affairs, and for a time the acting secretary, was given the job.

On December 27, late in the evening Washington time, the core group held its first telephone conference, with Grossman in the chair and Chester participating from Canberra. The other participants were the Indians and Japanese. Naturally the three relevant ambassadors had consulted and caucused in Washington in advance. Every day for the vital initial period of nearly two weeks, the core group consulted by telephone conference and coordinated their aid efforts.

A senior US official at the time told me: 'We were interested in the countries that could do the mostest the fastest. We weren't trying to make any big political point.'

Nonetheless the political point was made. The US called on its two great Pacific allies, and the two great Pacific democracies, Japan and Australia. It also called on Asia's biggest democracy, India, with whom it was already well on the way to forming a new strategic relationship.

The most notable absentee was China, which did not have the allies, the money, the navy or the regional trust to make a significant contribution. Indeed, the tsunami showed the limit of Chinese influence. None of the regional organisations was effective either. It is a contention of this book that the most effective regional organisation in the Asia-Pacific is the US alliance system, and the tsunami demonstrated this.

Nonetheless, other US allies were a little peeved. Canada's then prime minister, Paul Martin, rang Bush to complain about being excluded. But Bush and his team rightly saw that the group would be most effective if in the first emergency days it was restricted to the region, and to countries that could take decisions and take action quickly.

Blair argued that coordination should have gone through the UN and the G8 (Group of Eight Leading Industrialised Nations), of which Britain is a member. On December 31 the core group did hold a video conference involving Powell and the UN Secretary-General Kofi Annan. After this, core group meetings routinely involved senior UN representatives.

In truth the UN had no capacity to act in the first days. One Australian official told me: 'All this talk about UN capability is crap. The core group countries had forces steaming to the crisis while the UN was still on holidays.'

Eventually the core group wound itself up. Each of its members had pretty well worked out what it was going to do long term by then. The UN resumed its nominal coordinating role. The US had given the tsunami enormous priority, diverting military units that were steaming to Iraq to render assistance in Aceh. A summit was held in Jakarta in early January. Canberra urged the Americans to consider sending Bush himself. It would have been a powerful gesture but a logistical nightmare and it would have diverted precious resources away from the effort to help tsunami survivors.

Core group members gave some consideration to whether they should keep themselves involved in some kind of group but decided against it. The US, Japan and Australia already had a range of trilateral arrangements and the US was steaming along a separate route with India.

The lessons of the core group are important.

First, the main objective was to render as much assistance as possible as quickly as possible. In achieving this objective the Australian-US closeness built up under the alliance was helpful.

Second, this was effective, regional multilateralism and it had nothing to do with the UN. If the UN had been involved from the start, everything would have been slower and less effective.

Third, when the chips are down the region can count on the US and Australia, and their friends and allies.

Fourth, Australia got enormous good publicity in the US for its efforts, front page on the main newspapers, all over the TV screens. Australia's per capita contribution was by far the greatest and its absolute contribution comparable to that of the US.

Fifth, Australia and the US both showed themselves to be compassionate societies. I was based in the US during this period and society was completely obsessed with the tsunami, which was on the TV 24 hours a day and chased everything else off the front pages. The response in Australia was even stronger.

Sixth, Australia and the US both substantially improved their standing in Indonesia.

Seventh, Indonesia showed itself flexible and pragmatic, and concerned primarily with the welfare of its own people by welcoming foreign troops onto its soil.

Eighth, the core group provided a model which may well be followed in the future.

The Asia-Pacific Partnership on Clean Development and Climate will be less universally praised. This brief account will not seek to evaluate the science behind the Kyoto Protocol on Climate Change. It will examine how the Australian-US partnership helped Washington and Canberra respond in a way which both saw as serving their national interests and their political interests.

The Howard government contains more than a grain of scepticism about the science behind the idea that global warming produced by human activity is inevitably heading the world towards catastrophe. However, it has, at least formally, come to the view that global warming caused by human activity, specifically the emission of greenhouse gases, is a reality. Many take the view that even if this is true, the Kyoto remedies won't be effective and would impose costs that would make it more difficult for societies to cope with climate change. As a high energy-producing and energy-exporting first world nation, with a substantial immigration program contributing to population growth, Australia is almost uniquely designed to be disproportionately damaged by a Kyoto-style regime of compulsory targets.

This is particularly so because some of the biggest greenhouse gas emitters apart from the United States, such as China and India, while signatories to Kyoto, are not bound by any Kyoto targets. Thus if the implementation of Kyoto by Australia resulted in, say, the closure of an Australian coal mine and its place was taken by a Chinese coal mine, the consequence would be extremely perverse. The Chinese coal mine would use less clean technology than the Australian mine it replaced. So the net result would be a loss of economic activity and jobs in Australia, and a net rise in greenhouse gas emissions globally.

The Howard government responded to all this with some sophistication. When Robert Hill was environment minister, Canberra negotiated relatively generous Kyoto targets. In the first couple of years of Kyoto's implementation Australia was one of the few nations to meet its targets even though it had not signed and was not bound by Kyoto.

The Howard government's view was that it would prefer not to sign up to Kyoto but if there was an overwhelming global sign-up it would be impossible for Australia to stand in isolation against it. Then the Bush administration withdrew from the Kyoto negotiations. The Bush administration has been much demonised for this and it certainly handled the diplomacy of it all very clumsily. But in substance its position was no different from the Clinton administration's position. Under Clinton, the US Senate had voted unanimously against Kyoto and Clinton left office recommending to Congress that it not ratify Kyoto. The difference in style here is instructive. Clinton was always willing to keep talking even if the talk meant nothing. He was a master of tactical ambiguity and endless procrastination. The Bush administration preferred strategic clarity. It's not going to string anyone along if it knows that in the end the answer will be no.

For the Howard government, the Bush administration's rejection of Kyoto meant that Canberra had the international political space to follow its preferred course, which was also to reject the treaty. The Howard government may have been right or wrong about this, but even Howard's most severe critics should acknowledge that he was implementing what he believed to be in Australia's national interest. And he only had the capacity to do so because of Bush's decision.

Both Howard and Bush had similar policy problems and political problems about Kyoto. That was the old dilemma of being seen to fight something with nothing. The Bush administration itself was moving to a position similar to Canberra's – that global warming was real but Kyoto was not the way to handle it. Nothing was more natural, therefore, than that they should collaborate in an attempt to address these two problems. Both governments were following more or less parallel paths in their deliberations. A few points were pivotal. The foreign minister, Alexander Downer, had dinner with the environment minister, Ian Campbell, and Campbell's parliamentary secretary, Greg Hunt, in the parliamentary dining room in Canberra. Before Hunt went into parliament he worked for Downer and the two are close. Hunt, like his boss, Campbell, accepted that greenhouse was real and something had to be done about it, but not Kyoto.

Downer was inclined to be more sceptical. The first step to getting anything done was forming a whole-of-government consensus in Australia. Of course, Howard was the final arbiter but Downer was key to the process, both because of his status as a senior minister and his closeness to Howard, and because any effort would have to be international and would require a lot of diplomatic grunt. Downer took some convincing and was briefed by the CSIRO and the Bureau of Meteorology.

To be effective any response would need to involve the big greenhouse gas emitters, the US, China and India, none of which was covered by Kyoto targets. It would have to solve the problem of Australia looking isolated or excluded because of Kyoto, and the politics and diplomacy would have to work.

Washington faced similar concerns and had come to similar conclusions. Bush's personal adviser on climate issues, Jim Connaughton, visited Australia in March 2005. He had been working on an idea to form an Asia-Pacific Partnership which would eschew Kyoto's binding targets. He planned to approach India, China and South Korea. Japan was not on his initial list. Tokyo has a great attachment to the Kyoto process, simply because it began in Kyoto and bears that beautiful city's name. Kyoto may well be the most sublimely beautiful man-made environment in the world and the creators of the Kyoto Protocol were smart to harness the prestige of that name to their project. As a result, Tokyo doesn't like to do anything which would seem to diminish Kyoto.

Connaughton had a series of dinners in Australia. He dined with Campbell, who quickly bought on to the project. He dined with Downer. Downer stressed the need to get Japan on board and the two brainstormed ways of making the proposed partnership look Kyoto-friendly. Downer also suggested an inaugural summit, which he offered to host. He further argued that the initiative would look better in Asia, and be easier to sell, if Australia rather than the US were seen to take the lead. Downer judged it important that the process not be confined to environment ministers, who very often cannot really commit their governments. It needed the clout of foreign ministers and if possible energy ministers.

Connaughton's key meeting, however, was with Howard, with Campbell also in attendance. It took place in the meeting room next door to Howard's office in Parliament House. Connaughton presented Howard with a letter from Bush outlining the rationale for the group. As you might expect, Howard, well prepared by his ministers and bureaucrats and alive to the politics and the policy considerations of the situation, endorsed the concept with enthusiasm. This was a breakthrough for the Americans as Howard was the first non-US head of government to do so.

As a result, in the arcane Sir Humphrey Appleby terminology of international diplomacy, a 'non-paper' was produced. A non-paper is a paper with notionally no official status. It can therefore be disowned but everybody knows it is the official view. The non-paper was circulated internationally to potential members.

Australian diplomacy went into high gear. Downer raised the initiative with his Indian counterpart on a visit to India. On that trip he also saw the Indian environment minister. Campbell went to New York for the UN's annual Commission on Sustainable Development and held private meetings with his counterparts from all the potential member countries. The Australian Greenhouse Office, Australian embassies in Asia and the ambassador for the environment, Jan Adams, all worked the idea hard. Getting India and China involved was the turning point.

Their deliberations were hard-headed, self-interested and globally enlightened. India and China, as we have seen, though nominal signatories to Kyoto have no targets or commitments to meet under it because they are developing countries. There is supposed to be a second stage of Kyoto when developing countries will sign up to targets, but New Delhi and Beijing reject targets absolutely. On the other hand, each is experiencing real and troubling particle pollution in their big cities, each believes the greenhouse effect is real and each is chafing under the high price of oil. Kyoto unrealistically asks them to forfeit economic growth. The Asia-Pacific Partnership offers them accelerated technology development and the substitution of clean for dirty technology. Its critics may well be right that this stress on new and better technology will not be enough, but it is much better than nothing, and Kyoto has zero chance of getting the developing world to agree to permanent poverty through forfeiting energy consumption associated with economic growth.

The hardest trick, and the last, was to get Japan to sign up to the new body. But once India and China and South Korea were on board the Asia-Pacific Partnership had impressive Asian credentials. It could be sold as Kyoto plus rather than anti-Kyoto. Japan was moreover reluctant to say no to close allies such as the US and Australia. And finally Japan was unlikely to get anywhere near meeting its own Kyoto target, so the partnership option made a lot of sense. Still, there was a lot of resistance within the Japanese system, a worry that Japan might be seen as betraying Kyoto. In the end, and at the last minute, the decision went right up to Japanese Prime Minister Junichiro Koizumi.

Koizumi is close to both Howard and Bush, with whom he shares pretty much a global world view, even a global ideology. And Koizumi, by modern Japanese standards, is decisive and a risk-taker. Led by their prime minister, the Japanese decided they wanted to be in.

As a result the first summit of the Asia-Pacific Partnership on Clean Development and Climate was held in Sydney in early 2006, representing nations which account for more than 50 per cent of global greenhouse emissions. It offered a real chance to do some good and it would be more difficult as a result to present either Australia or the US as isolated on climate change issues.

Both the core group on the tsunami, and the Asia-Pacific Partnership flow from a high level of trust between Washington and Canberra, a similar global outlook, and a desire by the two governments to help each other where possible in political and policy matters. Australia is a much smaller economy than the US, but it is the 13th largest economy in the world. That is hardly negligible. And Canberra can bring to the table generally excellent relations in Asia. These are considerable assets. The US and Australia don't always see eye to eye but when they do they are diplomatic force multipliers for each other. These two episodes, so different, are a further illustration of the breadth of the alliance relationship and its impact internationally.

Chapter 19

THE AMERICANISATION OF AUSTRALIAN POLITICS

Australia and the United States both held national elections in 2004. There were a lot of similarities. Both incumbents, Howard and Bush, were re-elected with increased margins of support. Iraq played a much bigger role in the US election but it is fair to see a validation of Howard's handling of Iraq in the Australian election. What the elections also disclosed was the growing similarity of Australian and US politics.

There are huge differences between Australia and the US, not least sheer scale. But whereas 30 years ago Australian politics was often discussed with a British comparison in mind – Conservative versus Labour, trade unions central, parliamentary seats the test not notional popularity – now it is the US to which we most often compare our politics, and for good reason.

The 2004 election in Australia disclosed four hugely important social and political dynamics in Australia which closely mirror similar dynamics in the US and are leading to the Americanisation of Australian politics, while the US election had some remarkable similarities to Australia's and may well point to aspects of our future.

It could be that these elections are signs of the two societies becoming more alike. I am not talking, of course, of the mere fact that Australian politics is becoming more presidential, with more power focused on the prime minister and more attention focused on the leaders during the campaign, to the point where an election is really more a prime ministerial campaign – that is a campaign for two individuals for the prime ministership – rather than a parliamentary campaign. That trend is nearly universal in Western societies. It is other dynamics from 2004 which are more revealing.

The 2004 election in Australia was not very edifying. It was not a disgraceful campaign. It did not turn on race or religion, or blaming a minority or any such noxious practice. But it was not a high-quality campaign. The single debate between Howard and Latham was poor compared with the three presidential and one vice-presidential debates in the US. Howard deserves censure over this. When he was Opposition leader in 1987 and Bob Hawke refused a televised campaign debate with him he flayed Hawke for his alleged cowardice. Now he ruthlessly exploits the advantage of incumbency to minimise the exposure of the Opposition leader.

Australian democracy would benefit from three, or at least two 90-minute televised debates for the prime minister and Opposition leader, and one for their deputies. In this aspect at least, US political culture is clearly superior to Australia's.

But the deeper failure of the Australian election was the way it failed to deal seriously with most of the long-term issues which confront us, such as the ageing of the population. Similarly, while Canberra had 800 troops in the Iraq theatre for the whole of the campaign, nobody on either side talked about this much at all.

The fact that the campaign was undramatic and banal was not necessarily a bad thing. Australia is the undramatic country, that is part of its national genius. This often annoys the class of political commentators, single-issue activists and political academics who yearn for something more compelling. But the better governed a society is the more likely its politics are to be bland and quotidian in their concerns. In itself, that is most often a good thing.

But it was the lack of substance that was worrying, the failure of the political class to address real problems with coherent policies in the context of an election campaign. Both Howard and Bush are big-government, big-spending conservatives. Howard at least can claim to have kept the budget in surplus, but he didn't confront recession as Bush did, a devastating terrorist attack on his own soil or the need for military commitments on the scale that Bush felt necessary. Nonetheless the nature of the spending commitments by both sides in the Australian campaign was troubling. All Western societies face a huge demographic challenge. They are growing older. They are not having enough babies even to replace themselves. To confront this they must do five things: attract good quality immigrants; pursue policies to encourage fertility; raise productivity in order to raise economic growth, so as to become richer before becoming older; encourage savings and later retirements so that people provide for their own futures; and rationalise the use of scarce services, especially health care, to discourage overuse while providing for the needy.

The Howard government came up with the Medicare Safety Net which is classic middle-class welfare. Middle-class welfare increases the size of government. It provides services notionally for free so there is no price signal or rationing. A safety net with a low threshold directs welfare dollars to the rich who can afford lots of medical procedures and quickly pass the threshold.

Labor's Medicare Gold was even worse, one of the most irresponsible policies in recent decades. To provide a non-means-tested, open-ended guarantee of private hospital treatment to everyone over a certain age is almost the perfect model of how not to deal with an ageing society. In this sense it was more a European welfare state-style promise than a classically American measure, but in the US the political power of the ageing has seen them ratchet up entitlements to unsustainable levels. The ageing are particularly powerful in the US because overall voting rates are so low. Seniors vote in much higher proportions than other age cohorts and much of US politics has been skewed to accommodate them.

The chief stylistic innovation of the Australian campaign was Mark Latham's attempt to make his unremarkable personal story the centrepiece of his campaign, with 'a place called Green Valley' substituting for Bill Clinton's more euphonious 'a place called Hope'. Howard is a keen student of American politics and an expert exploiter of the US security connection, but he is less a cultural and political Americaphile than many on the Labor right. Like others on the Labor right, Latham had a devotion to the study of Richard Nixon, and was a student of the one-time Clinton strategist, Dick Morris. He particularly tried to ape Morris's 'triangulation' strategy in which Clinton as president rose above party differences to seek a middle way, and in which he emphasised many small symbolic issues, such as supporting the wearing of school uniforms. Latham's version was to support reading to children, as though the other side of politics opposed this.

That the Australian people rejected all this falderol may suggest they are more mature voters than their American counterparts. On the other hand, Clinton 'triangulated' after he had become president and in a time of peace and prosperity. His innovations in that line don't seem to have become permanent features of American politics.

None of this, however, constitutes the four underlying social dynamics which the election revealed, which are bringing Australia much closer to the US in the style and substance of its politics. These four decisive trends are the Americanisation of the middle class, the emergence of a Christian right, Australia's distinctive national security dynamics and the acceptance of ethnic diversity.

The Americanisation of the middle class is evident in every capital city and indeed in the coastal growth belts of the sea-changers. Consider Sydney. Parramatta, which had been marginal for a long time, fell to Labor on the narrowest of swings. But Greenway, the seat encompassing Parramatta's poorer, newer, more troubled sibling further west, Blacktown, was taken by the Liberals. And the Liberals' Jackie Kelly easily held her seat of Lindsay, which encompasses Penrith. When I was a kid growing up in Sydney's western suburbs Parramatta, Blacktown and Penrith were the three great centres of western suburbs working-class culture. It would have been unthinkable in those times for the Libs to hold Blacktown and Penrith.

What's going on? Labor's shrewdest political head, Senator Robert Ray, commented on election night that he didn't think such seats were lost to Labor forever. But, for the purposes of this chapter, that's the very point. They're no longer safely Labor. They're detribalised and middle class, not only in income level but in social and political outlook.

When I was a kid I watched a lot of American sitcoms on TV and frankly marvelled at the size of the houses, which were always two storeys and seemed to me like mansions.

'Does everyone in America live in mansions, are they all rich?' I'd ask my parents about shows such as *My Three Sons*, *Father Knows Best* and *Leave it to Beaver*. No, no, they'd assure me, these houses are unrepresentative. Most Americans don't live like that.

My parents, I now believe, were a little misinformed. When I first visited the US, in the early 1980s, I found that the middle class did very well indeed. For a time on that visit I stayed with some Irish friends of my parents in Chicago. The husband had worked in the building trade but was now a boiler attendant and the wife worked part-time – hardly plutocrats. But their home was straight out of *Father Knows Best* land. It was a split-level, brick house in a leafy, affluent suburb. It had a huge formal lounge at the front and a vast basement that the family had turned into a TV room, as well as a separate dining room, eat-in kitchen and four bedrooms upstairs. The family ran two vehicles – a pick-up truck with a baseball bat in the cabin for protection, and a family sedan. These people certainly didn't think of themselves as poor, or even particularly working class. Of their four kids, two were working, one was at college and one was at a Catholic high school (although he was on a football scholarship). They were as likely to vote Republican as Democrat. Though I don't know whether they voted for Ronald Reagan or not, they had about them many of the characteristics of the so-called Reagan Democrats – socially conservative ethnic voters of working-class background (traditional Democrats in other words), who were aspirational economically and patriotic in national security matters, and therefore potential

Republican voters on issues of social values and national security. The Reagan Democrats, of course, were the forerunners by 15 years of the Howard battlers.

It seems to me now that in Parramatta, Blacktown and Penrith, and in many other areas of Australia, we have reproduced this aspirational ex-working, now middle, class. It's evident in a seat like Aston in Melbourne, a seat full of McMansions which voted Labor all through the 1980s and is now more safely Liberal than a traditional Liberal stronghold like Kooyong.

When I was growing up, the average Aussie home had three bedrooms, a bathroom, a kitchen with space for a table and a lounge room, and it was often made of fibro. Now, in great swathes of Australia, the McMansions have transformed all that. You see it, socially if not yet politically, even in a suburb on the northern fringes of Melbourne like Craigieburn, a new suburb full of beautiful new McMansions.

There is a lot of nonsense talked about McMansions, especially by the most affluent people in the best parts of Sydney and Melbourne, who live in beautiful homes themselves but think there's something wrong with ordinary people wanting the same. The McMansions are energy-inefficient in a characteristically American fashion and that should be addressed, but other than that I think the McMansions are a sign of a magnificent, democratising social movement in Australia. The sight of them fills my heart with joy. McMansions are available to average-income Australians and, in great contrast to the average house of my childhood, they are typically two-storey, four bedrooms, a big formal lounge at the front, separate dining, a family room and often another sitting room upstairs. Typically they have an ensuite bathroom for the main bedroom, a second bathroom upstairs and a downstairs toilet. And of course big garages for lots of cars.

They are the ordinary houses of ordinary, successful Australians, yet they are also the mansions I used to marvel at on American sitcoms. Australia is now a very wealthy, middle-class society. Total private wealth in Australia is now well over $5 trillion, which means, per capita, we're worth $250 000. Even more startling is that 40 per cent of Sydney households have air-conditioning. When I was a kid I knew that air-conditioning was only for rich people.

What this means is this new middle class, in the new McMansion suburbs, often very distant geographically from the old city centres, have a lot of property to protect. This reinforces their social conservatism. They think of themselves as successful and they certainly want success for their children. This makes them partial to private education. Naturally they are keen on any transfer payments they can receive from the government, which they don't see as welfare but as a return on their taxes or sensible support for families. They tend to be patriotic on national security and conservative on crime and law and order.

At its broadest this is a very American mixture. More narrowly, it should reinforce the already strong support for the Australian-US alliance. The alliance is a symbol of security, and newly affluent people with substantial property but also substantial debts value security very highly indeed.

The second great dynamic disclosed by the 2004 election is the birth of a Christian right. Australia has been pregnant with a Christian right for years, but they could never quite get their act together. The year 2004 may have seen it at last come into the national life in a formidably organised way. The long-term former senator from Tasmania, Brian Harradine, was really a Christian right politician but made no effort to take his movement national. Fred Nile has been a Christian right presence in the NSW Parliament, but his appeal has been too narrow. But at the 2004 election Family First scored about two per cent of the vote nationally and won one senator. It was a pity for Family First that the numbers did not precisely fall to give it the balance of power, which would have guaranteed it a high profile. Family First is the right name for a movement like this. It carries an ideological message – support for families – but is inclusive, reassuring.

There is nothing remotely threatening about a political movement which takes its inspiration from Christian values. Indeed we are only a couple of generations removed from the time when all mainstream political movements did. Family First emerged from the Assemblies of God church. One of the most powerful social trends in recent years in Australia, and one which is very reminiscent of an earlier trend in the US, is the growth of Bible-based, evangelical Christianity. It is by far the most vital segment of Christianity in Australia. You see it all over the Gold Coast and in the fast-growing McMansion suburbs of all our big cities. The Hillsong Church in Sydney's Hills district is not only a huge church but has become something of a national institution, regularly attracting the most senior politicians from both sides to its functions.

The American Christian right is much demonised in the Australian media, but while it has its extremes, within the US it is for the most part a perfectly normal, mainstream force. It has not turned the US into a theocracy nor curtailed civil liberties. It has injected a strong, values-based discussion into national politics. And with its independent publishing and broadcasting arms, and its market power, it has acted as a force for diversity, creating alternatives to the left liberal orthodoxy of the east and west coast media establishments.

There are about 50 million evangelical Christians in the United States (a much bigger proportion than in Australia). They are highly committed, with a high church-going rate, generally a high rate of voting in elections, and their churches have become centres of social and political as well as religious organisation. Australian Bible-based churches are also highly committed, which is evident in the rapid growth of Christian schools. They are a social movement just beginning to seek political expression. That can only be good for Australian democracy. It also reinforces a distinctive similarity between Australia and the US.

The 2004 election was also one which came after the government had, every year for several years, increased the size of the immigration intake and retained it as totally racially non-discriminatory. John Howard, who made foolish remarks in the late 1980s questioning the rate of Asian immigration, now sends out letters written in Chinese to that 15 per cent of his Sydney electorate which is of Chinese origin. He believes Asian immigrants in particular, with their small business proclivities, stress on education and conservative family values, are a natural constituency for the Liberal Party.

In the 2004 National Rugby League grand final all the points for the winning Bulldogs side were scored by Muslims (Hazem El Masri and Matt Utai) which, quite naturally, nobody noticed. In the US, as in Australia, professional sports have been a powerful force for integration because they are based entirely upon performance. What is interesting is that the Howard government chases the immigrant vote, not through the politics of identity, but through normal economic self-interest. It does not oppose any aspect of the make-up of modern Australia. This is similar to the way Bush chases the Hispanic vote.

The Cronulla riots in Sydney at the end of 2005 and the subsequent reprisal attacks don't deny that reality. Of course there are some problems with young men feeling affronted, but Australian society is not yearning for a pure Anglo-Celtic past. There is a broad acceptance of ethnic diversity and a desire to make it work. An earlier Australia might have recoiled from diversity itself after the Cronulla riots. Now people look for solutions – they stress tolerance, they also want more effective, if necessary tougher, law enforcement. But no one is seriously arguing to reinstate racial discrimination in immigration policy, for example.

And the final dynamic of the 2004 election is that national security was a big underlying issue, even though it didn't figure heavily in the campaign. This is probably the first time since the Vietnam years when national security, broadly defined, has been so much on people's minds so that one of the standard tests for a leader was the poll question as to who would handle national security better. That too obviously plays into support for the US alliance.

The US presidential election of 2004 also disclosed some interesting similarities to Australia, and perhaps some trends for our future. One was the sheer power of incumbency. By the beginning of 2006, in the 61 years since World War II, federal government in Australia had changed hands only five times – 1949, 1972, 1975, 1983 and 1996 – which yields an average term of 12 years. If you look at the US parties – Republican and Democrat – there have been only seven changes of party control of the White House since 1932. These occurred in 1952, 1960, 1968, 1976, 1980, 1992 and 2000. By 2006 that's seven changes in 74 years, yielding an average term of about 10 years, eerily similar to Australia's.

One of the most telling aspects of the US presidential campaign was that John Kerry, the furthest-left Democrat candidate for the presidency since at least Michael Dukakis in 1988, pledged to keep in place all of Bush's tax cuts up to those for people earning $200 000. In other words, Kerry judged that everybody earning up to $200 000 was a target voter for him. Kerry won a lot of votes and came close to the presidency. There is a lesson here for Labor. If it is going to succeed in the newly affluent McMansion suburbs it has to show that it's in favour of economic success, that it's friendly to small business, low tax and low interest rates.

The flip side to Kerry's pitch for the economically successful was Bush's pitch for the votes of racial minorities. He failed in his effort to break through with African Americans, winning only 11 per cent of their votes. But he won 45 per cent of Hispanic votes nationally, a staggering result. Hispanics, who make up nearly 15 per cent of the US population, and are its biggest minority, are also by far its fastest growing demographic, both because of high fertility rates and continued immigration from Latin America. If the Hispanic vote becomes basically a one-for-one split between Democrats and Republicans this makes life extremely difficult for Democrats. Bush won a similar share of the Asian vote, a smaller minority than the Hispanics but important nonetheless (indeed the first Punjabi to enter Congress did so in 2004 as a Republican from Louisiana).

The lesson here for all centre-right parties is obvious. They must contest the immigrant communities. If a centre-right party retreats into a politics-of-identity exclusiveness, it cuts itself off from what are generally the fastest growing sections of the society, certainly in the US and Australia. The challenge for the centre-right is always to combine their traditional patriotism with a convincing welcome for new immigrants who commit to the country. Republicans targeted Hispanics on social issues, on which they are more conservative than most Americans, and Asians on economic issues. New immigrant groups are often socially conservative, and if they're successful immigrants they are often economically liberal, a combination which yields receptive ground for centre-right parties.

In the US, Democrats target rich people and Republicans target immigrants. That's much more akin to the realities of contemporary Australia than the old capital/worker divide and a union-based traditional Labor Party.

The US election also reminded us that voters prefer candidates with executive experience in office. Every successful presidential candidate since 1964 has been an incumbent president, an incumbent or former vice president or a state governor. Our equivalent is a preference for federal cabinet experience. Every prime minister since World War II has previously been a federal cabinet minister except for Gough Whitlam and Bob Hawke. In 1995 the Liberals returned to their last remaining substantial former cabinet minister in John Howard.

There are huge differences between Australia and the US. It is a mistake for Australians to think Americans are just like us, just as it would be a mistake for Americans to think that we are just like them. But the whole world these days is influenced by US social and political trends. And probably there is no country in the world in which these trends play out in a more similar fashion to the US than Australia, notwithstanding all the differences between our societies. Even Canada, the US's nearest neighbour, having a huge neighbour to look after it, lacks the US's security imperatives, whereas Australia lives in an uncertain strategic environment and must devote serious attention to national security.

Understanding the US political process is important, therefore, not only for our dealings with the United States, but also as one part of understanding ourselves.

Chapter 20

THE FREE TRADE AGREEMENT: MAKING DOLLARS AND SENSE

The Free Trade Agreement (FTA) between Australia and the United States lay, at one point in May 2004, like a patient etherised upon a table, somewhere between life and death. Mark Vaile, Australia's trade minister, thought this time it must die. Vaile, a good, knockabout, hard-working politician from northern NSW, was in Washington, staying at the stylish but small Hey Adams Hotel on Lafayette Square.

Every day, all day and often all night, for two full weeks and the three weekends that bounded them, he and a team of officials, led by the formidably brainy Dr Ashton Calvert, then head of the Department of Foreign Affairs and Trade, went at the final negotiations with an American team led by Bob Zoellick, then the US trade representative, who in the second George W Bush administration became deputy secretary of state.

Zoellick was an old, old friend of Australia. A founding member of the Australian-American Leadership Dialogue, he had invested countless hours in the relationship. His Australian connection went back to college. Zoellick, tall and lean and intense and every inch the obsessive workaholic, was a long-distance runner at college. As a youngster, he was inspired by a book, *Young Men in a Hurry*, which included a portrait of the Australian distance champion Ron Clarke, who tragically never won a gold medal.

Zoellick was a classic over-achiever. Married without children, he had been under secretary of state when his mentor, James Baker, was secretary of state under George Bush snr in the late 1980s. As a committed Republican he didn't work for government while Clinton was in power, but spent those years shuttling between a variety of think-tank, corporate and academic roles. He was a good pick for USTR because he had both strategic vision and an inexhaustible appetite for detail.

Trade negotiations are often marathons and the FTA was no exception. Often the negotiating teams would pull all-nighters, ordering in soggy pizzas, stale Chinese takeaways and endless Diet Cokes. Trade policy is the enemy of health.

Zoellick had first proposed an FTA with Australia way back at the beginning of the 1990s. In those days Australia was not interested. Canberra had its own FTA with New Zealand, but apart from that, its big trade partners, Japan, South Korea, China and most of the other Asian countries, did not go in for FTAs. Canberra did not want to be in a position where it was discriminating against its biggest trade partner, Japan, in particular, by having a preferential deal with the US. Australia was committed to the Asia-Pacific Economic Cooperation forum's ideals of open regionalism: the idea that trade agreements should be non-exclusive, where any trade liberalisation you engaged in was extended to everybody.

When Vaile first became trade minister in 1999 he raised the idea of a US FTA with his department but the bureaucrats were against it at that stage. It was better, they said, to pursue global trade liberalisation through the World Trade Organisation (WTO). But then came the monumental failure of the WTO meeting in Seattle in 1999. It was clear to Vaile that Australia might wait another decade for meaningful action from the WTO. Meanwhile its big trade partners were doing their own FTAs. Japan did one with Mexico and was talking about lots of others. China agreed one with the ten nations of the Association of Southeast Asian Nations (ASEAN).

In a perfect world it would be better to have liberalisation globally than between a few nations at a time. But alas the world is not perfect. There was a real danger of Australia becoming isolated as the Polly Pureheart of free trade, with an agreement only with New Zealand, while everyone else was sleeping around.

At the same time, Howard and Downer saw the election of Bush in 2000 as offering an opportunity to pursue an FTA with the US. They thought this would have both economic benefits and strategic consequences. This too was a change of doctrine. For decades it had been deep Australian doctrine to keep trade and strategic matters strictly separated. This was to avoid what was essentially a National Party impulse to use the US/Australian military joint facilities in Australia as bargaining chips for access to the US market for Australia's agricultural produce.

But times had changed. It would be far too crude to say that the FTA was a reward for participating in the Iraq war but it was certainly fair to say the FTA emerged naturally out of the strategic closeness of the two governments. It is also the judgment of many that it would not have happened without the Iraq commitment. This is illustrated by the fate of New Zealand. Wellington put in a huge effort trying to convince Canberra to approach the US jointly for an FTA with both Australia and New Zealand, just as it had negotiated the North American Free Trade Agreement simultaneously with Canada and Mexico.

Canberra was having none of it. Howard has worked quite hard on the New Zealand relationship and kept it in surprisingly good shape. But there was no way he was ever going to blur the distinction between Australia as an ally of the US, and New Zealand as a friend but not an ally.

When New Zealand bugged out of the ANZUS alliance in the mid-1980s by banning the visit of US nuclear powered or armed ships, it set up a tremendous tension within the Australian Labor Party, many of whom, especially the Left, wanted to adopt New Zealand-style policies. Bob Hawke, Kim Beazley and Bill Hayden did sterling work fighting off the New Zealand temptation. But if

Wellington could ever establish that it got the benefits of alliance without having to meet the obligations of alliance, this would inevitably set off a new dynamic in Australian politics.

Therefore, whatever soft soap Australians use with New Zealanders, it is generally the Australian position that allies and non-allies are two distinct species when dealing with the US. Canberra rebuffed Wellington's proposed joint approach, and New Zealand's efforts to interest the US in an FTA on its own have gone nowhere.

To this day, Vaile believes the FTA would not have been possible without Zoellick's personal commitment to the Australian relationship, and this was certainly at least as much strategic as commercial. Indeed, even the formulation the two sides used – that the FTA would elevate the economic relationship to the same level as the strategic relationship – stresses the link between the two.

In an interview with me when he was US trade representative, Zoellick did allude to the strategic dimension of free trade: 'First of all, trade is about openness. And free trade is about freedom. The values that are associated with free trade are the values that terrorists are trying to destroy. It is also true at another level. I don't take the view that poverty causes terrorism because that's an insult to a lot of poor people, and many terrorists come from affluent backgrounds. But societies that become fragmented and impoverished do become breeding grounds for terrorism.'

Zoellick always stressed that the FTA was being pursued for trade and economic reasons, but he acknowledged the importance to the process of the background of the security relationship between Australia and the US: 'I've got a lot of respect and appreciation for the solidarity the US and Australia have shared over the last 100 years. This is not conditioned on security, but we're proud of the friendship and we want to build on it. I went to the Australian War Memorial and you could not fail to be moved by the record of Australian heroism there. This means something to me and to the president.'

Not that the economic relationship is at all anaemic. Although the US is generally Australia's second, third or fourth largest export market (the figures vary from year to year), a reasonable case can be made that the overall US economic relationship is the largest that Australia has.

In fact, the Australian government has put out official statements saying just that. Documents for the 2004 AUSMIN (Australia-United States Ministerial) meeting issued by Canberra declared: 'The United States is Australia's single most important economic partner.'

This is a reasonable judgment, but the results are not absolutely clear-cut. In 2003 the US was Australia's third-largest merchandise trade partner. But it was our largest services trade partner and total two-way trade was $40 billion (all these figures come from the Department of Foreign Affairs and Trade).

What is interesting is just how huge the Australian commitment to the US economy is. The US at 300 million people is 15 times Australia's population and an even higher multiple in terms of the size of its economy. Yet in several measures of economic interaction we commit in absolute terms roughly equal resources with the US. For example, the US is the largest foreign investor in Australia, larger than Britain or Japan or anyone else. In 2003 it had $71 billion invested in Australia. But Australia had a staggering $78 billion invested in the US. Australia was the tenth-largest foreign investor in the US.

There is a similar relationship in tourism. In 2004 about 400 000 Americans visited Australia and the US market is one that should register solid growth for tourism to Australia. But an astounding 375 000 Australians visited the US in the same year, almost a match in absolute numbers. (No Australian forgets the most poignant case of such a numerical equivalence – Australia and the US suffered approximately the same number of battlefield dead in World War I.)

Rather surprisingly, the US is one of the fastest growing markets for Australian tertiary education and in 2005 there were 9000 US students enrolled in Australian universities.

It is a reasonable judgment to make, therefore, that the US is Australia's 'single most important economic partner'. Our biggest merchandise trade partners, Japan and China, do not have the same size of trade in services or the same level of investment in Australia that the US does.

But surely China is the future and America is the past in economic terms?

This is not so, even in proportionate terms or in terms of growth. Although China typically grows at a higher rate each year than the US, the US economy is so vast that the absolute amount it grows by each year is greater than the amount the Chinese economy grows by. Thus in 2005 the US gross domestic product was US$12 400 billion. In 2005 its economy registered 3.2 per cent growth, having grown the previous year by 4.4 per cent. Although China's growth in both those years was about 9 per cent, in absolute terms this was a smaller dollar amount of growth than that registered by the US economy.

It is an abiding tenet of the Howard prime ministership that the US is not declining, absolutely or relatively, that it will remain central in Asia, and that the US and Australia are destined to grow more important to each other, not only strategically but economically.

In an interview for this book, Howard said: 'I don't buy (US decline). I remember all those books a few years ago about the end of the American century and how Japan was going to rise. But I don't believe in long-term US decline, I really don't. They have a lot of assets in their favour. They are a society that is still firmly rooted in individual initiative and private property ownership. The Free Trade Agreement's greatest contribution will be the way it brings the service sectors of the economies together. In a globalised economy the melding of the services sectors of Australia and the US will become much stronger.'

Certainly much of the publicity concerning the FTA that Vaile and Zoellick finally negotiated focused on the increased access for Australian agricultural products into the US. Ironically, Australia did not fill some of the agricultural quotas it was given in the first year of operation of the FTA because it could get higher prices for its products in Asia. But the trade professionals believe that the most important gains in the FTA are in gaining national treatment in large parts of the services sector (meaning that Australian services will be treated the same as services provided by US companies) and in gaining access to the US government procurement program, so that Australian firms can sell directly to the US government at federal and state levels (the states had to sign on to this individually and most US states subsequently did so), and in investment liberalisation.

During the negotiations the Australians were particularly upset, one might almost say bitter, that they could not gain any extra access for Australian sugar. Zoellick had to make very fine judgments. Generally, US agriculture was a friend to the Bush administration. Generally, although they always wanted their subsidies, US agriculture would support US administration efforts at trade liberalisation, at least as long as it did not involve them in making unilateral concessions, especially vis-à-vis the European Union. Australia is a major agricultural producer in global terms and therefore was capable of providing real competition. Zoellick had to work out how many and which agricultural constituencies he could annoy with greater Australian access and still get the deal past Congress. In his view, sugar had to be out.

What made the Australians bitter during the negotiations was the knowledge that the United States was planning to include sugar in the deal it did with five central American nations, the Central American Free Trade Agreement (CAFTA). The Australian argument was that as Australia is one of the US's closest allies, anything the US does for anyone else it should be able to do for Australia. The Americans' argument was that these impoverished central American nations were meant to be helped through CAFTA in a way that was almost equivalent to aid. And they didn't have many products they could sell to the US anyway.

Vaile fought hard over sugar. It was nearly a deal breaker, and Vaile told me there were 'several near-death experiences'. He and Zoellick, though good friends, had some volcanic shouting matches. Vaile went to the final measure of getting Howard to raise the subject of sugar with Bush in a phone call. Bush similarly raised something from the American side with Howard. On this occasion neither leader could help the other. The Pacific partners agreed to disagree. Australia got no extra sugar access.

The process of the FTA was a fascinating exercise in Australian diplomacy. It was not just a whole-of-government enterprise, but a government-plus-business alliance. It was as close as you get to an Australia Inc operation. Australian businesses in the US were mobilised and they allied with US businesses which had Australian connections.

Lobbying Congress was as important as negotiating with the administration. The Australians wanted better working-visa access. Zoellick was clear he didn't have authority for that. Such authority rested with Congress. Eventually, in 2005, well after the FTA was implemented, that came out of Congress. Australians are eligible for 10 500 E-3 visas a year. These are available to people with tertiary qualifications and job offers in the US. They include spouse work rights and can be renewed indefinitely every two years, so long as the visa holder stays in employment. This is as good a deal as anyone gets in the US.

One Australian intimately involved with the whole FTA process told me part of its complexity was that it really constituted a sequence of four negotiations. First was convincing the Bush administration to begin negotiations at all. That was a high hurdle because the administration realised that once negotiations began something would have to come out at the other end, even if it was failure. To try to do a deal and then perhaps lose it in Congress would be intensely embarrassing.

Once that hurdle was jumped, there was the negotiation on the substance of the agreement, an immensely complex business. Then there was the negotiation of the final text, which in a sense opened up all the issues again. And then there was the negotiation to get the votes in Congress.

Here Australia's good name in the US was crucial. The former deputy secretary of state, Rich Armitage, told me that he and his boss, Colin Powell, volunteered to talk to any senator or congressman that Zoellick wanted them to in order to help sell the deal. In the end, in an atmosphere hostile to new trade deals, the FTA passed both houses of Congress with record votes, an eye-popping result.

In Australia the politics centred on the Labor Party which, with the minor parties, could have held up the enabling legislation in the Senate. There was a fierce internal battle in the Labor Party. The anti-FTA position was actually hurt by then leader Mark Latham's weakness on the alliance. Labor could not be seen taking another gratuitous anti-American position. The pro-FTA position had two key allies – Kim Beazley, with his immense residual authority, and the state Labor premiers, all of whom, influenced by their respective business communities, supported the FTA.

Latham did have one moment of glory, when he insisted on two minor amendments as his price for allowing the enabling legislation to go through.

The Howard government wanted the FTA and the kudos it would bring, but it thought it had a big vote winner if Labor rejected the FTA outright. The government would have gone around every electorate in Australia identifying factories and farms which could have benefited from greater access to the US market. Labor understood the politics of this as well.

Vaile's three weekends in Washington saw him make the short walk each Sunday morning from the Hey Adams up to Washington's grand and dignified old Byzantine-style Catholic cathedral, St Mathews, just off Connecticut Avenue near Dupont Circle. The Americans respect church-going and even workaholic Zoellick was prepared to schedule a break on Sunday mornings.

The Australians had scheduled a week in Washington, and Calvert was then supposed to go on to Tokyo for a meeting of the Trilateral Security Dialogue with Armitage and the Japanese vice foreign minister.

At the end of the first week, Calvert approached Vaile.

'Minister', he said, 'do you mind if I stay on for the rest of these negotiations?'

'Ashton', Vaile replied, 'I can't do it without you.'

Often when they would get back to their hotel in the middle of the night, Vaile and Calvert and the other senior Australians would have a debriefing session. Room service at this ungodly hour could only rustle up a bowl of soup and a bread roll.

Ah, minister', Calvert would remark, 'it's time for our daily soup and human-rights-convention mandated bread roll.'

Finally, on the last night, the Americans were refusing to budge on an insistence that extra protection to the intellectual data in drugs be given. They had wanted this all along. The relevant advisers in the Australian party were adamant to Vaile that this would affect Australia's cherished generic drugs policy. Vaile was talking every night to Howard. He rang the prime minister again on the last night and told him: 'This could destroy the deal.'

Howard had invested a great deal in the FTA and a failure would have been an embarrassment. But he was clear, it was a concession too far: 'We can't do this.'

Vaile went back to Zoellick with the news. But the deal didn't die. The ether wore off, the patient got up and walked. Zoellick concluded the deal without the concession.

It was a marathon negotiation. In the first year, the merchandise trade figures didn't move in Australia's favour. But this is a deal for the long run. It's a bit like a military action. It sets up an undeniable opportunity. Australian business has to take it.

Chapter 21

LORD OF THE SKIES: A FIGHTER PILOT'S STORY

Air Commodore Mark Binskin had a single sign on his desk the day I met him at Williamtown Royal Australian Air Force base near Newcastle. It bore his name, and just two other words: 'Fighter Pilot'. It's what he wanted to be all his life. It's what he's become, except now he's a leader of fighter pilots. For a time he was a leader and wielder of almost unimaginable airpower.

For an incredible period Binskin served as the first ever non-American Director of the US Central Air Force Combined Air and Space Operations Centre, based in Qatar (it was formerly in Saudi Arabia). It's a long-winded title but in essence Binskin's job was simple. He had to plan and approve every combat operation by the US-led coalition in Iraq and Afghanistan. It was one of the toughest jobs an air force commander can have because it was in reality 24 hours a day, seven days a week, with life-and-death responsibility. Binskin would take a few hours to sleep during each 24-hour period but he was always called back if an operation was going to involve deadly fire.

In that infinite wilderness of acronyms which makes up defence organisations the world over, Binskin was called director KOC – director of the coalition operations centre. He had a couple of layers of decision maker above him but he could authorise the deadly use of force from the air. Except in immediate self-defence, no one below him could do that.

Some men have it in them to fly. It seems to be born in them. As kids they draw pictures of planes and dream about them at night. In the day they look up at the sky and know that that's where they are meant to be. That's how it was with Binskin. At age 18 he joined the navy and became a naval pilot. When the navy got rid of its aircraft carrier and all of its other aeroplanes Binskin transferred to the air force, which was, for everyone who did it, a tricky, complex, bureaucratically problematic operation. To make it work you had to be very determined, and you had to be very good. As a result of being very good Binskin has logged nearly 4000 hours in single-seat fighter aircraft.

When I met him Binskin was commander of Australia's Air Combat Group. He has since moved on from that position. The air combat group comprised all the air force's F/A-18 hornet fighters, its F-111 strategic fighter/bombers and its PC9 forward air control aircraft.

For a small nation it's a lot of air firepower. But short of Australia going to war it's hard to imagine Binskin ever having to shoulder more responsibility than he did in Qatar. An Englishman had held the same job on a 'shadow' basis with an American in the driver's seat but Binskin was the first non-American to hold the KOC position completely on his own, and with complete responsibility. The US has a lot of allies around the world but the closeness of the US-UK-Australia connection is evident in Binskin's position. After Binskin finished his tour of duty the position reverted to an American. Since then it has rotated between Americans, Brits and Australians. And no one else. This is allied inter-operability and trust at the highest level.

Before he went to Qatar, Binskin had a substantial history of involvement with the Americans. He had twice been posted on exchange programs with American forces, once with the US navy in California flying F-18s, and once with the US air force in Arizona flying F-16s. Such exchanges are an integral part of maintaining inter-operability. They also promote the personal connections that can be crucial in later operations.

He was seconded to the US navy in 1984 and to the US air force from 1988 to 1990. It was to be his first experience of commanding American pilots: 'We send pilots to the US marines and the US navy and they send pilots to us. Being able to plug and play, as we call it, with your ally's tactics is vital. I arrived in Arizona and was promoted to squadron leader. Normally the exchange is at instructor level. The (US) commander treated me as an American pilot. He made me leader of A Flight. We had about 20 planes in A Flight.'

He took home another personal memento from America: 'My eldest son was born there.'

Binskin went to Qatar at the end of 2003 and spent just under four months as director KOC. The conventional part of the war was over in both Iraq and Afghanistan and in both countries the mission was nation building and counter-insurgency. The insurgency in Iraq was much less intense then than it was to become.

At the KOC headquarters, Binskin had 300 people, mostly Americans, many of them colonels, working directly under him. He oversaw intelligence, surveillance, reconnaissance, combat operations, combat plans, strategic development and air mobility and transport. He had direct line responsibility to a US air force general though he remained technically under Australian command.

He was bound under Australian rules of engagement at all times. He also had US planes and UK planes under his control so he had to make sure that there was no compromise of US or UK rules of engagement for those pilots. There are some differences in Australian and US rules of engagement. Australian rules, for example, ban the use of land mines as well as cluster bombs, both of which are permissible in US rules of engagement.

I asked Binskin what he would have done if there had been a conflict between what he needed to do as director of such a large American force and his Australian rules of engagement: 'If it had come up I would have tried to resolve it another way. But I always could have stepped aside. But it didn't come up because as allies we share the same basic values.

'In any event we were in the nation-building phase. We went through a painstaking process before we dropped any weapons. We insisted on minimum collateral damage and certainly no more damage than benefit.'

Just before Binskin arrived, in September/October 2003, there had been a lull in insurgency activity in Iraq. Then in October coalition forces lost about 100 personnel. In November and December the insurgency gained more momentum. There was intense coalition activity analysing where the insurgency was strongest, where the pockets of insurgents were hiding. This led to a lot of coalition air strikes on terrorist targets, but, Binskin said: 'We tried not to get in the faces of people who were trying to get on with their lives.'

Afghanistan was different. There was still a lot of Taliban activity in the eastern part of the country, which was substantially inaccessible to coalition helicopters and where artillery was ineffective. So the coalition relied on its fixed-wing assets.

Binskin's outfit was running about 270 sorties a day, a high percentage were transport, intelligence and reconnaissance.

'It required working also very closely with the British. When I went in-country (to Iraq or Afghanistan) I was literally in and out in a day. I would go in at the level of chief of operations, at the level of Jim Molan. He went in when I went home and the coalition land forces were restructured. The US and the multinationals hadn't quite got together while I was there. They did get together later.

'We were very conscious of our impact on people's lives. One F-15 was carrying a lantern pod and cruised at about 3000 to 4000 feet to monitor improvised explosive devices (IEDs – the famed roadside bombs and booby traps that killed so many Americans, and Iraqis). It saw everyone jump in a car and it turned out to be a family stopped for a kid to have a leak. So we told the F-15 to sit a little higher, disturb them a little less.

'We did a lot of non-kinetic impacts.'

This little bit of jargon means the military did a lot of things that didn't involve weapons. The military uses the word kinetic to mean when one thing hits another, like a bomb or a bullet. Non-kinetic operations are often psychological operations, but the word psychological has all kind of unpleasant connotations in military history. Non-kinetic sounds much more neutral, much less sinister.

Binskin describes one of his non-kinetic operations: 'In Afghanistan we had a call from a provincial reconstruction team in a camp just north of Kandahar. It was cold and wet and the food was not fantastic, and they were having a bit of trouble from their itinerant workers, guys from many different countries who were basically on the brink of a mutiny. All we had available was a B-1 (bomber) so we sent it over at 3000 feet, at supersonic speed with its after-burner going. It was not in a built-up area.'

The sound was huge and frightening. This was Binskin's own little bit of shock and awe, simply a demonstration of power: 'We got a phone call a little later saying thanks very much, we won't have another problem with these guys for three or four months.'

This sort of effects-based operation had much wider application: 'Sometimes that's all you need, you just show the stick. But you have to be prepared to use it too because they get to realise if you only show it.'

Binskin said he got four or five hours sleep a day, seven days a week: 'You tend to burn out in that job after about four months. Whenever an engagement with weapons was on I was called back, even if I was sleeping. A day off was going into Iraq or Afghanistan.'

Why was this level of manic involvement necessary? Why couldn't the machine run with the deputy doing Binskin's job. Binskin offered an answer in two parts: 'You've got to consider the potential impact of some sort of adverse situation. When something pops up as a critical issue it has to be handled, but the rest of the operation still has to run. Also, from its rules of engagement the US needs at least a one-star officer (brigadier or above, equivalent to Binskin's air force rank at the time) to authorise a weapons operation.'

Despite all his exposure to the Americans, Binskin still had to navigate some cross-cultural issues. He had to make sure, for example, that what he was saying was clearly understood by his American subordinates. Australian slang is rich and inventive and no one uses it better than the military but it's a bit much to expect other nations' service personnel to be able to speak it.

'You have to be careful how you use certain terms. After I arrived it took me about a week to settle in, but really it was fairly easy. There was a little bit of shock on the part of the ground forces that they were talking to an Australian. It took a little working out but after a week or so they accepted my street cred in fast jets and on my previous exchanges (in the US) I'd made a few good friends and so we had common contacts.

'Every morning we'd have a brief at KOC. I'd have a bagel with Vegemite and coffee. They didn't take to the Vegemite – an alliance can only go so far. We all watched the rugby together (Rugby World Cup) and the Brits didn't let me forget that the whole time I was there (the Brits beat Australia). There were times when there were very tense situations and you could use Australian humour to break the tension and bring the team together.'

Binskin sees his deployment as part of a long history of intimate Australian-US cooperation: 'We and the Americans do share a lot of values. We mainly support each other. We're the Americans' only major ally never to have attacked them. From the air force point of view it's a very close relationship, going back to World War II and on through Korea and Vietnam. So tactics and the way we work are very close. But inter-operability is not static – tactics, technique and procedure, these things evolve every couple of years, so you really need to keep that contact going continually. Our guys who go over there from Australia bring a lot of things with them from Australia and contribute ideas and techniques. Of course the US is such a big operation, if you went to an east coast squadron it may not operate exactly the same as a west coast squadron.'

Binskin had little contact with his fellow Australians in the Middle East although he was conscious every moment that for many Americans he was the face of the Australian air force and he was constantly being evaluated in that light: 'I rarely ran into the other Australians. But in Baghdad even if I was up for US meetings I'd always stay with our guys just to get an idea of how they were going.'

Technically, perhaps the most difficult task Binskin faced was trying to find a way to reduce the threat from the IEDs. It was also one of his most important efforts: 'The counter-IED operations were most significant. We also spent a lot of time on critical infrastructure – roads, electricity etc. In Iraq there was a lot of concern about moving forces by road, also to some extent in Afghanistan.'

He is honest about the coalition's inability to blunt the effects of the IEDs: 'We were probably not as successful against the IEDs as we could have been because of all the coordination efforts, especially with the smaller ground forces. For ground commanders it (IEDs) was their main problem. And it was a bugger of a problem.'

The intricacy of the operations Binskin oversaw was exhaustive, as well as exhausting: 'We had combat air capability 24 hours a day but rather than have them just sitting and orbiting we'd have them do infrastructure and road patrols. They'd report back information which would be passed to ground commanders who would then react. If they saw something the first move would be to send jets overhead and then 10 or 15 minutes later you'd have the ground force there. Often you'd show the air force just as a show of force. It was three-dimensional chess but there were a lot of moving parts.'

For many things, planning was critical: 'We'd ask the question – can we achieve this objective with minimal collateral? We got very good at taking out buildings on the edge of town without hurting anyone in the town. We'd get information about where terrorists were meeting and we could process the information fully (and order a response) within 30 minutes. There would be full weapons-effect planning, database imagery, rules on how up-to-date the imagery was, (check) the relevant weapons spread and aircraft for time-sensitive targeting.

'A lot of the engagements were non-kinetic, like getting the (unmanned) predator overhead to film a terrorist meeting. The predator would be 10 000 feet up. You can't hear it and it's pretty hard to see at that level.'

And the morality of it all, the conflict, the casualties – how does Binskin feel about all that? I didn't ask him to make political judgments, he's a soldier and within reason must do as his government tells him. But how did he personally feel about everything he did and saw and supervised in Iraq and Afghanistan?

'I felt very good about the work I was doing. I would have liked to stay for another month or two. I felt we were trying to do the right things the right way, focusing on nation building.'

Chapter 22

LABOR AND AMERICA: OUT-THOUGHT, OUT-MUSCLED, OUT-VOTED

When on June 3, 2004, in the deceptively tranquil setting of the White House Rose Garden in Washington, DC, George W Bush thrust his burning Damoclean sword into the viscera of Mark Latham's leadership of the Labor Party, turning the sword with maximum force to cause maximum pain and damage, the president knew exactly what he was doing. He was very well prepared.

The occasion was a joint press conference by Bush and a visiting John Howard. Before the president meets a foreign leader he has what is known as a 'pre-briefing' from the relevant senior US officials. In this case, Bush had a pre-briefing with the secretary of state, Colin Powell, the assistant secretary of state for East Asia and the Pacific, the much-liked Asia veteran Jim Kelly, the national security advisor, Condoleeza Rice, the NSC's Asia director, Mike Green, and one or two others.

The officials' staffs had prepared a briefing paper for the president. Such a briefing paper is a work of art. It cannot be too long or the president won't read it or remember it; it cannot be too short or it will lack critical information and not convey to the president the themes he should stress with his foreign visitor.

The Americans are just like any other government. They want things from foreign leaders and they use presidential conversations to try to get them. The US briefing paper for the visit of the Australian prime minister focused on the business between Bush and Howard. But it also contained a summary of Latham's commitment to bring Australian troops home from Iraq by Christmas. It also sketched Australian reaction to this and the drop in Latham's poll numbers following the Labor leader's promise to bring the troops home. Bush knew that Latham's position on troops home from Iraq, which had once seemed popular, was a grave danger for the Labor leader heading into an Australian election. And Bush very much wanted Howard to win. Indeed on Australia's election night the White House was monitoring the Australian results constantly. The US ambassador to Canberra, Bush's friend, the formidable fellow Texan, Tom Schieffer, was constantly on the phone to the White House. When Bush rang to congratulate Howard on election night Howard was astonished at how much detail Bush had on the Australian vote, likely two-party preferred projections and the rest.

However, in Washington on the day of Howard's visit, Bush and his officials did not discuss the idea of having a shot at Latham at the press conference. Instead, they discussed the items of substantial business Bush would transact with Howard. Nonetheless, once the press conference began, Bush did his best to help Howard by lavishing praise on him.

Bush said: 'It's my honor to welcome back to the White House my friend and our ally Prime Minister John Howard. He is a close friend of mine. I appreciate the frequent discussions we have. I value his advice. I appreciate his clear vision. Our two nations were allies in every major conflict of the last century. We've each lost citizens in the first war of the new century...'. And so on.

Interestingly, Bush made a claim for the unique standing of the contemporary alliance: 'Australia and the United States have never been closer. Our closeness is based on a shared belief in the power of freedom and democracy to change lives. As the prime minister said, the war on terror is not a contest of civilisations, it is a contest of convictions.'

Even without the explosive attack on Latham's leadership that followed, pictures of Bush saying such things beaming back to

Australia would have been helpful politically to Howard. The Bush administration has never been particularly popular in Australia. But the alliance is overwhelmingly popular. A prime minister who looks as though he can handle the alliance effectively gets a big mark up from the electorate. An Opposition leader who looks as though he can't handle it at all gets a big mark down.

As so often happens with what turn out to be strategic communications from political leaders, Bush's attack on Latham turned on a matter of chance. I have seen this happen time without number. Once at an AUSMIN (annual Australia-United States Ministerial) conference in the mid-90s I interviewed the then US defense secretary, William Cohen. Officials gently told me my time was up but like all journalists I asked for one more question. I asked whether Australia was spending enough on defence equipment to maintain inter-operability with the US, without which the alliance would be compromised. Cohen replied that this was a huge challenge and clearly implied Australia needed to spend more. It was a front-page story and everyone naturally assumed that sending that message, publicly as well as privately, was Cohen's main purpose. But if I hadn't asked that last question it never would have come up. In 30 years of journalism I have seen that sort of thing happen again and again.

This day in Washington the press conference was to be limited to four questions, two from Americans and two from Australians. The Australians split the questions between a broadcast journalist and a print journalist. Mark Riley from the Seven Network asked Bush about the two Australians then in detention in Guantanamo Bay – Mamdouh Habib and David Hicks. Steve Lewis from *The Australian* was chosen by his colleagues to ask the print journalists' question. With only one question between them Lewis and his colleagues caucused about what it should be. Lewis thought it should be about Latham's commitment to withdraw the Aussie troops. His colleagues agreed. But they might just as easily have decided to ask about relations with China, or tensions at the UN. A little piece of Australian-US history would then have been different.

To this day Howard says he did not know Bush was going to attack Latham, and that he had certainly not asked Bush to make such an intervention. Howard told me: 'I don't believe Bush himself knew he was going to say it until he was asked the question. His (Bush's) analysis was absolutely right. I think Latham would have been of catastrophic consequence for the alliance. Emboldened by office, he would have gone in full bore. The view at the time was that office would moderate him. I don't think it would have. Thank God it didn't happen.'

In any event, Lewis asked Bush for his reaction to the plan by Australia's alternative prime minister to have the troops home by Christmas. Bush replied: 'I think that would be disastrous, it would be disastrous for the leader of a great country like Australia to say we're pulling out. It would dis-spirit those who love freedom in Iraq, it would say that the Australian government doesn't see the hope of a free and democratic society leading to a peaceful world. It would embolden the enemy, who believe that they can shake our will. See, they want to kill innocent life, because they think that the Western world, and the free world is weak. That when times get tough, we will shirk our duty to those who long for freedom, and we'll leave.'

Footage of those remarks was played on just about every Australian news broadcast imaginable. It was one of the most devastating presidential interventions in Australian politics ever. The first question to ask is: was it proper? It was open to Bush to say something like: 'our position is well known and I don't want to get drawn into Australian politics'. Instead, Bush went in hard. One consideration must be that Latham, and Labor generally, had lost the moral standing to criticise Bush for speaking ill of them when they had spoken so ill of him. Latham, admittedly before he became Opposition leader but quite recently, had described Bush as the most incompetent and dangerous president in decades. In a formulation insulting to both Americans and Australians he had described Howard as an 'arse-licker' for the way he related to Bush, and said the Liberals generally were a 'conga-line of suck-holes' while the Bush administration was dangerous and flaky.

Of course there is not a real symmetry. Latham's criticisms of Bush had little or no political impact on Bush. Bush's criticisms of Latham had a devastating impact on Latham. Still, Australian critics of the US cannot have it both ways. It cannot be perfectly acceptable for Australian political leaders to criticise Bush in scatological language yet wrong for Bush to criticise a proposed radical change in alliance policy by Australia in the midst of an allied military deployment.

Many in the Labor Party were angry with Bush for interfering in Australian politics and perhaps this feeling was shared fairly broadly among political, academic and media elites in Australia. But the average voter focuses little on politics. Only a little while before election time do they start to take an interest. And as the polls and the academic studies show, the alliance has deep and wide support, far beyond those normally interested in politics. If you give the electorate reason to doubt that you can manage the alliance you give a naturally cautious electorate a very good reason to vote for the other side.

Labor had mismanaged alliance issues at several levels and for several years. Often a position which is superficially popular may be bad for you at a deeper level if it cuts across the alliance. In March 2004, Latham had made his troops home by Christmas commitment in a radio interview without proper consultation with the wise heads in his party, such as Kim Beazley or Kevin Rudd, or most of the state premiers, who could have told him of the danger of where he was heading.

On the government side it was the foreign minister, Alexander Downer, who first saw the significance of Latham's words. Downer has been second in importance only to Howard in running the national security debate. After rather a lot of stumbles in his early years as foreign minister, he has become an effective minister and in Australian history will be seen as one of the more consequential foreign ministers. Politically, he is effective both on offence and defence.

In defensive mode he can bland-up an issue, responding with jargon, plausible circumlocutions or just endless, reasonable, pedantic explanation, without ever losing his temper. On offence, he can spot an opponent's weakness and speak with sufficient force and clarity to cut through to the public. When he needs to affect public opinion on a foreign policy issue he will hole-up in his office and speak to at least one high-rating talkback radio station in each capital city. When foreign policy is running hot he has no difficulty organising appearances on such shows. In an afternoon he can talk to a million Australians, many of them people who don't consume much other political news. Both he and Howard have perfected this technique.

In any event it was Downer who prosecuted the line that Labor's policy was to 'cut and run' from Iraq. Downer believes that this ended Latham's honeymoon with the electorate and first germinated big doubts about Latham's fitness to be prime minister. It may be the single most important political intervention Downer has made.

But Labor, and not just Latham, had mismanaged the American relationship on at least two other levels. One was in allowing so much hostility, so much of it unnecessary, to grow up between itself and the Bush administration. A number of Latham's most senior colleagues told me frequently while he was leader how worried they were about his potential to damage the alliance and take Australia in dangerous directions in national security. There are dangers here for Australia more generally, not just for Labor. Australia needs both sides of mainstream politics to be able to manage the alliance. That doesn't mean agreeing with the Americans on everything. Kim Beazley has opposed the Iraq operation from day one, but few people suggest that the nation couldn't trust Beazley with the alliance.

Labor was so damaged on alliance issues by the time of the 2004 election that Latham didn't mention Iraq in his policy speech until the bottom of page 13 of a 16-page speech. Labor didn't buy a single ad on Iraq, and throughout the campaign the polls showed Howard enjoying a huge lead on national security.

The other problem was that Labor could not find and stick to a clear position on Iraq. This is in part because of the intellectually crippling obeisance most of the party pays to the United Nations. Iraq played a big part in destroying Simon Crean's leadership, essentially because Crean's position on Iraq was that whatever the UN said he would support. Yet for a long time there was a real chance the United States would get explicit UN Security Council endorsement for a military operation to disarm Saddam Hussein. This meant that Crean always looked as though he was keeping his options open rather than making an independent judgment.

The intellectual problem for Labor in this was that it was thus always arguing process and only seldom, and often contradictorily, arguing about the substance of Iraq. The public didn't follow all the ins and outs of this – such as Crean's crazy position at one stage that he could still possibly support an invasion if it was opposed by one unreasonable Security Council veto but not by two – but they could see that Labor's position was confused and vacillating. The government, like it or loathe it, at least had the advantage of clarity. This is one of the severe intellectual problems for those who routinely put the UN at the centre of their foreign policy. Supporting the UN is no substitute for making hard policy choices, hard choices of strategy, politics, ethics and morality, which important issues demand. And the world body itself has neither the moral, intellectual nor political authority to make such choices anyway.

Latham in his book, *The Latham Diaries*, published after the election and his resignation from the Labor leadership, took a more extreme anti-alliance position which his party thoroughly repudiated. It is impossible to know what attitude he would have taken to the alliance had he won government.

There is no reason, given its history, that a competently led Labor Party should feel intimidated over the alliance, although its history should also teach the party some lessons.

Labor, under John Curtin, pioneered strategic cooperation with the US. After World War II it failed, with Ben Chifley as prime minister and the erratic Dr HV Evatt as foreign minister, to get a security treaty with the United States that it very much wanted. However, the tempo of signals intelligence cooperation between the US and Australia, which to this day remains a central pillar of the alliance, accelerated rapidly under Chifley, especially in 1947 and 48, although this was mainly the doing of the UK.

The 1950s and 60s were grim years for Labor, substantially because of the split in the party in the mid-50s over communism and the best way to fight it. The most dedicated anti-communists left the ALP or were expelled from it and formed the Democratic Labor Party. The DLP had its share of extremists and cranks but it was mainly made up of good Labor people who believed the party had given too much influence to those trade unions which were communist-controlled. Those days seem infinitely distant now and it requires serious historical reading, and the exercise of political and historical imagination, to recall that for much of the Cold War the Soviet Union did well against the West, and for a long period each year more of the world slipped under the rule of tyrannical and totalitarian systems. It is also sobering to recall how many in the West, including Australia, succumbed to the totalitarian temptation and became supporters of the Russian or Chinese gulags, or some other brand of communism which was similarly predicated on the falseness of Western democracy.

The defection of the Soviet spy, Vladimir Petrov, the top KGB man in Australia, in the early 1950s, just before the great Labor split, and the wildly erratic response to it by Evatt, then the Opposition leader, was a crippling blow for Labor. The split kept Labor out of office until 1972. Even the hugely controversial Vietnam war led to a landslide against Labor in 1966. The execrably mediocre Liberal prime minister John Gorton scraped back into office in 1969, beating Gough Whitlam by emphasising security issues in the last days of the election campaign.

As Kim Beazley has pointed out, Labor's victory under Whitlam in 1972 was accompanied by a view in the electorate that the policy differences between Labor and the government had narrowed in the preceding years. Labor won office, as always, from the centre. The Australian electorate is cautious and the chief lesson of those years for Labor is the extreme danger it runs whenever it allows a perception to arise, among even a significant minority of the electorate, that it is suspect on security.

In Whitlam's brief period in office, 1972 to 75, the ill-disciplined anti-American outbursts of some of his ministers, such as Jim Cairns and Tom Uren, did a great deal to contribute to the savage defeat in 1975, when the Liberals won by the greatest parliamentary margin in Australian history. Whitlam himself, while having plenty of disagreements with the Americans, was committed to the alliance. But his cabinet, and his party, was such a mess that he felt he could not discuss numerous national security issues in cabinet because the far Left ministers would leak the details of such discussions.

The most effective template for modern Labor dealing effectively with the alliance was provided by Bob Hawke as prime minister and Kim Beazley as defence minister. In the next chapter this book critically evaluates the narrow and ineffective defence of Australia doctrine which Beazley developed as defence minister. However, there has never been any suggestion that Beazley overall was not an effective defence minister, or that he did not understand the alliance and could not manage it effectively.

It is easy to forget the pains to which Hawke went to distinguish his government in style and substance from the Whitlam government, especially in national security and alliance matters. An interview Hawke gave to *The Australian* newspaper on April 18, 1984 is typical. He declared: 'We would be at greater risk if we eschewed the relationship with the US. We are an aligned nation and we have been since the last war. Labor and non-Labor governments alike, without exception, have maintained that relationship.'

It was a huge achievement of Hawke's to make pragmatic centrism, rooted in the US alliance, the natural position of Labor. Keating, too, highly esteemed the American relationship. It was central to his Asian diplomacy, for which he is chiefly remembered in foreign policy. Perhaps Keating's most lasting achievement in foreign policy was the formation of the annual summit of the Asia-Pacific Economic Cooperation (APEC) forum. He achieved this by convincing the former US president, Bill Clinton, of its merits and getting Clinton to convene and host the first APEC meeting. Keating's main argument in Asia was with Malaysia's redoubtable prime minister, Dr Mahathir Mohammed. Dr Mahathir promoted an East Asian Economic Caucus against APEC. The main difference between them was that the EAEC excluded the US and APEC included it. By its last years in office, the Keating government's formal position was that it would not attend an EAEC meeting even if it were invited, being fully committed to APEC with the Americans.

Part of the problem for modern Labor is that both Hawke and Keating out of office have become vociferously anti-Bush, if not anti-American, and this has confused the emotions of the Labor Party. Instead of looking at the record of Hawke, who never let an opportunity pass to schmooze with his good friend the then secretary of state, George Schultz, they look to his post-office interviews, which often, like Keating's, display a China-centric view of the world.

This suggests a wider problem in Australian politics. Because parts of the media, the academic world, and the non-governmental organisation activists are so hostile to the US, there is a lot of cheap applause to be had for anyone who denounces Washington. But it seems this cuts no ice with the wider electorate. With both Crean, and to a much greater extent Latham, Howard was able to play the politics of the alliance in such a way as to create doubts about Labor's ability to handle it in office.

This is also a danger in long-term Opposition. Alliance issues are not easy to manage from Opposition in a time of high military activity – ask the British Tories. There is no reason to think the great Labor mainstream tradition – the heritage of Hawke, Beazley, Rudd and many others – could not manage the alliance perfectly well. But by electing two leaders, Crean and Latham, who were weak on national security and had not apparently thought deeply about it, Labor created huge problems for itself. The rule for an Opposition in national security is to look respectable and make the government pay for its mistakes. It is clear the alliance is a bedrock sentiment of the Australian people. Once an Opposition starts to fool around with the alliance, it is asking for trouble.

Chapter 23

WHY DOES EVERYONE HATE AMERICA, BUT LOVE IT TOO?

The paradox of anti-Americanism was encapsulated for me by an Indian newspaper editor. We were both attending an editors' conference in Seoul, South Korea, and discussing Korean anti-Americanism, which can at times be truly virulent.

'We have a saying in India', my Mumbai friend said.

'Yankee go home! But take me with you.'

The paradox of course is that people sometimes loathe America at the very same time as they want to be Americans, or at least to have what Americans have. And many in the developed world, who may have no wish to live in America, want Americans to pay attention to them, from politics to the arts, from higher education to high fashion.

Everyone in the world has an opinion on America. That is part of the reason for this book. America in some way has become the modern universal. Writers have been grappling with this since the 19th century, but only since World War II, the last 60 years, has it emerged as the dominant feature of modernity.

Evelyn Waugh got close to it when he remarked that for the Irishman there are only two final realities – hell, and the United States.

Samuel Huntington, in his book, *Who Are We: The Challenges to America's National Identity* (Simon & Schuster, 2004), argues that every culture needs a sense of the Other to define its own identity. For many people around the globe, the US is the Other, because, through the vast reach of US popular culture, they feel they understand the United States, even if it doesn't understand them.

But the US is more than just the Other. People around the world also feel some sense of participation in America, in its society and politics. This is a mysterious and difficult process to get hold of. It's not that people feel they are Americans exactly, but virtually everyone with a TV has grown up with some sense of American myth and identity as a core part of their childhood. And for those without a TV, the exotic lure of the riches and technology of America make it in some cases perhaps an even greater presence in the mind.

For America is the universal currency of our age. Everything is measured against America, and America is measured against everything. At some level, a surprisingly large number of people feel that America is responsible for everything.

On Boxing Day 2004 a dreadful tsunami devastated Asia. Nowhere was more savagely hit than the Indonesian province of Aceh. The loss of life was horrendous, many tens of thousands wiped out, whole villages reclaimed by the sea, much of the province flattened by the relentless power of the giant wave.

The American response, like the Australian response, was swift, generous and effective. But the tragedy also gave rise to one of those revealing moments – a moment which should become iconic. CNN, with the usual newshound keenness, had got its cameras into Aceh and the scenes of destruction were appalling. One man, a wretched and deeply distressed survivor, had lost most of his family. He turned to the camera and cried out 'Where is America?'

Sometimes the ordinary man or woman sees the deep pattern of things more accurately than do intellectuals. It is revealing that the Acehnese survivor did not cry out: Where is the United Nations? or Where is China? Still less did he ask for the operational arm of international Islamic solidarity. He knew that there was one power that could help him, that would help him, that in some sense was responsible for him, just because of the ultimate responsibility of great power and of leadership in our world, and of its own professed universal values. Perhaps his cry also implied that the United States should not have allowed the tsunami to occur. That may seem irrational or unfair, but there's a sense in which people can feel that the US is responsible for the order of the world – and how could the US let that order produce an Indonesia with a province so unable to withstand a tsunami, or with so little warning.

These are deep and strange waters, but because of America's power, and because of its role as the universal of our time, everyone's response to America is caught up in their own visceral emotions, the most primordial of their feelings about God, man and the universe.

This short chapter cannot possibly exhaust so complex, paradoxical and confusing a question as anti-Americanism. It can only offer a few clues about the main lines of anti-Americanism and ask what the situation is in Australia.

First, what is anti-Americanism? It is not criticism of US society or policy, particularly its foreign policy. I have written countless newspaper columns and not a few books critical of aspects of American foreign policy. Like everyone else on the planet I feel free to give America's leaders plenty of advice about how to handle the world. And I am certainly not anti-American.

Anti-Americanism can take three main forms. The first is a double standard. This means applying standards to US behaviour that the critic does not apply to others.

The second is exaggerated hostility to the US, regarding small mistakes as giant crimes, regarding the United States as inherently evil, regarding it as the source of everyone else's problems. Of course the US has done some evil things and is the source of some problems, but where the conviction of US guilt and responsibility goes beyond the factual evidence, where the rhetoric is more emotional than analytical, then there is a form of pathological anti-Americanism.

And the third main form of anti-Americanism is the characterisation of US society itself and its leaders. Certainly American society, and America's leaders, are imperfect but where the characterisation of them is unremittingly hostile, more negative than a balanced appreciation of the facts warrants, that is anti-Americanism.

So what causes anti-Americanism?

A large part of it is just the size and power of the United States. Depending on exchange rates, the US accounts for one quarter to one third of the global economy. It is the richest nation the world has ever seen. It is impossible to be that powerful and that rich without exciting envy.

There is an element of envy in both European and Arab anti-Americanism. Anyone who has spent any time among foreign affairs officials has come across the settled European conviction that European diplomacy and statecraft are more subtle and sophisticated than American diplomacy and statecraft. This is a conviction held all over Europe, yet the facts don't bear it out.

America is the most meritocratic society on Earth. Of course it is not perfectly egalitarian and the wealthy have much greater opportunity than the poor. But, especially in government service, anyone who can get a good education can compete meaningfully for position and promotion. The top of big US government institutions, like the State Department or the Pentagon, are typically peopled by seasoned veterans with numerous university degrees, command of one or more foreign languages, who have lived and studied abroad. These institutions have been dominant in the world for at least 60 years. The people at their apex are immensely sophisticated and cosmopolitan. The idea that there are rednecks and hicks and naïve fools at the top of such US institutions is absurd. The notion doesn't survive a moment's thought, but it has a substantial hold on the European mind.

The other question about European sophistication is what has it ever delivered? In the 20th century European sophistication, diplomacy and statecraft brought us two world wars and two of the most hateful and murderous ideologies in human history – Nazism and communism.

Arab anti-Americanism is a bit different. Of course some Arab hostility to the US derives from the plight of Palestinians and America's strong support of Israel. But there are independent cultural factors at work as well. As Huntington has pointed out, the Arab ideologue feels that he is the inheritor, in Islam and in Arab culture more widely, of the most exquisite and deeply true civilisation that mankind has known. Yet no Arab society has really been successful in its encounter with modernisation. International power lies disproportionately with the Americans. What can be the explanation of this disjuncture between reality and the proper order of things? It can only be conspiracy and the perverse machinations of the international system. In this cosmology there is often an assumption of near-omnipotence of the United States in the international system. The United Nations itself is often seen as a tool of American power, even when it directly opposes US policy.

The radical Islamist has another complaint against the US – its hedonistic lifestyle. As Bernard Lewis, the legendary scholar of the Middle East, has pointed out, when the ideologues of the Iranian revolution describe the United States as the great Satan they are speaking, from their point of view, very nearly literally. It is the US, with its materialism and its pornography, which tempts the faithful away from the true and proper life.

There are many trends in Western thought, too, which give rise to anti-Americanism, and many of these come from the US itself. No international polemicist is more consistently anti-American than the US academic Noam Chomsky, and imitation of Chomsky among the Western left is widespread. Thus many of the fiercest critics of the US often derive much of their critique from the United States itself, from Chomsky, or Michael Moore, or journals, from *Mother Jones* and *The Nation*, to *The New Yorker*, and from the endless American books about the military/industrial complex, the perfidies of Bush, and the like. The exaggerated critique of US society and policy is itself an American specialty. Chomsky's writing in particular is notable for its emotional intensity, its rhetorical excess and its lack of factual analysis. It is ideological writing in that it proceeds from a certain view of the world and interprets events to fit that view. Anti-Americanism can be seen as quite a coherent ideology. Like many ideologies it is a closed system. Contrary evidence doesn't penetrate.

Thus in Turkey I've been told by intelligent young people that Washington is preparing to attack their country militarily. But why would it do that I ask. In Indonesia I've been told that the US navy was behind the Bali bombings in 2002. But where's the evidence for that, I vainly protest. Ah, comes the reply, we have read sources you have not. In Sydney I've been told that the Americans invented AIDS to weaken Asia. That is utter madness, I feebly respond. In London I've been told that Americans don't get the full range of facts and news that Europeans do, and the American media is scared to criticise its government or offer tough scrutiny of US policy. But have you never read *The New York Times*, I ask. Have you ever seen Maureen Dowd's columns or those of Paul Krugman? They present Bush and his administration as little better than criminals and this is in the most influential general newspaper in America.

Of course the US has a robust conservative media as well, from *The Wall St Journal* to Fox News to talkback radio. But most big city broadsheet newspapers – *The New York Times*, *LA Times*, *San Francisco Chronicle*, *The Philadelphia Inquirer*, *The Boston Globe*, *St Louis Post-Dispatch* and countless others – are, like most high-end political magazines, such as *The New Yorker*, *The Atlantic Monthly* and many others, broadly left liberal in their views. The same is true of most free-to-air television networks and CNN. America's media is a cacophony of contradiction, not a choir of conspiracy.

All of which leads me to the conclusion that the human mind craves the explanatory comfort which a conspiracy theory offers. The beautiful simplicity of all conspiracy theories, which reduce the complex to the intellectually manageable, always holds a measure of attraction. Most of the building blocks of conspiracy theory, countless untested, unsourced, essentially crazy assertions, flow and swirl with manic energy across the internet and across the planet every hour of every day.

Which brings us to the perplexing connection between anti-Semitism and anti-Americanism. Criticism of Israel certainly is not anti-Semitism. Anti-Semitism is like anti-Americanism, a critique which goes beyond the facts, an attribution of inherent evil, a blaming of many unconnected misfortunes on the single cause – those are features of anti-Semitism.

Anti-Semitism has a very long history in Europe, and a more recent history in the Arab world. It is not the purpose of this chapter to explore the rights and wrongs of Israel and its policies. But an element of independent anti-Semitism exists in the Arab world. The *Protocols of the Elders of Zion*, the notorious czarist forgery, circulates in many Arab lands. An Iranian president can court domestic popularity by denying that the holocaust ever took place. Anti-Semitism has never really been extirpated in Europe. Because the United States is the greatest Western power, and because Israel is so much a representative of Western power in the Middle East, and because the two are such close allies, anti-Semitism and anti-Americanism cross-fertilise.

Then there is the intellectual fashion which has swept across Western universities these last four decades. Western universities are diverse and many strands of opinion on all sorts of issues are to be found in them. But it is amazing how pervasive a certain orthodoxy has become among the humanities departments. A certain kind of post-modern irony, paradoxically combined with an intense moral outrage at any defence of Western tradition, has made the ultra-critical position the dominant view in many university humanities departments. In this ideology it is the height of moral good form to challenge what is still viewed as Western orthodoxy. Western societies, Western structures and above all Western history are seen as inherently unjust and oppressive. Their faults are not incidental, nor even stages along the universal search for the good life. Their faults are what define them, and the pose of the perennial challenge to Western authority is the new romanticism, endlessly pursued.

Sexism, racism, militarism, imperialism, classism, ageism, religious medievalism and fundamentalism – these evils (although the word evil is tremendously unfashionable as it has too many echoes of traditional Christian morality) are regarded as inherent in the identity of the West. The great intellectual quest is therefore to subvert the West, or at least to subvert the unjust structures of the West.

One of the problems with this line of thinking is that there are no commonsense limits. Human life and human civilisation are always a question of a dynamic balance and the constraints of commonsense. Any idea which is taken to its extreme conclusions is invariably destructive. You could mount a fair case in Victorian times that there was benefit to be had in subverting sexual prudishness. But when subversion just goes on progressively forever, ultimately you reach a stage where there are no standards at all: no standards of human behaviour or restraint, nothing more really than a nihilistic rage and quest for ever-greater intensity, an urge merely to personal power and gratification.

As the pre-eminent Western power, the US is the natural recipient of all this hostility, so that even the most oppressive regime on Earth, Afghanistan under the Taliban say, will not earn the ire the United States earns. Whereas any imperfection in an ally of the US is regarded as a further sign of the essential corruption of the Western system.

In foreign relations the key term of abuse in all this ideology is empire, which in the post-modern universe unites racism and sexism and militarism and everything else. The United States never had much of an empire and always expected those few foreign territories it ruled to achieve self-government or independence. But because the US intervenes often in international affairs – even if this intervention is saving the lives of Muslim Kosovars or bringing aid to tsunami-ravaged Indonesia – everything it does internationally is evidence of its deep imperialism. The fact that it doesn't look like imperialism is an added bonus, because then the academic theory of economic empire can deliver the pleasure of conspiracy theory, revealing the hidden, inner truth, the structural pattern, of the world. In today's world, when the European Union, Japan, China and many other nations are such strong foreign investors it is even more difficult to sustain the idea of economic empire, but few things are more tenacious than unfalsifiable theory.

Because the US is the modern universal, anything you don't like about modern life you can find in America and attribute to it. This explains why all fundamentalisms are anti-American. Even American Christian fundamentalism exists in opposition to modern America as it really exists.

All the types of anti-Americanism described above are to be found in Australia, although none in terribly intense form. There is no strong tradition of anti-Semitism, for example, in Australia. There was some anti-Semitism in Australia but it did not stop John Monash becoming the supreme military commander in World War I, nor Isaac Isaacs becoming the first Australian-born governor-general. In contemporary Australia echoes of foreign anti-Semitism filter into our debate, but not much more that. Probably the strongest strand of anti-Americanism is the post-modern academic variety, which is well represented at universities and in parts of the media, especially the Australian Broadcasting Corporation (ABC).

And of course in the normal way the popularity of any particular administration in Washington waxes and wanes. The Pew polls demonstrate that the Bush administration is unpopular internationally, including in Australia. It's hard to know what such poll ratings mean. The administration of Ronald Reagan was exceptionally unpopular in the early 1980s when it installed medium-range nuclear missiles in Western Europe to counter Soviet military deployments. There were huge anti-American demonstrations in Europe, but the missiles were deployed and governments which allied themselves with Washington were mostly returned to office. The US was wildly unpopular in the Vietnam period, but no ally broke its alliance with the United States over disagreements on Vietnam policy.

But the truly fascinating thing about today's politics is how little impact all the efflorescence of anti-Americanism has had on Australian support for the US alliance. The distinction between the elites and the people is often a dangerous rhetorical device and can be quite dishonest. But there does seem to be a remarkable contradiction between the views of the academic and media leaders and the ordinary people on questions relating to the US alliance. Partly as a result, academic commentators have little influence in this area of policy.

Only a tiny minority of mainstream broadsheet newspapers or ABC journalists, and hardly an academic, was sympathetic to Australia's participation in the Iraq war. The Labor Party opposed it and was committed, under Mark Latham's leadership, to withdrawing Australian troops from Iraq as soon as possible after election.

The electorate was thus given a clear choice on this issue at the 2004 federal election and the Howard government was returned with an increased majority. All through the election the authoritative Newspoll showed voters preferring Howard, giving him a huge margin as the leader who could best handle national security. It could be argued that Iraq did not figure heavily in the election. But that was an even more comprehensive victory for Howard's position. Both sides of politics polled these issues relentlessly. If there had been any potential gain for Labor in campaigning on Iraq it would have done so.

Public opinion polling is difficult to do effectively in foreign policy. There are many reasons for this. The Australian public, like most publics around the world, are not generally thinking about foreign affairs. It's difficult therefore to get at what they really think, or what convictions in foreign policy they hold dearly and what answers might merely reflect the passing breeze of whatever happens to be in the news that day. It's also exceptionally easy to get distorted results by asking loaded or inadequately designed questions. Political parties pay great attention to this because their electoral success or failure depends on it. The parties find all the time that the public's attachment to the US alliance is deep and broad. The former Labor leader and former foreign minister, Bill Hayden, recalled in his memoirs flirting with a position similar to the one New Zealand adopted of banning port visits by nuclear-armed or nuclear-powered American ships. Hayden found out quickly that if it came to a choice between him and the US alliance, the public was not going to choose him.

The most reliable and neutral published poll on the alliance was that of the Australian Strategic Policy Institute (ASPI) in Canberra in 2005. It was titled Representative Views, and was based on the Australian Electoral Study, a big survey done after every federal election. The raw data and conclusions are staggering. Some 84 per cent of Australians believe the US alliance is important to the country's security. A minuscule 6 per cent believe the US is a threat to Australia's interests. According to ASPI's analysis of the poll data, Australians actually have a higher level of trust and confidence in the US in terms of its security commitments to Australia than they did in the 1970s. The authors conclude that attachment to the alliance is very widespread across the whole community, although the less tertiary education you have, the more you tend to value the alliance.

Polling on foreign affairs always produces paradoxes. One of them in this bundle of data is that 52 per cent supported the way Howard had handled Iraq, but 60 per cent, looking back, did not believe that the Iraq war was worth it.

That is a paradox more than a contradiction. Two explanations suggest themselves. One is that the people accept that Howard acted in good faith on Iraq, given everything that could be known at the time, but that now it's clear Saddam Hussein did not have weapons of mass destruction the war was not worth the suffering it caused.

Another explanation of the paradox is that while they have come to feel in retrospect the war was not worth it, the public placed a high value on the alliance-management dimension of the decision to support the Americans. That would certainly be in character with Australian history.

It would seem that Australians will share in a degree of both popular and elite anti-Americanism, disparaging the Texan accent, feeling that our soldiers are better than American soldiers, believing darkly that Phar Lap was assassinated, and putting up with commentators who see the US as the source of all evil. But they don't take any of this very seriously.

What they do take seriously is their own security, and they know that this is greatly enhanced by the US alliance. They seem to know this in a hard-wired, deep conviction way that would be extremely difficult for any political movement to shift.

They may also feel that while it's perfectly fine to bitch about the Americans, at the end of the day, as the former British prime minister, Jim Callaghan, put it, they're the only Americans we have. They may even feel, as I do, that the world would be an infinitely worse place without those Americans.

Chapter 24

SECRETS OF THE ALLIANCE: ROOSEVELT, SPENDER AND SCANLAN

Imagine a president who could say: 'If a nation shows that it knows how to act with decency ... then it need fear no interference from the United States ... (but) brutal wrongdoing, or an impotence which results in a general loosening of the ties of civilised society, may finally require intervention by some civilised nation ... the United States cannot ignore this duty.'

Surely these are the words of George W Bush or some latter day neoconservative supporter of his? In fact they come to us from more than a century ago, from the US president who was more important to Australia than any other in our history – Theodore Roosevelt.

But his true historic importance to Australia is almost a secret. If Roosevelt is remembered at all in the history of the Australian-US relationship, it is for his dispatch in 1908 of the Great White Fleet to visit Australia (so-called because of the colour of the ships, not the colour of the crew). But the Great White Fleet was not his most significant contribution to Australian history, or to Australian security. Nonetheless, the fleet was significant. Roosevelt himself thought that building up the US fleet, and sending it all around the world to show its prowess (a significant technical feat for that time, as no fleet so large had sailed so far without significant mishap), was one of his most important accomplishments as president.

It was also a singular moment in the development of Australian strategic thinking and diplomatic policy. The Australian prime minister of the time, Alfred Deakin, insisted on the British diplomatic service, which then had responsibility for Australia's diplomatic communications, transmitting the invitation officially to Washington, while he also made sure the Americans knew of it by many other channels.

The British Foreign and Colonial Office was furious with Deakin and strongly opposed the idea of the fleet visit. So did the British navy. They thought it betokened unwelcome Australian independence and might be considered a slight on their then military alliance with Japan. But Deakin stuck to his guns and the visit was a monumental success. The American fleet, when it sailed into Sydney, attracted the largest crowds ever assembled in the history of Australia to that point.

The welcoming crowds prefigured the Australian-US alliance to come and they were in a sense an outcome of Roosevelt's most important strategic contribution to Australia.

Roosevelt's chief contribution to Australian history came before he became president. It was the 1898 Spanish-American war which resulted in the US defeating Spain and taking possession of its Pacific colony, the Philippines. This single American action has underwritten Australian security for more than a century, for it resulted in the US becoming a great Pacific power, and therefore a great naval power, and therefore a great Asian power. Nothing, nothing at all, has been more important in securing Australia's existence as an independent nation.

Roosevelt at the time was assistant secretary of the navy. More than any other American, with the exception of William Randolph Hearst, whose newspapers strongly supported war with Spain (particularly after a mysterious explosion sank the *USS Maine* in Havana harbour), Roosevelt was responsible for bringing the Spanish-American war about. He was also the critical player in making sure the US took possession of the Philippines.

TR was an extraordinary force of nature. He was an intellectual, a boundless outdoorsmen and naturist, a hunter, a soldier, a politician, a prolific author, a rambunctious and devoted family man, and altogether the single most prodigious human being ever to hold the office of president. Above all he was the first president to conceive of the US as a great global power, and to consider that managing global geo-politics was an essential task for a president.

The exuberance and irreducible optimism of Roosevelt were his most attractive characteristics. Once after a birthday celebration, he was standing on the sidewalk making a great and jolly commotion. A little distance down the street, a passerby asked one of his friends, what's all that racket about?

Why, replied the friend, that's just the president introducing some fellows to the stars.

In 1897 and 98, Roosevelt was merely assistant secretary of the navy but his tenure of that position was the most significant in the history of the US. President William McKinley (whom Roosevelt would later serve as vice president and succeed in office on McKinley's assassination) liked Roosevelt and spent happy hours in his company. There was an anti-Spanish rebellion roiling away in Cuba and Roosevelt constantly urged decisive military intervention on McKinley to free Cuba of Spanish rule and to fulfil Roosevelt's strategic vision of expelling European power from the Americas.

As assistant secretary of the navy he constantly advocated war against Spain in all forums available to him and he campaigned relentlessly to build up the American fleet. In 1897 he worked out a comprehensive battle plan for the US to use in war against Spain and presented it to McKinley. It involved the simultaneous deployment of three fleets – one to blockade Cuba, one to harass the Spanish coast, and the Asiatic squadron to defeat the Spaniards in the Philippines. Roosevelt's plan was substantially followed by the US in 1898.

Roosevelt, whose energy was neurotic but endless, successfully intrigued to have the legendary George Dewey appointed commander of the US Asiatic Squadron. This would be a decisive appointment.

Although only assistant secretary of the navy, Roosevelt was driving policy through his sheer energy. His boss, the kindly and elderly Secretary Long, took an afternoon off on February 25. Big mistake. While he was away Roosevelt, as acting secretary, issued countless orders for war preparation, refurbishing of ships, calling men off leave and the rest. Although Long was more than a little annoyed the next day, he didn't reverse Roosevelt's orders.

Most important of all, however, in his afternoon of delirious authority, Roosevelt sent a cable to Dewey. As Nathan Miller recounts in *Theodore Roosevelt – A Life* (William Morrow, New York, 1992), Roosevelt ordered Dewey to concentrate the US fleet in Hong Kong and be ready to lunge immediately at the Spanish fleet in Manila. Roosevelt's cable said: KEEP FULL OF COAL. IN THE EVENT DECLARATION OF WAR SPAIN, YOUR DUTY WILL BE TO SEE THAT THE SPANISH SQUADRON WILL NOT LEAVE THE ASIATIC COAST AND THEN OFFENSIVE OPERATIONS IN PHILIPPINE ISLANDS.

The cable was decisive in the US occupation of the Philippines. When war was declared Dewey, a dynamic and proactive naval leader, sailed to Manila and sank the entire Spanish fleet.

The historian Howard Beale in *Theodore Roosevelt and the Rise of America to World Power* (Johns Hopkins University Press, 1984) declared that: 'The Assistant Secretary had seized the opportunity given by Long's absence to ensure our grabbing the Philippines without a decision to do so by either the Congress or the President, or at least of all the people. Thus was important history made not by economic forces or democratic decisions but by the grasping of chance authority by a man with daring and a program.'

Roosevelt is a perfect illustration of the falseness of the larger theories of history, which see the inevitable unfolding of universal laws or social evolution. Roosevelt proves that nothing is inevitable and very few things are impossible.

A short consideration of such a decisive episode in history does not pretend to evaluate its morality or fairness or even how it related to the politics of its day. All the relevant facts are available in any of the big Roosevelt biographies. But they may as well be secrets for all the consideration they get as vital elements of Australian history. In the Roosevelt biographies these events are told entirely by Americans for Americans, whereas Roosevelt's decisive Pacific and naval transformation are important events in Australian history as well.

To understand Australia at all it is necessary to study British and Irish history, and Aboriginal history and Asian history. It is also absolutely necessary to study American history, especially the history of America in Asia.

The second great secret of the alliance is the role of Percy Spender. No one named Percy can expect to get a fair go in the contemporary study of history and Spender is certainly denied a fair go. Yet he is by far the most important foreign minister in Australian history and the true father of the Australian-US alliance.

It is a great strength of the Australian Labor Party that it takes history so seriously. It is always writing histories about itself, and it recognises the importance of controlling history as a political weapon. This is all to the credit of the Labor Party. It is especially assiduous in creating its own heroes and celebrating and enlarging their myth.

But Australian history is often greatly distorted by Labor mythologising, and nowhere more so than in the case of the wartime prime minister, John Curtin, and the US alliance. When he was challenged on the US alliance during the run-up to the 2004 election, the party's foreign affairs spokesman, Kevin Rudd, a former diplomat and one of the party's most intellectually substantial figures, frequently replied by saying that Labor had founded the US alliance under Curtin in the war.

But such a claim is truly nonsense. One might just as well argue that Deakin founded the alliance in 1908 with the visit of the Great White Fleet, or that Billy Hughes founded the alliance in World War I when Australian and American troops fought side by side. Curtin was a very important figure in the wartime alliance which Australia had, by virtue of its association with the British, with the

United States. But after the end of the war Australia clearly did not have a military alliance with the US. Curtin was a good man and a good wartime prime minister, and he forged an effective relationship with the US general, Douglas MacArthur, to whom he effectively handed over military control of Australia during the war. In the latter stages of the conflict, however, Curtin worked hard to try to re-establish an imperial defence order centred on Britain. Moreover, he desired to create in Australia after the war (Curtin died in its final stages) 'a second Britannia in the Antipodes'.

After the war the Chifley government did intensify signals intelligence cooperation with the US, but this was entirely as a subset of the British commitment to the UKUSA agreements.

The Chifley government also tried, as a matter of policy, to secure from the US a serious, written, treaty-level commitment to Australia's security and if possible a wider Pacific security treaty. In this ambition it failed utterly. Part of the problem was the foreign minister, Doctor HV Evatt. Irascible, erratic and by the end a bit mad, Evatt is the most wildly overrated foreign minister in Australian history. Probably it would have been impossible for Australia to have gotten a security treaty out of the United States in the period 1945 to 49 under any circumstances, but Evatt's abrasive and at times delusional personality certainly didn't help.

There was no formal Australian-US alliance between 1945 and 49, and Labor spokesmen are wrong to claim that Labor founded the alliance. However, the claim has its political uses, and not just for the Labor Party. One of the reasons that the alliance is so easily successful in Australian politics is that both sides can claim to have founded it, Labor through Curtin, and the Liberal and National parties through the signing of the ANZUS treaty in 1951

But the ANZUS treaty, the alliance between Australia and the US, belonged more than anyone to Percy Spender, the Liberal external affairs minister from 1949 to 51.

Spender, too, is not necessarily the most attractive of individuals, but he was smart, a shrewd judge of personality, a clear and independent strategic thinker, and above all he got things done.

Spender was directly responsible for the three great signature achievements of Australian post-war diplomacy – the ANZUS alliance, the Colombo Plan, and the commitment of troops to the Korean war.

In an interview in Paul Kelly's marvellous single volume account of Australian 20th century history, *100 Years – The Australian Story* (Allen & Unwin, 2001), Kim Beazley said: 'I think you've got to give Spender almost the entire credit for the (ANZUS) treaty.'

Beazley was right. Spender gets the credit for the most important security treaty in Australian history. It is thus a singular dereliction that there is no biography of him. Spender wrote his own memoirs and they are not too bad. They are straightforward, cheery books, weighed down by that slightly pedantic style that very few lawyers can avoid altogether. They give the essential information but they offer few piercing insights, or deeper perceptions of colleagues or international interlocutors, and there is nothing memorable in the prose. That is why there should be a biography of Spender. He clearly possessed all the analytical and even intuitive political skills to bring off such a giant venture as ANZUS, but either couldn't or wouldn't do justice to these gifts in his memoirs.

The story of Spender making the commitment of Australian troops to Korea almost has a touch of Roosevelt about it. Spender, like Roosevelt, was an activist with a plan. He could see the declining strategic relevance of the UK in Asia. He became external affairs minister straight after the 1949 election. In his first speech to parliament as minister he declared his intent to pursue a Pacific security treaty. He said: 'What I envisage is a defensive military arrangement between countries that have a vital interest in the security of Asia and the Pacific.'

Above all he wanted the United States, whose 'participation would give such a pact a substance that it would otherwise lack'. But time and circumstance were not yet with Spender. In him, Australian history would bring together opportunity, skill and determination, and this would produce ANZUS, but not quite yet.

In January 1950, not long into his all-too-short term as external affairs minister, Spender attended a conference in Colombo, Ceylon (now Sri Lanka). Although a new minister, he took a leading role in the creation of the Colombo Plan. Spender understood the strategic importance of Asia to Australia, especially of southeast Asia. The Colombo Plan was designed to help development in the region, but it also had important social and political consequences for Australia. This plan, of assistance to southeast and south Asia, led to thousands of Asian students coming to Australia for university training. With the White Australia policy still intact, they broke down some of the racial barriers which had been a part of the national identity. As well as contributing to development in their own countries, these students, who mostly had enjoyed themselves during their stays, furnished an enormous reservoir of goodwill for Australia and knowledge of the country in the region for decades to come. Many of them became political, professional or business leaders in their own countries. The Colombo Plan was one of the greatest acts of enlightened self-interest ever undertaken by Australia.

When North Korea invaded South Korea in June 1950, Australia, like the UK, reacted in support of the US effort to drive the North Koreans back. At first this involved the commitment of a very small number of ships and planes. Menzies was against sending ground troops, as was the UK at first. In late July, Menzies had been in London and boarded a ship for New York. Spender got word, after Menzies had boarded his ship, that the British were going to change their position and commit ground troops to Korea. Spender had been vigorously lobbying Menzies to send Australian ground forces, but Menzies had resisted his lobbying.

Now, Spender thought, if the British send ground troops Australia inevitably will as well, but the look of the UK going first would be awful. It would seem as though Australia was just making a decision as part of the British Commonwealth. Australia would get no independent credit from Washington for its decision. So while Menzies was on the ship Spender rang the acting prime minister, Arthur Fadden, and demanded that Australia commit ground troops immediately, before London, which might make its decision the next day. It was impossible to have such a sensitive policy discussion with Menzies by radio phone on the ship. Fadden was in a funk and very reluctant to pre-empt Menzies. But Spender overcame his resistance with persistence and sheer will. Finally Fadden caved-in and the announcement was made that Australia was committing ground troops. Menzies was not best pleased at first but happy to take the credit, which was substantial, with Washington.

The Cold War provided the context for the negotiation of ANZUS. The Korean commitment was a big psychological factor in Australia's favour. Other Cold War dynamics were even more important. The US wanted a generous peace treaty with Japan in order to revive Japanese society and its economy and turn Japan into a Cold War ally. Canberra said it could accept this if it got a clear security commitment from Washington.

Menzies had been indifferent to Spender's idea of a treaty because he believed it might not be achievable and it might offend London. From the Australian side, Spender drove the process. One critical encounter occurred when Spender went to see the US president, Harry Truman.

Truman loved nothing in life more than his daughter, Margaret, who was by way of being an amateur singer of some note. The newspapers had panned a recent concert she had given. Spender judged his man perfectly. Instead of beginning with a self-indulgent strategic lecture, or an abrasive list of demands, Spender began by disparaging the wickedly unkind newspaper reviews. Truman went off like a firecracker, damning the newspapers and forming a small, temporary but real bond with Spender. Truman used up most of their meeting on this and felt somewhat in Spender's debt. He asked if there had been anything specific Spender wanted to discuss.

At that point Spender made his pitch for a Pacific alliance. Truman remembered the Aussies with affection from his service in

World War I, where he had formed the highest opinion of their fighting capabilities. Spender had recruited Truman to his idea.

As so often happened, one link in the relationship led on to another. Spender then negotiated the details of the ANZUS alliance, which was formally signed in San Francisco in September 1951. It would be foolish to overstate the importance of this one meeting, but in the United States the attention and goodwill of the president are crucial. All the facts about Spender are in the standard histories of the alliance, but it is an indictment of the popular study of history, as well as the conservative side of politics in Australia, that there has been so little exploration, much less celebration, of his mighty achievements in his short time in office. They changed Australia forever.

Presidential attention and goodwill were also important in the third semi-secret of the alliance, the Australian-American Leadership Dialogue

It was a brilliant New Year's Day on Sydney Harbour on January 1, 1992 when the businessman Phil Scanlan met the then US president, George Herbert Walker Bush, father of President George W Bush.

Bush snr would go on to be defeated by Bill Clinton in the presidential election of November 1992. His visit to Australia as president was the first by a serving president for 25 years. However, Bush snr's visit in office has been followed by Bill Clinton visiting while in office, and George W Bush doing the same, perhaps now setting a useful precedent.

Scanlan, a tall, thoughtful, perennially cheerful Sydney businessman, who, unusually, had studied at both Harvard and Oxford, and was married to an American television journalist, happened to be sitting opposite Bush on the harbour cruise because then NSW premier, Nick Greiner, a friend of Scanlan's, had invited him. Like Spender, Scanlan was not going to waste the opportunity of a presidential interview. The alliance has progressed in part because individuals have taken opportunities. Scanlan struck an opportunity with the president.

The two men discussed the melancholy fact that Bush would be the last of the Pacific-war generation who would rule America. Bush had served as vice president in the Reagan cabinet alongside George Schultz, the secretary of state, and Caspar Weinberger, the secretary of defense. They had all fought in the Pacific in World War II. They knew Australia very well. But Bush snr was the last of them. Now the two societies faced the challenge of renewing connections at the highest levels, not only the connection of political leaders but of leaders across social and business and intellectual fields as well.

Scanlan won from Bush presidential support, later expressed in presidential letters, for what would become the Australian American Leadership Dialogue. Scanlan's idea was deceptively simple. Each year he would convene a group of senior Americans and senior Australians, drawn from politics, business, civil service, academia and later the media. They would engage intensively on traditional strategic issues as well as social issues. There would be a few ground rules. The delegations from both countries must be bipartisan – this didn't belong to any government or any one political party. The proceedings would be completely off the record, not for attribution of any kind. Everybody would attend in their private capacity and there would be a kind of collegiality, a virtual equality, about the proceedings. Sessions would commence with short scene-setting contributions, not with formal or lengthy papers. The emphasis would be on dialogue, a free flow back and forth, an honest, frank and intellectually high-powered exchange of ideas and assessments.

This may sound simple. It is exceptionally difficult to bring off. Attracting high-level Americans to participate in the first meeting was a huge challenge. The type of Americans Scanlan wanted typically budget their days in 15-minute intervals. Just getting through to them is generally difficult. The quality of the proposed discussion would have to be very good to attract them a first time, and even better to keep them coming back. To bring them all the way to Australia on a regular basis would be close to miraculous.

And then the thing would require funding. Taking the Australians to the US in the first year, bringing the Americans back subsequently. A lot of people would need to be convinced that it could work, that it was worth their time and that it was worth their money.

Scanlan put in 18 months of prodigious work, using every Australian and American contact, and every contact of a contact, he had, to get the right people together. He also raised enough money to make it work. Scanlan has never taken a cent in salary from the Dialogue and he maintained his full-time corporate role all the while, but he put in much more than a full-time effort bringing the Dialogue together without any staff resources, except the endless devotion of his wife, Julie, and the energetic help of his kids.

Scanlan invited me to join the first session of the Dialogue, to be held in the Four Seasons Hotel in Washington's Georgetown in mid-July 1993. The Australian group was an eclectic mix. I was the only journalist at that first meeting. We went to New York first for a couple of days of briefings with various high-powered Americans Scanlan had lined up. The politicians included Kim Beazley, then deputy prime minister, and Nick Bolkus, then immigration minister, and from the then Opposition David Kemp and Warwick Smith, who would both go on to hold ministerial office under Howard. Labor's Kevin Rudd was there, at that stage working for Queensland's Wayne Goss. Dick Woolcott, the former head of the Department of Foreign Affairs and Trade, and Professor Ross Garnaut, author of the seminal report on Australia and northeast Asia, were among the delegation.

After our New York experience we hopped on a bus and drove down to Washington. It was like a campaign bus, but with both sides of politics, or perhaps like a very senior school excursion.

The meeting was to take place over a whole day in the basement of the hotel. It's always easier to get people from the side of US politics which is out of office rather than the side which is in, but Bill Clinton's assistant secretary of state for east Asia, Winston

Lord, was there, as well as Phil Lader, who would go on to be White House deputy chief of staff, and Joe Duffy, the head of the US Information Agency.

On the Republican side, though we didn't know it at the time, we had the nucleus of the future George W Bush administration. There was Dick Cheney, fresh from his term as defense secretary, Rich Armitage, Paul Wolfowitz, Bob Zoellick, and Karl Rove, all of whom would go on to high office under George W Bush. There were a few important congressmen. At later Dialogues, a regular participant was Porter Goss, who would go on to become director of the Central Intelligence Agency.

I found myself at lunch, an informal buffet in the garden near the basement, sitting next to Brent Scowcroft, the former national security advisor, who, in the American way, was perfectly friendly but most happy to forego small talk and continue discussing the strategic subjects of the morning..

At that first meeting the morning was devoted to international strategic issues in the Asia-Pacifc region and the afternoon to domestic policy issues. Much of the morning discussion focused on China, Japan and APEC (Asia-Pacific Economic Cooperation forum).

The Dialogue was to become a quite pivotal institution in the Australian-US relationship over the next 15 years, to the extent that at the AUSMIN (Australia-United States Ministerial) meeting in 2004 it was cited in official pre-meeting documents as one of the key connections between the two societies. While always flexible on detail, it is notable how closely Scanlan has stuck to his original vision – the meetings are off the record, the delegations are bipartisan, as well as discussing security issues the group always has a substantial discussion around issues concerning the maintenance of a cohesive, racially inclusive society. Discussion is honest, sometimes brutally so. It's not a mutual admiration society. Everyone is polite, as is the American way in particular, but everybody is there to communicate real messages, and also of course to listen and learn.

From that first meeting Armitage and Zoellick became stalwarts of the Dialogue. When he was deputy secretary of state, Armitage, to avoid any question of conflict of interest, took leave and paid his own fare in order to attend a Dialogue in Australia.

Over the years Scanlan introduced more media players – Tom Friedman and RW 'Johnny' Apple from *The New York Times*, EJ Dionne from *The Washington Post* and many others. Each year some new players were added and some old players dropped out. State premiers were brought in and out. It has grown bigger and bigger, and Scanlan has had to take tough decisions to keep it manageable. He convinced successive Australian prime ministers Keating and Howard to do private sessions exclusively for the visiting Americans. A small group session with the prime minister makes a trip to Australia worthwhile for almost any American.

Part of the elan of the Dialogue comes from forcing people from different occupational cultures to mix. Foreign and defence ministers, and their shadows, chiefs of the defence force and secretaries of policy departments in Canberra have often revelled in the strategic discussions. But they have also listened, and participated in Dialogue sessions about business, or about social issues, immigration, education – areas that the two societies, with all their similarities and differences, can usefully talk to each other about.

The second Dialogue, in 1994, was almost as important as the first, to see which Americans would come and what value the Australians could offer. One highlight that year was an informal address by Sabam Siagian, the former newspaper editor who was Indonesia's highly successful ambassador to Australia at the time. Sabam has given me permission to reveal what he said to the group. Sabam, though he began in his folksy, amusing style, had some serious stuff to say. His basic message was that long-time Indonesia president, Suharto, had to go, his days as Indonesia's leader were drawing to a close, Indonesians wanted democracy, it was coming down the turnpike. Whether it would be peaceful change depended substantially on how long Suharto determined to cling to power. An orderly transition, within the constitution, would be best.

It was an electric moment. Both the Americans and the Australians were transfixed. Sabam had invested enormous trust in us by being so frank. He also forced senior Americans to focus on Indonesia and to contemplate the coming changes.

Armitage himself a few years down the track provided a similar moment of high-voltage concentration. It was 1999, the Dialogue was being held in Sydney. The discussion centred on US and Australian policy towards China. Everyone was grappling with the same problem – how to integrate China successfully into the international system, how to help it continue its economic development and encourage greater pluralism, how to manage US-China relations and what role Australia should play, and how to avoid military conflict over Taiwan without sacrificing the rights of the Taiwanese.

Armitage wanted us all to understand the gravity of this issue. Some Australians seemed a little complacent that we could happily ride out any difficulties between the US and China. God forbid that there should ever be military conflict, Armitage said, or words to that effect, but if American soldiers were fighting and dying for the freedom of an island democracy in the Pacific, and Australia decided to do nothing 'how could that alliance endure?' In other words, the United States would expect Australia to help in any conflict with China over Taiwan.

Armitage repeated exactly these remarks to the media the next day, so their substance is known. Inside the room there was intense reaction. Australians had got used to speaking bluntly at times about America's shortcomings. Here was an American with a confronting message about the choices that could face Australia. Armitage's comments not only led to a tough-minded discussion within the Dialogue room, they also led to a thorough review of China policy within the Australian government, and a more concerted effort to run a proactive China policy designed to avoid such a conflict. They are also thought by some to have helped Howard decide to include a public call in his next meeting with senior Chinese for them not to use force on Taiwan.

The most remarkable session of the Dialogue I ever attended was in Washington, DC, in July 2002. It was held in the Eisenhower Building, in the precincts of the White House. The bipartisan Australian and American group walked over to the White House, early in the morning, from the St Regis Hotel. One after another Dick Cheney, Paul Wolfowitz, Condoleeza Rice, Karl Rove and a number of other administration figures had half-hour sessions with the group. These consisted of a 15-minute talk and then 15 minutes of discussion. To coordinate a group like that – to get all their schedules into sync, to get them to make the commitment of time, to get them to each show up on time and each leave on time – is only possible when the principals themselves have a deep commitment to the relationship. In the lead-up to the Iraq war the session was an opportunity to hear American views from the top, and to express Australian views back into the process.

That year Zoellick, then the US trade representative, gave the main Dialogue dinner speech, in the grand atmosphere of the State Department at a glittering dinner for several hundred Washington movers and shakers, plus the Australian delegation, and began a brilliant campaign to convince Australian and US opinion makers of the desirability of a free trade agreement between the two nations. This was several months before the formal commencement of negotiations between the two governments. Zoellick has told me that he believes the networks established by the Dialogue were crucial in bringing about the Australia-US FTA.

The Dialogue is now an established institution and is even branching out with an annual west coast Dialogue in California. It now has one administrative staffer, but Scanlan and all the other principals, the American and Australian boards, do everything on an honorary basis. It is the most significant exercise in private diplomacy ever undertaken in Australian history.

It has become a prestigious institution in itself and now everyone wants to be part of it. In a way it has not only derived prestige from the alliance it has contributed prestige to it. Its continued ability to attract the top Americans, and to give them sufficient intellectual value that they keep coming back, is a rare accomplishment. The Dialogue is deeply Australian but unselfconsciously so. It is quite unique. There are other bilateral dialogue groups but they are almost all dependent on government money and don't have anything like the drive, horsepower or independence of the Australian-American Leadership Dialogue. It answers a specific Australian need and was not modelled on anything from elsewhere, though of course there would be nothing wrong with creative borrowing. It has led to numerous imitators and almost all such efforts, however imperfect, are useful.

It has led to high-powered people on both sides of the Pacific working at problems and issues in the context of the alliance. It has also engendered countless friendships. It has become a substantial part of Scanlan's life work and such an institution could only be created by someone with the drive and energy, the talent and the sheer persistence to keep relentlessly at the task of institution building. It is confidential, but not exactly a secret, a unique Australian-American creation.

Chapter 25

THE NEW ALLIANCE

So where does the alliance go from here? Perhaps the intimacy under Howard and Bush is as good as it gets and the alliance can only go backwards. But that is too negative a view. The alliance is resilient and adaptable. It will always take on a little of the character of the particular leaders in office at any given time. But it is almost certain always to be important, unless the character of Australia, or America, changes fundamentally.

It is unlikely that all future prime ministers and presidents will be as close as Howard and Bush. But the Howard government has been shrewd in trying to institutionalise as much as possible of the new intimacy – through the new intelligence relationships, through the Australian equity stake in the Joint Strike Fighter, through the Australian military personnel deployed into the key US military commands, through the habit of visits by serving presidents, and of course through the Free Trade Agreement. Nonetheless the alliance always needs political nourishment and attention from the highest level.

Australia has global security interests and the alliance is now a global partnership. Australia also has vital Asia-Pacific interests and the alliance has always been about the Pacific. In the post-9/11 environment it is quite likely that many of the threats which confront both Australia and the US will be, as the boffins put it, 'asymmetric'. They will be threats not from superpowers but from weak ones, they will be the deadly warfare of weakness. Terrorists, failed states, weak states, rogue states, international criminal groups – and the interaction of all of these in the age of increasingly easy nuclear weapons technology may provide even existential threat levels.

This is profoundly different from the dominance of conventional state threats when the alliance was conceived in the late 1940s and signed in 1951.

But the alliance is dynamic, and it needs to be. It is a living, intelligent entity and it must be adaptable and proactive. It needs to embody the greatest range of consultation and cooperative effort possible from both sides. Australia can only command that sort of attention, and all the operational and other benefits that go with it, if it has something to offer – relevant capabilities, important insights, a willingness to act, a willingness to share risk.

None of this abridges Australia's national independence. Here is a paradox. The US alliance is a fundamental element of Australia's international posture. It is a key part of the story Canberra tells the world about what Australia is and the values it professes. It is also a key part of the story Australians tell themselves about themselves.

Yet this does not make Australia any less independently or authentically Australian. The US alliance is a vector of Australian power. It is not by any remote stretch the limit of the nation's power but it is an important dimension of its national power. It is, literally, a force multiplier, not only militarily but economically and diplomatically. No nation lives in complete isolation. Few try to – perhaps only North Korea, and even Pyongyang values its relationship with China.

The most successful nations tend to have the most friends, and the most successful friends.

I remember attending a regional security conference in Jakarta once and a distinguished Australian professor commented to me: 'You know, really in the last few years we've done quite a lot without the Americans. And we've disagreed with them on a lot of things. Really we've been quite independent.'

The professor, erudite, calm and charming, is a generally sensible man but I couldn't believe how negative, more than that, how anachronistic and perfectly antique his words were, and what a chip on the shoulder they betrayed – as if Australia, as proud and good a nation as the world knows, needs to prove its independence to anybody, least of all itself. And there again was that adolescent and belittling assumption that the only way we prove ourselves independent is by disagreeing with the Americans, as if it's impossible to independently agree with the Americans. For as long as I can remember there have been things we disagree with the Americans about and things we agree about.

Because of the alliance our disagreements become in a sense more important, or at least more consequential, in that the Americans pay some attention to them, more, say, than they do to disagreements they might have with New Zealand.

If Washington pursues a perfectly good policy then a good Australian government will independently agree with it on everything. If it runs a perfectly bad policy a good Australian government will independently disagree with it on everything. Neither the alliance, nor Australia's independence, mandate agreement or disagreement.

Of course, Australia will do some things for the sake of the alliance which it wouldn't otherwise do, but it shouldn't do any bad thing for the sake of the alliance. If a cause is just Australia might commit to it because the Americans are leading the charge and Canberra wishes to offer them support, and calculates the balance of Australia's interests in terms of alliance management, whereas if this cause were led by a nation Australia cared less about, or didn't have such an important alliance with, the balance of its interests might be different and Australia might make a different decision. Naturally Australia would not commit to a bad cause because of alliance solidarity. But the history of Australia's alliance commitments with the Americans, this book contends, involves no commitments to bad causes, although it may well have involved commitments to badly executed causes.

Most of the time Australian governments agree with the US because it proceeds from the same core values as Australia does and it has the same core objectives. In its views of this region, it is in constant dialogue with Canberra, so that Australia has a role in shaping its views and objectives.

In the end, the future of the alliance is not certain because nothing is certain in this fallen world. But the ongoing commitment of American leaders is very strong.

Take Condoleeza Rice. She was a Soviet expert, with little Asian or Pacific exposure. But she has become a steadfast friend of Australia. She charmed Australia on a visit in early 2006. On that visit I asked her how important the alliance was. She declared: 'The Australia-US alliance is extremely important to the United States. It's one of our most important and most enduring alliances. It's important because we have economic ties. It's important because we have ties of friendship and values. And it's important because whenever there's a need to defend freedom throughout the decades the US and Australia have done it together. So this is an extremely important relationship to us and one we value greatly.'

I would not bet against the alliance. It has come up trumps too often. Its enduring power does derive from shared interests and mutual benefits, but at the deepest levels it derives from the fact that for all our differences, the values we share as nations are so great. Naturally this does not limit the friendships we have with other nations, with whom we also share values. Friendship is highly expandable, it is never a zero sum.

One of the alliance's great virtues is that the Americans listen to Australians. Of course, the Americans themselves are highly self-critical, highly dialectical in their own arguments. They are an empirical, problem-solving people. Their high-blown rhetoric, to which they are much more prone than Australians, is always tested and evaluated against reality. Nonetheless, they will certainly listen to an ally as well.

At one of the early meetings of the Australian-American Leadership Dialogue, I was blasting away at what I saw as the ham-fistedness of US policy in Asia, giving the Americans both barrels on the basis that if you don't tell them what you think there's no value in talking to them at all. At the end of my intervention, one of the Americans spoke, answering some of my points.

And then I saw the huge, bald-headed form of Rich Armitage lumber across the room in my direction. I'm going to be severely rebuked here, I thought. But Armitage merely dropped a note on my section of the long conference table we all shared. I opened it and read: 'Dead on in all respects'. He had come to the same conclusion as me about US policy in Asia at that stage, and perhaps he thought there was some utility in his colleagues hearing it from a non-American voice. In any event, as ever, Armitage, like America itself, was prepared to listen.

Australia brings its own unique strategic personality to the alliance. Howard's calculations on Iraq were profoundly east Asian in their priority on alliance management. Australia is also characteristically southeast Asian in its ease with ambiguity. It is utterly Anglo-Saxon in its empiricism and pragmatism and very American in its sense of being a new world nation where everyone writes their own script, and in glorying in its military traditions. It's easy to overlook just how unique this combination is. It's a strategic personality that has served Australia well, and the alliance is a central part of that.

Having prospered in its first six decades, the Australian-US alliance seems to grow more robust with time. It has brought great benefits to Australia, and great benefits to America. It has also brought benefits to Asia, where it is a vital interest anchoring the US in the region, promoting a stability which the region could not ensure itself.

The alliance has always been a two-way street. Australians have been assertive, critical and demanding, as well as fraternal and supportive. It enjoys the widest support in Australia, and no discernible opposition in America. It is a sturdy creature, now. In a naughty world, it is a candle in the darkness.

INDEX

N.B. Due to the frequent references to John Howard and George W. Bush, their names do not appear in the index.

ABCA 160
Abrams tank 135, 136, 137, 138
Abu Ghraib prison 65, 83, 113, 122, 138
Aceh (Indonesia) 186, 236, 238–42, 291
Afghanistan 25, 34, 37, 38–9, 40–56, 83, 90, 93–4, 99, 106, 109, 125, 139, 143, 152, 156, 160, 164, 167, 188, 271, 273, 274–5, 277, 278, 297
Albright, Madeleine 32, 57–8, 66
air warfare destroyers (AWDs) 129, 138–9, 212
al-Qaeda 37, 43, 47, 48, 49, 51, 54, 56, 63–4, 93, 94, 127, 169, 176, 178
al-Zarkawi, Abu Musab 93, 127
Ansar al-Islam 63
anti-Americanism 15, 79, 88, 183, 269, 287, 288, 290, 293–6, 298–9, 301
anti-semitism 296, 298
Anzac Day 142, 145–6
ANZUS 16, 35, 36–7, 39, 108, 158–9, 179, 189, 191–2, 263, 307–8, 310, 311
Armitage, Richard 16, 18, 33, 40, 63, 79–81, 101, 168–9, 211, 240, 268–9, 314, 315, 316, 323
Association of Southeast Asian Nations (ASEAN) 262
AUSMIN 98, 100, 160, 166, 171, 186, 265, 281, 314
Australia, politics 249–60, 279–89

Australia-UK relationship 103–4, 107
Australian Labor Party 131, 132, 134, 139, 146, 147, 232, 250, 251–2, 269, 279–89, 299–300
Australian Secret Intelligence Service (ASIS) 103, 104
Australian Special Air Service Regiment (SAS) 19, 27, 40, 37, 39, 40–56, 69
Australian Strategic Policy Institute (ASPI) 140, 300

Baker, James 81
Bali bombings 37–8, 90–1, 131, 143, 173–4, 182–3, 185, 233, 235, 295
Beazley, Kim 79, 131, 132, 134, 139, 146, 147, 263, 269, 283, 284, 286–7, 288, 308, 313
Berger, Sandy 62
Binskin, Air Commodore Mark 156, 208, 271–8
Blair, Tony 20, 23–4, 35, 62, 65, 104, 150, 166, 167, 229, 237, 241
Bolger, Jim 159
Bolton, John 77
Bremer, Paul 67–8, 113, 114

Calvert, Ashton 19, 261, 269–70
Campbell, Ian 244–6
Campbell, Kurt 148, 149–50, 165
Canada 107, 108–9, 152, 155, 160, 168, 221, 222, 241, 259, 263
Casey, General George 112, 114, 116, 117, 120–1

CENTCOM 43, 154, 207
Central American Free Trade Agreement (CAFTA) 267
Chen Yonglin 195–6
Cheney, Dick 19, 20, 27, 28–30, 33, 74, 77–8, 81–2, 89, 169, 234, 314, 317
Chester, Doug 240
Chifley, Ben 285–6, 307
China 16, 28, 31, 92, 108, 140, 175, 187, 188–205, 220, 223, 224, 225, 241, 243, 245, 246–7, 262, 266, 281, 288, 291, 298, 314, 316, 320
Chirac, Jacques 29, 61, 193
Clarke, Richard 63–4
climate change 243, 247
Clinton, Bill 32–3, 34, 43, 58, 61–2, 63, 78, 81, 83–4, 89, 149, 165, 166, 169, 171, 177, 179, 180–1, 228, 244, 252, 262, 268, 311, 313
Connaughton, Jim 245–6
Cosgrove, General Peter 110, 122, 141–2, 144–5, 180, 232, 233, 238
Crean, Simon 285, 288
Cuba 304
Curtin, John 15, 134, 285, 306–7

Darfur 224, 226
Dauth, John 162, 221, 222, 223
Deakin, Alfred 15, 303, 306
Defence Imagery and Geospatial Organisation (DIGO) 103
Defence Intelligence Group 103
Defence Intelligence Organisation (DIO) 103, 137, 145
Defence Signals Directorate (DSD) 103
Dewey, George 304–5
Dibb, Paul 132, 139
Downer, Alexander 13–14, 19, 20–1, 22–31, 32–5, 36, 38, 57–8, 65, 66–8, 79, 130, 172–3, 176–7, 179, 184, 189, 190–3, 221, 227, 235, 240, 244–6, 263–4

East Timor 42–3, 67, 104, 122–3, 131, 134, 136, 141–2, 143, 148, 169, 177–82, 185, 224, 235
Evatt, HV 286, 307

Fadden, Arthur 310
Family First 255–6
Feith, Doug 78

Fiji 134
Five Power Defence Arrangements (FPDA) 104
foreign policy, Bush 74–85
France 25, 29, 61, 62, 135, 146, 193, 223
Franks, General Tommy 11–12, 20, 66, 67, 72, 116
free trade agreement (FTA) 13, 17, 33, 165, 189, 260, 262–3, 264, 266–70, 317

Garner, Jay 66, 82, 116
Germany 29, 61, 62, 108, 146, 147
Gilmore, Commodore Steve 156, 207–13
Gore, Al 32
Grossman, Marc 238, 240
Gulf war 37, 42, 60, 64, 78, 88, 207, 211

Haass, Richard 165–6
Habibie, BJ 177–8
Hadley, Stephen 80, 83, 239
Hanson, Pauline 143, 174–5, 177
Hawke, Bob 15, 42, 134, 144, 232, 250, 259, 263, 187–8
Hearst, William Randolph 303
Hill, Robert 82, 100, 130–1, 132, 139–40, 243
Hollingworth, Peter 145
Hong Kong 92
Houston, Air Marshall Angus 10, 156
Hughes, Billy 306
Hunt, Greg 244–5

Ibrahim Al-Jaafari 68
India 200, 202, 224, 237, 241, 242, 243, 245–7
Indonesia 13, 17, 43, 66, 88–9, 122–4, 125, 136, 172–87, 190, 195, 224, 233, 237–8, 242, 291–2, 295, 298, 315–16
Indyk, Martin 61
INTERFET 123, 141, 179, 180
Iraq 11, 12, 18–26, 30–1, 57–73, 84–5, 92, 93, 111–27

Jalal Talibani 68
Japan 80, 92, 105, 108, 175, 189, 194, 195, 199–204, 224–5, 240–1, 242, 245, 247, 262, 266, 298, 303, 310, 314

Jeffrey, Michael 145
Jiang Zemin 28, 30

Katrina (hurricane) 150, 229
Keating, Paul 134, 174, 287–8, 315
Keelty, Mick 232–3
Kerry, John 148–9, 165, 166, 170, 228, 258
Kosovo 23, 94, 179, 226
Krauthammer, Charles 78
Kristol, Bill 78
Kyoto Protocol 243–7

Latham, Mark 250, 251–2, 269, 279, 280–5, 288, 299
Leahy, General Peter 10, 137
Lewincamp, Frank 145
Lewis, General Duncan 41, 51, 52, 145, 231
Libby, Scooter 19
Libya 217–19, 223

MacArthur, General Douglas 15, 107
McKinley, William 304
McNarn, General Maurie 10–11, 70–2, 145
Mahathir, Mohammed 66, 288
Malaysia 56, 66, 89, 104, 125, 237, 288
Marcos, Ferdinand 89, 95
Martin, Paul 241
media 21–2, 25, 30–1, 44, 47, 64, 88, 121, 199, 207, 222, 229–30, 233, 256, 283, 288, 295, 298, 299, 312, 315, 316
Medicare 251
Menzies, Robert 309–10
Middle East 26–7, 43, 61–2, 64, 83, 92, 94–6, 99, 112, 154, 156, 214, 217, 220, 221, 223, 276, 294, 296
Molan, Major-General Jim 111–27, 156, 208, 274
Miller, Major-General Tom 116
Morris, Steven 60

9/11 terror attack *see* September 11, 2001
Negroponte, John 112, 114, 116, 124
Nelson, Brendon 130–1
New Zealand 46, 52, 104, 107, 108–9, 120, 134, 135, 152, 155, 158–9, 179, 200, 222, 262, 263–4, 300, 321

Nidal, Abu 63
Nixon, Richard 252
North Atlantic Treaty Organisation (NATO) 29, 36, 43, 93, 105, 112, 158, 225
North Korea 27–8, 30–1, 101–2, 108, 158, 220, 309, 320
Nuclear Non-Proliferation Treaty 102

Office of National Assessment (ONA) 74–5, 103, 104, 230–1, 232, 234
O'Hanlon, Michael 148–50
Operation Anaconda 40, 41–2, 44, 46–7, 49–55, 56

PACOM 43, 154, 207, 238
Petrov, Vladimir 286
Philippines 80, 89, 95, 181, 183, 187, 202, 303–5
Pine Gap 108
Plame, Valerie 19
Pollack, Ken 61, 62
Powell, Colin 18, 33–4, 66–7, 74, 79, 80, 81–2, 89, 112, 165–6, 240, 241, 269, 279
Prins, Gwyn 166–8
Proliferation Security Initiative (PSI) 101, 158

Rice, Condoleeza 19, 27, 28, 74, 80–2, 83, 162, 240, 279, 317, 322
Richardson, Dennis 232–3
Roosevelt, Teddy 15, 302–6, 308
Rove, Karl 82, 239, 314, 317
Rumsfeld, Donald 20, 39, 77–8, 80–2, 83, 91, 98–9, 100, 124, 239
Russell, Sergeant Andrew 47
Rwanda 224, 226

Saddam Hussein 11, 18, 19, 21, 22, 25, 30, 57–64, 68–9, 73, 78, 83, 84, 88, 89, 92, 93, 94–5, 101, 121, 164, 183, 206, 207, 210–11, 225, 265, 300
Sanchez, General Ricardo 112–14, 122
SAS *see* Australian Special Air Service (SAS)
Scanlan, Phil 311–13, 314–15, 317, 318
Schultz, George 288, 312
Schroeder, Gerhard 29, 30
September 11, 2001 34, 35–6, 38, 43, 58, 63, 82–3, 90–1

signals intelligence 102–4, 107, 109, 128, 286, 307
Singapore 92, 104, 140, 187, 202, 203, 208
Smith, Mike 35, 217, 313
Somalia 94, 125, 134, 136
South Korea 27–8, 66, 92, 105, 175, 198, 202, 245, 247, 262, 290, 309
Spain 74, 303–5
Spender, Percy 306–11
Summers, Larry 176–7

Taiwan 92, 189, 191, 192, 198, 200, 204, 224, 225, 316
Thailand 175, 181, 202, 237
Thawley, Michael 18–19, 26, 163, 239, 240
Tink, Colonel Rowan 41, 44–5, 46–7, 50–5, 156
Truman, Harry 310–11

UKUSA 107–9, 156, 307
United Kingdom 107, 132, 152
United Nations 23, 31, 66–7, 214–27, 241
  Security Council 23–4, 28–9, 63–4, 65, 95, 106, 114, 199, 223–5, 226, 230, 238–9, 285

Vaile, Mark 261, 262, 264, 266, 267, 269–70
Varghese, Peter 234

Wallace, Brigadier Jim 133
Wallace, Trooper John 49–50
weapons of mass destruction (WMDs) 11, 27, 28–9, 30, 58, 59–63, 64–5, 76, 83, 89, 101, 120, 126, 132, 155, 158, 300
Weinberger, Caspar 312
Whitlam, Gough 15, 259, 286–7
Wolfowitz, Paul 27, 33, 38, 59, 64, 74, 78, 86–96, 239, 314, 317
Woodward, Edward 145
World Trade Organisation (WTO) 262

Yates, Steve 19
Yudhoyono, Susilo Bambang 17, 182, 184

Zimbabwe 219, 220
Zoellick, Bob 33, 80–1, 83, 166, 201, 261–2, 264, 266–9, 270, 314, 315, 317